"This series enkindles thoughtful discussion about the implications of the New Testament for lived Christian faith in the Church today. Its accessible format and multi-angled approach offer a model for teaching and ministry."

—**Katherine Hayes**, Seminary of the Immaculate Conception

"The Catholic Commentary on Sacred Scripture is an ideal tool for living our faith more deeply. This extraordinary resource should be on the shelf of every committed Catholic believer. I highly recommend it."

—**Charles J. Chaput, OFM Cap**, Archbishop of Philadelphia

"There is a great hunger among Catholic laity for a deeper understanding of the Bible. The Catholic Commentary on Sacred Scripture fills the need for a more in-depth interpretation of Scripture. I am very excited to be able to recommend this series to our Bible Study groups around the world."

—**Gail Buckley**, founder and director, Catholic Scripture Study International (www.cssprogram.net)

"The Catholic Commentary on Sacred Scripture is a landmark achievement in theological interpretation of Scripture in and for the Church. Everything about it is inviting and edifying. It is a wonderful gift to the Catholic Church and a model for the rest of us. Highly recommended for all!"

—**Michael J. Gorman**, St. Mary's Seminary and University, Baltimore

"This series represents a much-needed approach, based on good scholarship but not overloaded with it. The frequent references to the *Catechism of the Catholic Church* help us to read Holy Scripture with a vivid sense of the living tradition of the Church."

—**Christoph Cardinal Schönborn**, Archbishop of Vienna

"The Catholic Commentary on Sacred Scripture will prove itself to be a reliable, Catholic—but ecumenically open and respectful—commentary."

—**Scot McKnight**, *Jesus Creed* blog

"The Catholic Commentary on Sacred Scripture assists Catholic preachers and teachers, lay and ordained, in their ministry of the Word. Moreover, it offers ordinary Catholics a scriptural resource that will enhance their understanding of God's Word. Thus these commentaries, nourished on the faith of the Church and guided by scholarly wisdom, are both exegetically sound and spiritually nourishing."

—Thomas G. Weinandy, OFM Cap

T0311366

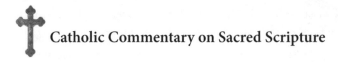 Catholic Commentary on Sacred Scripture

First and Second Thessalonians

Nathan Eubank

B
Baker Academic
a division of Baker Publishing Group
Grand Rapids, Michigan

Published by Baker Academic
a division of Baker Publishing Group
PO Box 6287, Grand Rapids, MI 49516-6287
www.bakeracademic.com

Printed in the United States of America

Library of Congress Cataloging-in-Publication Data
Names: Eubank, Nathan, author.
Title: First and Second Thessalonians / Nathan Eubank.
Description: Grand Rapids : Baker Academic, a division of Baker Publishing Group, 2019. | Series: Catholic commentary on sacred scripture | Includes index.
Identifiers: LCCN 2019005676 | ISBN 9780801049446 (pbk.)
Subjects: LCSH: Bible. Thessalonians—Commentaries.
Classification: LCC BS2725.53 .E93 2019 | DDC 227/.81077—dc23
LC record available at https://lccn.loc.gov/2019005676

Nihil obstat:
Reverend Monsignor Michael Heintz
Censor Librorum
October 22, 2018

Imprimatur:
Most Reverend Kevin C. Rhoades
Bishop of Fort Wayne–South Bend
October 22, 2018

19   20   21   22   23   24   25   7   6   5   4   3   2   1

For the seminarians
among my students.

Contents

Illustrations

Editors' Preface

The Church has always venerated the divine Scriptures just as she venerates the body of the Lord. . . . All the preaching of the Church should be nourished and governed by Sacred Scripture. For in the sacred books, the Father who is in heaven meets His children with great love and speaks with them; and the power and goodness in the word of God is so great that it stands as the support and energy of the Church, the strength of faith for her sons and daughters, the food of the soul, a pure and perennial fountain of spiritual life.

Second Vatican Council, Dei Verbum 21

Were not our hearts burning [within us] while he spoke to us on the way and opened the scriptures to us?

Luke 24:32

The Catholic Commentary on Sacred Scripture aims to serve the ministry of the Word of God in the life and mission of the Church. Since Vatican Council II, there has been an increasing hunger among Catholics to study Scripture in depth and in a way that reveals its relationship to liturgy, evangelization, catechesis, theology, and personal and communal life. This series responds to that desire by providing accessible yet substantive commentary on each book of the New Testament, drawn from the best of contemporary biblical scholarship as well as the rich treasury of the Church's tradition. These volumes seek to offer scholarship illumined by faith, in the conviction that the ultimate aim of biblical interpretation is to discover what God has revealed and is still speaking through the sacred text. Central to our approach are the principles taught by Vatican II: first, the use of historical and literary methods to discern what the biblical authors intended to express; second, prayerful theological reflection to understand the sacred text "in accord with the same Spirit by whom it was written"—that is, in light of the content and unity of the whole Scripture, the living tradition of the Church, and the analogy of faith (*Dei Verbum* 12).

The Catholic Commentary on Sacred Scripture is written for those engaged in or training for pastoral ministry and others interested in studying Scripture to understand their faith more deeply, to nourish their spiritual life, or to share the good news with others. With this in mind, the authors focus on the meaning of the text for faith and life rather than on the technical questions that occupy scholars, and they explain the Bible in ordinary language that does not require translation for preaching and catechesis. Although this series is written from the perspective of Catholic faith, its authors draw on the interpretation of Protestant and Orthodox scholars and hope these volumes will serve Christians of other traditions as well.

A variety of features are designed to make the commentary as useful as possible. Each volume includes the biblical text of the New American Bible, Revised Edition (NABRE), the translation approved for liturgical use in the United States. In order to serve readers who use other translations, the commentary notes and explains the most important differences between the NABRE and other widely used translations (e.g., RSV, NRSV, JB, NJB, and NIV). Each unit of the biblical text is followed by a list of references to relevant Scripture passages, Catechism sections, and uses in the Roman Lectionary. The exegesis that follows aims to explain in a clear and engaging way the meaning of the text in its original historical context as well as its perennial meaning for Christians. Reflection and Application sections help readers apply Scripture to Christian life today by responding to questions that the text raises, offering spiritual interpretations drawn from Christian tradition, or providing suggestions for the use of the biblical text in catechesis, preaching, or other forms of pastoral ministry.

Interspersed throughout the commentary are Biblical Background sidebars that present historical, literary, or theological information, and Living Tradition sidebars that offer pertinent material from the postbiblical Christian tradition, including quotations from Church documents and from the writings of saints and Church Fathers. The Biblical Background sidebars are indicated by a photo of urns that were excavated in Jerusalem, signifying the importance of historical study in understanding the sacred text. The Living Tradition sidebars are indicated by an image of Eadwine, a twelfth-century monk and scribe, signifying the growth in the Church's understanding that comes by the grace of the

Holy Spirit as believers study and ponder the Word of God in their hearts (see *Dei Verbum* 8).

Maps and a glossary are included in each volume for easy reference. The glossary explains key terms from the biblical text as well as theological or exegetical terms, which are marked in the commentary with a cross (†). A list of suggested resources, an index of pastoral topics, and an index of sidebars are included to enhance the usefulness of these volumes. Further resources, including questions for reflection or discussion, can be found at the series website, www.CatholicScriptureCommentary.com.

It is our desire and prayer that these volumes be of service so that more and more "the word of the Lord may speed forward and be glorified" (2 Thess 3:1) in the Church and throughout the world.

Peter S. Williamson
Mary Healy
Kevin Perrotta

Note to Readers

The New American Bible, Revised Edition differs slightly from most English translations in its verse numbering of Psalms and certain other parts of the Old Testament. For instance, Ps 51:4 in the NABRE is Ps 51:2 in other translations; Mal 3:19 in the NABRE is Mal 4:1 in other translations. Readers who use different translations are advised to keep this in mind when looking up Old Testament cross-references given in the commentary.

Abbreviations

†	Indicates that a definition of a term appears in the glossary
//	Indicates where a parallel account can be found in other Gospels
AB	Anchor Bible
ACCS	Ancient Christian Commentary on Scripture: New Testament
ANTC	Abingdon New Testament Commentaries
BBC	Blackwell's Bible Commentaries
BDAG	Frederick W. Danker, Walter Bauer, William F. Arndt, and F. Wilbur Gingrich, *A Greek-English Lexicon of the New Testament and Other Early Christian Literature*, 3rd ed. (Chicago: University of Chicago Press, 2000)
BECNT	Baker Exegetical Commentary on the New Testament
BZNW	Beihefte zur Zeitschrift für die neutestamentliche Wissenschaft
ca.	*circa*, around
Catechism	*Catechism of the Catholic Church*, 2nd ed. (New York: Doubleday, 2003)
CBQ	*Catholic Biblical Quarterly*
CCSS	Catholic Commentary on Sacred Scripture
CEB	Common English Bible
EBib	Etudes bibliques
ESV	English Standard Version
ET	English translation
FC	Fathers of the Church
HTR	*Harvard Theological Review*
IBC	Interpretation: A Bible Commentary for Teaching and Preaching
ICG	*Inscriptiones Christianae Graecae*, edited by Cilliers Breytenbach et al. (Berlin: Edition Topoi, 2016)
IG	*Inscriptiones Graecae*, Editio Minor (Berlin: de Gruyter, 1924–)
JBL	*Journal of Biblical Literature*
JSNT	*Journal for the Study of the New Testament*
JSPHL	*Journal for the Study of Paul and His Letters*
JTS	*Journal of Theological Studies*
KJV	King James Version
LEC	Library of Early Christianity
Lectionary	*The Lectionary for Mass* (1998/2002 USA edition)

LNTS	Library of New Testament Studies
LSJ	Henry George Liddell, Robert Scott, and Henry Stuart Jones, *A Greek-English Lexicon*, 9th ed. with revised supplement (Oxford: Clarendon, 1996)
LXX	Septuagint
MM	J. H. Moulton and G. Milligan, *The Vocabulary of the Greek Testament* (London, 1930; reprint, Peabody, MA: Hendrickson, 1997)
NABRE	New American Bible (Revised Edition, 2011)
NCBC	New Century Bible Commentary
NCC	New Covenant Commentary
NICNT	New International Commentary on the New Testament
NIV	New International Version
NovT	*Novum Testamentum*
NPNF¹	*Nicene and Post-Nicene Fathers*, Series 1
NRSV	New Revised Standard Version
NTL	New Testament Library
NTS	*New Testament Studies*
PG	Patrologia Graeca [= *Patrologiae Cursus Completus*: Series Graeca], edited by J.-P. Migne, 162 vols. (Paris, 1857–86)
RIChrM	*Recueil des inscriptions chrétienne de Macédoine, du IIIe au VIe siècle*, by Denis Feissel (Paris: Boccard, 1983)
RSV	Revised Standard Version
SP	Sacra Pagina
SPNPT	Studies in Platonism, Neoplatonism, and the Platonic Tradition
StPatr	*Studia Patristica*
TDNT	*Theological Dictionary of the New Testament*, edited by Gerhard Kittel and Gerhard Friedrich, translated by Geoffrey W. Bromiley, 10 vols. (Grand Rapids: Eerdmans, 1974–2006)
TS	*Theological Studies*
TynBul	*Tyndale Bulletin*
v(v).	verse(s)
WUNT	Wissenschaftliche Untersuchungen zum Neuen Testament
ZNW	*Zeitschrift für die neutestamentliche Wissenschaft und die Kunde der älteren Kirche*

Books of the Old Testament

Gen	Genesis	2 Sam	2 Samuel	Esther	Esther
Exod	Exodus	1 Kings	1 Kings	1 Macc	1 Maccabees
Lev	Leviticus	2 Kings	2 Kings	2 Macc	2 Maccabees
Num	Numbers	1 Chron	1 Chronicles	Job	Job
Deut	Deuteronomy	2 Chron	2 Chronicles	Ps(s)	Psalm(s)
Josh	Joshua	Ezra	Ezra	Prov	Proverbs
Judg	Judges	Neh	Nehemiah	Eccles	Ecclesiastes
Ruth	Ruth	Tob	Tobit	Song	Song of Songs
1 Sam	1 Samuel	Jdt	Judith	Wis	Wisdom

Sir	Sirach	Hosea	Hosea	Hab	Habakkuk
Isa	Isaiah	Joel	Joel	Zeph	Zephaniah
Jer	Jeremiah	Amos	Amos	Hag	Haggai
Lam	Lamentations	Obad	Obadiah	Zech	Zechariah
Bar	Baruch	Jon	Jonah	Mal	Malachi
Ezek	Ezekiel	Mic	Micah		
Dan	Daniel	Nah	Nahum		

Books of the New Testament

Matt	Matthew	Eph	Ephesians	Heb	Hebrews
Mark	Mark	Phil	Philippians	James	James
Luke	Luke	Col	Colossians	1 Pet	1 Peter
John	John	1 Thess	1 Thessalonians	2 Pet	2 Peter
Acts	Acts	2 Thess	2 Thessalonians	1 John	1 John
Rom	Romans	1 Tim	1 Timothy	2 John	2 John
1 Cor	1 Corinthians	2 Tim	2 Timothy	3 John	3 John
2 Cor	2 Corinthians	Titus	Titus	Jude	Jude
Gal	Galatians	Philem	Philemon	Rev	Revelation

Introduction to First and
Second Thessalonians

First Thessalonians

First Thessalonians is likely to be Paul's oldest surviving letter and, indeed, the oldest surviving Christian text, but the Paul we meet in its pages was already a veteran apostle.[1] Before he wrote any of the letters that would make him famous, Paul spent years preaching the gospel around the eastern side of the Roman Empire. About the year 49, Paul started a new phase of missionary activity, heading out on a westward journey that would lead him to the Roman province of Macedonia. Traveling on the Via Egnatia, a road running from Byzantium to the Adriatic coast, he came to Philippi, where he founded a church in the midst of significant opposition (1 Thess 2:1–2). He then went southwest to Macedonia's capital, the busy port city of Thessalonica.

Thessalonica (Thessalonikē in ancient Greek; Thessaloniki in modern Greek) was founded in 316 or 315 BC by Cassander, one of the Macedonian generals who vied for control of the pieces of Alexander the Great's empire after Alexander's death in 323.[2] Situated in a natural harbor on the Thermaic Gulf in the Aegean Sea and with the Via Egnatia offering relatively easy access to the east and the west, Thessalonica became a bustling center of commerce, and it remains so to this day. A series of shrewd political decisions led the city to enjoy a close relationship with Rome and its emperors. Rome granted Thessalonica a

---

1. For a recent attempt to figure out the order in which Paul's Letters were written, see Douglas A. Campbell, *Framing Paul: An Epistolary Biography* (Grand Rapids: Eerdmans, 2014). Campbell dates 1 Thessalonians to the early 40s, almost a decade earlier than most scholars.

2. Cassander named the city after his wife, Thessalonikē, who was Alexander the Great's half-sister. See Strabo, *Geography* 7.21.

Figure 1. Map of the Aegean Sea.

degree of independence as a so-called free city, and the city expressed its gratitude for Rome's benevolence by honoring and fostering the worship of Roman gods—including the emperors. To the reverence of all things Roman, the diverse inhabitants of the city added the worship of Greek and Egyptian deities.[3]

While in Thessalonica, Paul and his companions Silvanus and Timothy worked to support themselves (1 Thess 2:5–9) and preached about the "living and true God" and the Lord Jesus, who was crucified but rose again and will return triumphant (1:9–10). Some members of the city were persuaded, and a congregation of the Thessalonians was founded. After a relatively short period of time—perhaps a few months—Paul and his companions were forced to leave (1 Thess 2:17).[4] According to the book of Acts (17:5–10), they fled under cover of darkness after being accused of sedition against Caesar. The apostolic band went on to Beroea and then to Athens, but all the while Paul felt it had been too early to leave the fledgling congregation. The same people who forced Paul to leave were bound to give the converts trouble, and Paul was worried they would abandon their new faith (1 Thess 3:5). He tried repeatedly to return to

3. The work of Charles Edson is still helpful. See "Cults of Thessalonica," *HTR* 41 (1948): 153–204.
4. Acts 17:2 could imply that Paul was in Thessalonica for only two or three weeks, but Paul was in Thessalonica long enough to receive assistance from Philippi more than once (Phil 4:16).

support them, but without success (2:18). So, while still in Athens he decided to send Timothy back to Thessalonica in his stead (3:1–2). When Timothy returned he had good news: the Thessalonian church had endured persecution and the death of some members, but they were holding fast to the faith (3:6–9; 4:13–18). Overjoyed, Paul responded by writing a letter that later tradition would call "1 Thessalonians."[5]

In the letter Paul seeks to accomplish all the things he would do in person if he could go to Thessalonica: reestablish friendships, encourage the downtrodden, exhort them to increased faithfulness in certain areas, and provide new instruction on the fate of those who die before the Lord's return. At one point Paul breaks into a prayer that is an excellent summary of the purpose of 1 Thessalonians as a whole:

> Now may God himself, our Father, and our Lord Jesus direct our way to you, and may the Lord make you increase and abound in love for one another and for all, just as we have for you, so as to strengthen your hearts, to be blameless in holiness before our God and Father at the coming of our Lord Jesus with all his holy ones. (1 Thess 3:11–13)

Directly and indirectly, this prayer touches on four of the letter's main concerns:

1. *Expression of affection.* The prayer illustrates Paul's affection for the Thessalonians and his hope to be reunited with them. With the possible exception of Philippians, no letter of Paul's is as warm and affectionate as 1 Thessalonians. One way this is manifested is with the vivid language of family. Paul is known for addressing the members of his churches as family members ("brothers"), but 1 Thessalonians contains by far the greatest concentration of this language and the most vivid familial metaphors (see commentary on 1 Thess 2:9–12). Paul addresses them as brothers, of course, but he also describes himself as their father and as a nurse or nanny who cherishes them (2:7, 11). He compares the experience of being parted from them to being orphaned (2:17). In practical terms, Paul is helping them to see themselves as a part of a new family, something that would be a comfort in the midst of rejection by other inhabitants of their city.

2. *Concern for the converts' growth in love and holiness.* Though he was pleased with their progress (1 Thess 1:8), Paul felt there were deficiencies in their faith

---

5. Many today suppose on the basis of Acts 18:5 that Timothy rejoined Paul in Corinth and that Paul wrote 1 Thessalonians from there. Conversely, some ancient manuscripts of 1 Thessalonians label it as having been written in Athens, a view that is based on a plausible interpretation of 1 Thess 3:1–6. Either city is a possibility.

(3:10), areas where they needed additional teaching or encouragement to help them become "blameless in holiness" (3:13). A number of issues surface in the letter, but the most important are chastity (4:2–8), self-reliance (4:9–12), and grief (4:13–18).[6]

3. *Instruction on the return of the Lord and the resurrection of the dead.* The prayer that they would be found "blameless in holiness" when the Lord comes illustrates the †eschatological focus of the letter. Paul's missionary preaching in Thessalonica had strongly emphasized what we might call "advent" themes (see commentary on 1 Thess 4:15) regarding the necessity of being prepared for the coming of the Lord. After Paul left, it seems that one or more of the congregation died, and the new believers did not know how to fit this disturbing reality into their new faith, possibly because they had assumed they would all live to see the return of the Lord. In response, Paul offers further instruction, explaining that those who die before the Lord's return will be at no disadvantage (4:13–18; see also 5:1–11).

4. *Instruction to expect persecution.* There is no explicit mention of persecution in the prayer, but the reality of opposition to the faith pervades the circumstances around the letter and stands behind Paul's prayer to return. Persecution is what forced Paul to leave Thessalonica and is at least part of the reason why he was worried that the believers there would fall away in his absence (1 Thess 3:3). Even if there is a touch of hyperbole in the letter's descriptions of "great affliction" (1:6) and "much struggle" (2:2), whatever was happening seems to have been serious enough to force Paul out of the city and cause him to worry that the new converts would fall away. There was no official, systematic opposition to Christianity in this period, but it is not hard to imagine why Paul's message would have been incendiary. Paul identifies the converts as former pagans (1:9).[7] By switching allegiance from the gods of their families and city, the new Christians probably seemed odd, impious, and disloyal. Family and business relationships would have been threatened. Ordinary activities like sharing a meal could become a minefield of potential conflict because meat was often sacrificed to a god before being eaten.[8] According to the book of Acts, many residents of Thessalonica opposed Paul and his companions on the grounds that they were inciting revolt, acting against the decrees of Caesar, and claiming that Jesus, not

---

6. For other issues related to love of neighbor, see 1 Thess 5:12–15.

7. Acts 17:1–4 mentions that some Jews in Thessalonica were persuaded by Paul's message, but the letter's recipients are explicitly described as former idol worshipers. Nijay K. Gupta has argued that these former idol worshipers could include "God-fearers" ("The Thessalonian Believers, Formerly 'Pagans' or 'God-Fearers'? Challenging a Stubborn Consensus," *Neotestamentica* 52 [2018]: 91–113).

8. See, e.g., 1 Cor 8; 10.

Caesar, was the true king (17:6–7). Paul had no interest in armed conflict with Rome (see Rom 13:1–7), but it is possible that his teaching was perceived as seditious by those who considered activities like swearing fealty to the gods of Rome essential for a good citizen.[9] While in Thessalonica Paul taught the new converts to expect persecution (see 1 Thess 3:3), and afterward he encouraged them with the reminder that in their sufferings they were becoming like Jesus (1:6). At the same time, he understood all too well that sometimes the faithful crack under pressure, so he was anxious to offer support.

Second Thessalonians

Apart from a few exceptions in the nineteenth century, Paul's authorship of 1 Thessalonians has never been questioned.[10] In contrast, many New Testament scholars have serious doubts about the authorship of 2 Thessalonians, and only about half are confident that he is the author.[11] While scholars vigorously debate the issue, the faithful are often less interested in or sympathetic to questions about the authorship of biblical books. When I taught in a seminary, students tended to assume that trustworthy professors would not seriously entertain the possibility that a book of the Bible might have been written by someone other than the person traditionally thought to be the author. There are compelling reasons, however, for taking questions about authorship seriously rather than dismissing them out of hand. Most fundamentally, it is never a good idea to dismiss bona fide arguments without a fair hearing or to seek to shelter one's opinions from critical scrutiny. Indeed, though modernity has brought an unprecedented flood of investigations into the authorship of biblical books, learned Christians have debated questions of authorship since antiquity. In what follows, I describe the two main scenarios that scholars have proposed for the authorship of 2 Thessalonians, the first making Paul the author, and the second a later admirer.[12] Then I provide a brief assessment of the arguments.

9. Karl P. Donfried, "The Cults of Thessalonica and the Thessalonian Correspondence," *NTS* 31 (1985): 336–56. On Acts 17, see C. Kavin Rowe, *World Upside Down: Reading Acts in the Graeco-Roman Age* (New York: Oxford University Press, 2010), 91–103.

10. Some argue that 1 Thess 2:13–16 was added by a later editor. See commentary on that passage.

11. Based on Paul Foster's informal survey at the 2011 British New Testament Conference. See Foster, "Who Wrote 2 Thessalonians? A Fresh Look at an Old Problem," *JSNT* 35 (2012): 150–75, esp. 171.

12. For a full-length defense of the non-Pauline origin of 2 Thessalonians, including possible scenarios not discussed here, see, e.g., M. Eugene Boring, *I & II Thessalonians*, NTL (Louisville: Westminster John Knox, 2015), 209–27. For a full defense of Pauline authorship, see, e.g., Abraham J. Malherbe, *The Letters to the Thessalonians: A New Translation with Introduction and Commentary*, AB 32B (New Haven: Yale University Press, 2000), 349–74.

Scenario 1: Paul Is the Author

A short time after sending 1 Thessalonians—perhaps a few months later—word came to Paul that the Thessalonians had fallen prey to another †eschatological delusion. Whereas they formerly worried about those who died before the †parousia—that is, the Lord's return—they now believed that the parousia had already come and they had missed out on it (2 Thess 2:1–2). Moreover, some members of the congregation were refusing to work in defiance of Paul's earlier instruction (3:6–15; see 1 Thess 4:9–12). On top of all this, the converts continued to experience significant persecution (2 Thess 1:4–12). In response, Paul fired off the letter that we know as 2 Thessalonians. Only three chapters long, this short epistle deals quickly with all the problems that needed to be addressed, occasionally referring the Thessalonians to what had already been taught rather than explaining everything again (2:5). Because it was written so soon after 1 Thessalonians, it contains similar language and structure.

Scenario 2: Paul Is Not the Author

A generation or more after the death of Paul, an admirer of his wished to extend the apostle's wisdom to a new situation. Using 1 Thessalonians as a template, this admirer wrote a new letter, ostensibly addressed to the church in Thessalonica but in reality more of an encyclical intended for wide Christian readership. The author was steeped in Paul's thought and skilled at imitating his style, but he unintentionally left behind clues that would alert later readers to the fact that Paul was not the author.[13] Here are the telltale signs most often discussed.

1. Many scholars have thought that 2 Thessalonians has a cold, authoritarian tone in comparison to the warmth of 1 Thessalonians. Most notoriously, the author thanks God not because he wants to but because it is an obligation (2 Thess 1:3; 2:13).

2. Second Thessalonians uses vocabulary and sentence structures that some argue are different from Paul's own. For instance, the sentences tend to be longer than in 1 Thessalonians.

3. The possibility of forged letters surfaces two times in 2 Thessalonians, first in 2:2, when the author warns against possible forgeries ("a letter allegedly from

---

13. Biblical commentators have often claimed that writing in the name of others was seen as morally unproblematic, but recent studies have rightly challenged this. See, most recently, Armin D. Baum, "Content and Form: Authorship Attribution and Pseudonymity in Ancient Speeches, Letters, Lectures, and Translations—A Rejoinder to Bart Ehrman," *JBL* 136 (2017): 381–403.

us"), and then in 3:17, when the author takes up the pen to offer an authenticating sign to show that he really is Paul ("This greeting is in my own hand, Paul's. This is the sign in every letter; this is how I write"). These passages strike many scholars as the marks of someone who is trying too hard to sound authentic.

4. The two letters are often thought to contradict each other on eschatology. First Thessalonians teaches that Jesus will return at an unknown time "like a thief at night," surprising everyone (1 Thess 5:2–3). Second Thessalonians, in contrast, lists a series of events that must take place before Jesus returns (2 Thess 2:1–12). In 1 Thessalonians the parousia is viewed as imminent and unexpected; 2 Thessalonians was written later when it had become clear that the Lord was not going to come as quickly as previously assumed, so the author pushes it off into the middle distance and claims it will be preceded by clear warnings.

5. On a number of occasions 2 Thessalonians uses the very same words as 1 Thessalonians (compare 2 Thess 3:8 with 1 Thess 2:9).[14] Moreover, the letters are structured similarly, including the very unusual double thanksgiving (1 Thess 1:2; 2:13; 2 Thess 1:3; 2:13). The overlap between the two letters makes perfect sense if 2 Thessalonians was written by a later author who had a copy of 1 Thessalonians. He copied Paul's letter to make his new letter sound authentic even while contradicting 1 Thessalonians on matters of substance.

Assessment

Which scenario is more likely? Pauline authorship is certainly possible and was held by everyone until the nineteenth century. The question is whether scenario 2 is more plausible. The argument from the difference in tone is hardly worth considering. Paul was not obliged to take the same tone in every letter, and few, if any, of the passages alleged to be cold or authoritarian would have been read that way by an ancient audience (see commentary on 2 Thess 1:3).[15] The arguments from differences in vocabulary and sentence structure run the danger of being merely impressionistic if they are not backed up by rigorous analysis. Recent work in this area suggests that the vocabulary and syntax of 2 Thessalonians falls within the range of the letters commonly acknowledged to be Paul's.[16] The argument that the author is too concerned to prove his authenticity

14. See the table in Béda Rigaux, *Saint Paul: Les Épitres aux Thessaloniciens*, EBib (Paris: Lecoffre, 1956), 133–34.

15. In 1983 I. Howard Marshall noted the flimsiness of this argument; see *1 and 2 Thessalonians*, NCBC (Grand Rapids: Eerdmans, 1983), 34.

16. See the summary in Campbell, *Framing Paul*, 205–16.

in 2:2 and 3:17 is interesting, but these passages also make good sense on the assumption of Pauline authorship (see commentary on both passages).

Regarding the allegedly contradictory eschatological teaching in the two letters, it is important to remember that one person's contradiction is another's complementary perspective. First Thessalonians says that the Lord will come like a thief at night; 2 Thessalonians speaks of certain events that will presage his coming. We may find these two views contradictory, but the question is whether first-century followers of Jesus would have agreed. In the synoptic Gospels, Jesus combines these two supposedly contradictory perspectives. Like 1 Thessalonians, he affirms that he will return suddenly (Mark 13:32–37; see 1 Thess 5:2–3), like a thief at night (Matt 24:43–44; see 1 Thess 5:2), and that it is necessary to remain awake to watch for his coming (Mark 13:32–37; see 1 Thess 5:4–8). In these very same passages Jesus also says that certain events must take place before he comes and that these will serve as signs that the end is near (Mark 13:3–23; see 2 Thess 2:1–12). Like 2 Thessalonians, Jesus says that these events will include tribulations for the faithful and blasphemous activity in the temple (Mark 13:9–23; see 2 Thess 1:4–2:12). In short, the combined eschatological teaching of the two Thessalonian letters is precisely what we find bundled together in the Gospels. For the early Christians, the parousia was understood as a sudden calamity—especially for unbelievers (see 1 Thess 5:3–4)—but also as something that would be preceded by certain signs known to the faithful.

The overlap in wording and structure of the two letters (number 5 above) is more difficult to explain. It would make sense for a later imitator to lift phrases from 1 Thessalonians, but it is less clear why Paul himself would do so. One suggestion is that Paul simply repeated himself.[17] It would have been easy enough for Paul to repeat phrases like "brothers loved by the Lord/God" if they were still on his mind a short time after writing 1 Thessalonians (1 Thess 1:4; 2 Thess 2:13).[18] It is also likely that Paul or his scribe retained copies of his letters, so it is possible that Paul would have had ongoing access to 1 Thessalonians.[19]

In short, while there is at least one good reason to consider the possibility of non-Pauline authorship for 2 Thessalonians, most of the arguments advanced are surprisingly weak. I would therefore concur with those who continue to maintain that Paul was the author.[20] Regardless of what one makes of such arguments,

---

17. Rigaux, *Les Épitres aux Thessaloniciens*, 152.
18. Malherbe, *Letters to the Thessalonians*, 357.
19. Campbell, *Framing Paul*, 201–2.
20. In the commentary I note occasionally how certain passages would be understood differently if the letter had been written by someone else.

however, 2 Thessalonians will remain an object of study and prayer because the Church has received it as Scripture and understands it to be "inspired by God" (2 Tim 3:16). To paraphrase something Thomas Aquinas once wrote about the so-called deuterocanonical books of the Old Testament, some may doubt who the author is, but we do not doubt what it teaches.[21]

This commentary follows the approach of scenario 1, sketched above. A short time after sending 1 Thessalonians, word came to Paul that some of the issues addressed in the first letter needed further attention. Three main themes appear in the second letter.

1. *God's justice.* The new converts have been suffering at the hands of certain opponents, so Paul encourages them with the assurance that when Jesus returns, God will repay all people for their deeds, punishing evildoers and comforting the afflicted (2 Thess 1:5–10). Paul expects that in the judgment the Thessalonians will be found to have lived lives "worthy" of the kingdom of God, but he continues to pray that this would be the case (1:5, 11–12).

2. *The day of the Lord.* This remains in the future. As noted above, the Thessalonians have gone from thinking that the dead would miss out on the Lord's return to thinking that the Lord has already returned and they missed it (2 Thess 2:1–2). In response, Paul assures them that Jesus's return will be a glorious "manifestation" (Greek *epiphaneia*) they are sure not to miss, and it will be preceded by a final rebellion by Satan and those under his sway (2:3–12). In order to prevent further confusion, Paul charges the Thessalonians to hold fast to the traditions he gave them (2:15).

3. *The freeloaders.* When Paul was in Thessalonica, he found it necessary to emphasize the importance of work (1 Thess 4:11). Certain members of the new church seem to have been all too willing to rely on the charity of their new brothers and sisters. Upon hearing that the problem was ongoing, Paul penned his strongest statement on the matter, instructing the congregation to discipline the erring members (2 Thess 3:6–15).

The Beginning of Christian Literature

As noted above, 1 Thessalonians is often thought to be the oldest of Paul's surviving letters, and therefore the oldest surviving Christian text. Second Thessalonians may very well be the second oldest. Paul's Letters are the only ancient Greek letters that many modern readers have ever encountered, so it is easy to miss the ways in which they were very ordinary and the ways in

21. See Thomas Aquinas, *Principium biblicum* 2.1204.

which they show Paul's creativity. Here are two short, non-Christian letters for comparison. The first was written by a son to encourage his parents, who were worried that they would be caught up in a civil war:

> Esthladas to his father and mother, greetings and health. As I have often written you to be courageous and to take care of yourself until things have settled down, you would once again do well to exhort [*parakaleō*] yourself and those who are with you to be courageous. For I have just discovered that Paos is sailing up river in the month of Tubi with sufficient forces to subdue the mobs at Hermonthis and to deal with them as rebels. Take care of my sisters also and Pelops, Stachys and Senathuris. Farewell. [Egypt, 130 BC][22]

The second example also happens to be from a son to his mother:

> Apollinarius to Taesis, his mother and lady, many greetings. Before all I pray for your health. I myself am well and make supplication for you before the gods of this place. I wish you to know, mother, that I arrived in Rome in good health on the 25th of the month Pachon and was posted to Misenum, though I have not yet learned the name of my company; for I had not gone to Misenum at the time of writing this letter. I beg you then, mother, look after yourself and do not worry about me; for I have come to a fine place. Please write me a letter about your welfare and that of my brothers and of all your folk. And whenever I find a messenger I will write to you; never will I be slow to write. Many salutations to my brothers and Apollinarius and his children and Karalas and his children. I salute Ptolemaeus and Ptolemais and her children and Heraclous and her children. I salute all who love you, each by name. I pray for your health. [Rome, second century AD][23]

Readers familiar with Paul's Letters will immediately notice similarities. These letters, like Paul's and most others, begin with "Person A to Person B, greetings." After the greeting, many letters include a thanksgiving section in which the author reports thanking or praying to the gods on the recipient's behalf. In the second letter quoted above, the soldier tells his mother that he makes "supplication for you before the gods of this place." Paul's Letters typically include a similar thanksgiving section. Like 1 and 2 Thessalonians, both of these letters attempt to comfort the recipients with news that will ease their worries. Also like the Thessalonian letters, the first letter exhorts (*parakaleō*)

---

22. P.Dryton 36. Translation from Stanley K. Stowers, *Letter Writing in Greco-Roman Antiquity*, LEC 5 (Philadelphia: Westminster, 1986), 97–98.

23. P.Mich. 8 491 (A. S. Hunt and C. C. Edgar, trans., *Select Papyri*, vol. 1, *Private Documents*, Loeb Classical Library 266 [Cambridge, MA: Cambridge University Press, 1932], 303).

the recipients to a certain type of behavior (e.g., 1 Thess 4:1).[24] Finally, letters often conclude with greetings from those who are present with the author, as well as to those present with the recipient. We see such greetings in the second letter above and often in Paul's Letters (e.g., Phil 4:21–22).[25]

What would have stood out to the Thessalonians is the way Paul tinkered with letter-writing conventions. In the opening of the letter he changes the word "greetings" (*chairein*) to the related noun *charis* ("grace" or "gift") and adds the traditional Jewish greeting "peace" (Greek *eirēnē*), from the Hebrew *shalom*. The Pauline greeting "grace and peace" also appears in various forms at the conclusions of his letters, replacing the typical "farewell." The result is a subtle reminder at the beginning and end of his letters of God's generosity, a key motif in his thought. Paul's Letters are also unusual because he writes as part of a team, including Silvanus and Timothy in the opening introduction and frequently speaking in the first-person plural ("we"). Moreover, unlike most letters, these were written to be read aloud to a gathered assembly (1 Thess 5:27). Finally, the length and complexity of Paul's Letters along with the authority with which he speaks in them give his letters unusual gravitas. It has been suggested that all these factors came together to form a new epistolary genre, the apostolic letter.[26] With the benefit of hindsight, we can certainly say that 1 Thessalonians kicked off a tradition of Christian letter writing that continued in later New Testament books and the Church Fathers.[27]

The Thessalonian Letters in the Church

First Thessalonians has always belonged in the context of worship, beginning with Paul's command that the letter be read out loud to the gathered church (5:27). After the Thessalonians heard the letter, it is likely that they retained a copy for future reference. Paul and his coworkers may have also kept copies of these and other letters.[28] As the years went by, the Thessalonians may have traded copies of Paul's Letters with other churches, as the churches in Colossae and Laodicea were instructed to do (Col 4:16).[29] We don't have any direct evidence

---

24. Stowers (*Letter Writing in Greco-Roman Antiquity*, 96–97) gives this letter and 1 Thessalonians as examples of paraenetic letters—that is, letters written to commend certain types of behavior and to discourage others.

25. For a list of epistolary clichés running throughout 1 Thessalonians, see Malherbe, *Letters to the Thessalonians*, 90.

26. Boring, *I & II Thessalonians*, 38.

27. See, e.g., *1 Clement*.

28. Harry Y. Gamble, *Books and Readers in the Early Church: A History of Early Christian Texts* (New Haven: Yale University Press, 1995), 96–101.

29. Gamble, *Books and Readers in the Early Church*, 96–101.

of how 1 and 2 Thessalonians were used in the remaining decades of the first century, but from around AD 100 we find Christian writers using phrases that seem to have been gleaned from them, either directly or through the language of the letters passing into common Christian parlance.[30] For instance, the late first-century letter *1 Clement* describes how a bishop should act in a "blameless and holy way" (*amemptōs kai hosiōs* [44.4]), which is very similar to the description of the apostles in 1 Thess 2:10.[31] St. Polycarp, a bishop of Smyrna until his martyrdom in the mid-second century, wrote a letter to the church in Philippi asking them to "shun every kind of evil" (*To the Philippians* 11.1; see 1 Thess 5:22) and not to treat erring Christians as enemies (*To the Philippians* 11.4; see 2 Thess 3:15). Justin Martyr and Irenaeus of Lyon both discuss the coming of the lawless one (see 2 Thess 2:3–9), and Irenaeus is clearly well acquainted with 1 and 2 Thessalonians.[32] The oldest surviving collection of Paul's Letters, which dates roughly to around 200, includes 1 Thessalonians and probably 2 Thessalonians as well.[33] Both letters appear on all the earliest lists of the New Testament canon.[34]

The earliest and best commentary on the Thessalonian letters is that of St. John Chrysostom (d. 407). This commentary is actually a series of homilies, but Chrysostom lingers over Paul's every word and expects the listening congregation to do the same.[35] Chrysostom revered Paul for his pastoral wisdom, and this makes his homilies on the Thessalonian letters particularly good. Unlike some of Paul's other letters, 1–2 Thessalonians do not attempt a great deal of theological heavy lifting. They are primarily letters of consolation and moral exhortation, both of which Chrysostom delights in bringing to his congregation. In the years and centuries to follow, commentators on the Thessalonian letters such as Theodoret of Cyrus (d. ca. 457) and John Damascene (seventh–eighth century) owed much to Chrysostom's homilies. The present commentary turns to Chrysostom for help time and again.

From late antiquity into the medieval period, readers read 1–2 Thessalonians for pastoral wisdom. In 1564, the Catechism of the Council of Trent cited the

---

30. See Rigaux, *Les Épitres aux Thessaloniciens*, 112–20.

31. The words *amemptōs* and *hosiōs* never appear together in Greek literature until 1 Thess 2:10 and then *1 Clement*, according to the Thesaurus Linguae Graecae database.

32. Justin Martyr, *Dialogue with Trypho* 32.4; Irenaeus, *Against Heresies* 3.6.5.

33. Chester Beatty Papyrus 46. Not all of Papyrus 46 has survived, but it would have had room for 2 Thessalonians.

34. Both 1 Thessalonians and 2 Thessalonians are missing from the list given in the sixth-century codex Claromontanus, but this is usually thought to be accidental.

35. It is not clear if these homilies were preached in Antioch or Constantinople, nor is it clear that they were preached sequentially. See Pauline Allen, "John Chrysostom's Homilies on I and II Thessalonians: The Preacher and His Audience," *StPatr* 31 (1997): 3–21.

description of the apostles' behavior (1 Thess 2:1–12) as a template for how parish priests should behave. The Thessalonian letters have also been an important source of instruction on the obligation of Christians to work rather than relying on others (see especially 1 Thess 4:9–12 and 2 Thess 3:6–15). In the ancient Church these passages were important for monks who taught one another that loafing and taking handouts would be their spiritual doom. Above all, 1–2 Thessalonians have been read in the Church as advent letters; that is, they speak of the future coming of the Lord. Paul's prayers that God would find the Church worthy at the last judgment are echoed in various Church liturgies from the ancient Church to today (see Reflection and Application on 2 Thess 1:11–12). Late ancient and medieval Christians pored over Paul's description of the lawless one (2 Thess 2:3), debating whether this would be a particular individual, perhaps someone already alive, or whether this was a description of anyone who opposes God. The best-known and best-loved passage in these letters is 1 Thess 4:13–18, where Paul comforts the Thessalonians with the news that the dead in Christ are not lost but rather will be raised and reunited with the Lord and with the living.

Outline of First and Second Thessalonians

Outline of First Thessalonians

I. Address (1:1)
II. Thanksgiving (1:2–3:13)
    A. The Thessalonians' Reception of the Gospel (1:2–10)
    B. The Apostles' Behavior in Thessalonica (2:1–12)
    C. Second Thanksgiving for Enduring Opposition (2:13–16)
    D. Timothy's Good Report (2:17–3:10)
    E. Transitional Prayer (3:11–13)
III. Exhortation (4:1–5:22)
    A. Introduction (4:1–2)
    B. Fornication (4:3–8)
    C. Brotherly Love and Manual Labor (4:9–12)
    D. The Fate of Dead Christians and the Return of the Lord (4:13–18)
    E. The Suddenness of the Lord's Coming (5:1–11)
    F. Final Admonitions (5:12–22)
IV. Conclusion (5:23–28)

Outline of Second Thessalonians

I. Address (1:1–2)
II. Thanksgiving and Exhortation (1:3–3:5)
    A. Justice for Persecutors and Their Victims (1:3–12)
    B. Events Preceding the Day of the Lord (2:1–12)

Thanksgiving for God's Work in Thessalonica

1 Thessalonians 1:1–10

Ever since Paul was torn away from the new Christians at Thessalonica he longed to return to them and encourage them in their newfound faith. Here in the letter's opening we see him doing what he had wanted to do in person. He reassures them by reminding them of his ongoing prayers on their behalf. He also recounts the astonishing work of God among them that has enabled them to set out on a new way of life in service to God.

Letter Opening (1:1)

---

¹**Paul, Silvanus, and Timothy to the church of the Thessalonians in God the Father and the Lord Jesus Christ: grace to you and peace.**

NT: Acts 15–17; 2 Thess 1:1–2
Catechism: the Church, 751–52; grace, 1996–2005

Artists have often imagined Paul alone at a desk, pen in hand, thoughtfully   1:1
writing to his churches. Deservedly famous works such as Rembrandt's *St. Paul at His Writing Desk* or Valentin de Boulogne's *Saint Paul Writing His Epistles* continue to shape the way we imagine the apostle at work. Yet right from the beginning of 1 Thessalonians we notice a problem with the image of Paul as solitary genius, for this letter says that it is from **Paul, Silvanus, and Timothy**.

Figure 2. *Saint Paul Writing His Epistles* by Valentin de Boulogne (1591–1632).

Paul is working as part of a team here, as he does in five of his letters. The Latin name "Silvanus" almost certainly refers to the companion of Paul known as Silas in the book of Acts. According to Acts, Silas was one of the leaders of the Jerusalem church (Acts 15:22) who had accompanied Paul to Thessalonica (17:1–10). Timothy, the other coauthor mentioned in this letter, was one of Paul's closest companions. In his letter to the Philippians Paul says that Timothy served alongside of him "as a child with a father" (Phil 2:22). Paul also refers to him as a "beloved and faithful son in the Lord" (1 Cor 4:17), "co-worker" (Rom 16:21), and "brother" (1 Thess 3:2). It is with these trusted companions that Paul writes to the Thessalonians. Also, Paul would not have been holding the pen. Instead, he would have dictated to a scribe.[1]

Did Silvanus and Timothy help Paul compose the letter? Scholars are divided on this question. It is clear that Paul is the principal author. His name is listed first, and in 2:18 he refers to himself in the first-person singular ("We decided to go to you—I, Paul, not only once but more than once"). At the same time, the very fact that Paul singles himself out in 2:18 suggests that the rest of the letter is from Silvanus and Timothy as well. Moreover, Paul frequently mentions

---

1. The scribe could have been a fourth, unnamed person. See, e.g., Rom 16:22, where the previously unnamed scribe Tertius greets the Romans. Some have suggested that Silvanus himself was the scribe, noting that 1 Pet 5:12 names a Silvanus as the one through whom that letter was written.

coworkers who are with him without mentioning them as authors in the opening address.[2] He also dictated to scribes who were present but not listed as authors (Rom 16:22; 1 Cor 16:21; Gal 6:11). This shows that Paul did not list his companions as coauthors simply because they were nearby when he was writing. Though we will never know precisely what role Silvanus and Timothy played in composing the letter, we should presume that the Thessalonian Christians read it as if it were from all three men, but with Paul as the leading voice.

The letter is addressed **to the church of the Thessalonians**. In all of Paul's other letters, with the exception of 2 Thessalonians, Paul describes the church in terms of its location. For instance, in 1 Cor 1:2 he writes "to the church of God that is in Corinth." When writing to the Thessalonians, however, Paul describes the church in terms of the people who belong to it. His words could be paraphrased, "to the church that is made up of people who live in Thessalonica."

Paul describes the church of the Thessalonians as being **in God the Father and the Lord Jesus Christ**. Only here and in 2 Thess 1:1 does he describe Christians as being "in God," usually preferring to speak of being "in Christ" (Rom 6:11, 23; 8:1–2; 1 Cor 1:30; Gal 3:26). What does it mean for the church to be "in" God? The Greek could indicate that the Thessalonian church was *brought into being* by God the Father and the Lord Jesus. The Greek preposition *en* ("in") could also indicate that the church has its *location* in God and in Jesus. Regardless of how the phrase is translated, it is clear that God the Father and the Lord Jesus are responsible for the existence of this new church. The words "in God the Father and the Lord Jesus Christ" also show that for Paul those who are "in Christ" are also "in God."[3] A few verses later Paul gives thanks for the empowering work of the Holy Spirit, which has enabled the Thessalonians to become imitators of the apostles and of Jesus by rejoicing in suffering (1 Thess 1:4–6). Even though Paul does not manifest in his letters the fully developed doctrine of the Trinity that will be formulated and defined in later centuries, it is striking to note that in the very first chapter of what is arguably his oldest surviving letter, he speaks of God the Father (1:1); the Son Jesus, who was raised from the dead and who will return (1:10); and the Spirit, who empowers the Thessalonians to rejoice in the midst of suffering (1:5–6).

The words **grace to you and peace** are a celebrated example of Paul's ability to rethink everything in light of the gospel. As noted in the introduction, letters in Paul's day usually began with this formula: "the Writer, to the Addressee,

2. Rom 16:21–23; 1 Cor 1:1; 16:19–21; Phil 1:1; 4:21–22; Col 1:1; 4:7–14.
3. Michael J. Gorman, *Inhabiting the Cruciform God: Kenosis, Justification, and Theosis in Paul's Narrative Soteriology* (Grand Rapids: Eerdmans, 2009), 115.

"Church" (*ekklēsia*) in Scripture

BIBLICAL BACKGROUND

What does Paul mean when he speaks of the "church" (Greek *ekklēsia*) of the Thessalonians? In Paul's day, *ekklēsia* was a common word referring to a congregation of people. It could describe official assemblies, but it was also used to describe crowds, as in Acts 19:32, where *ekklēsia* refers to a confused jumble of people in Ephesus who "had no idea why they had come together."

The word *ekklēsia* is common in the Greek translation of the Jewish Scriptures known as the †Septuagint (commonly abbreviated LXX, the Latin numeral for seventy) as a translation of the Hebrew word *qahal*, meaning "assembly." The term is commonly used to refer to the assembly of the people of Israel, called "the *ekklēsia* of the Lord" or "the *ekklēsia* of the people of God" (see LXX Deut 23:1–2; Judg 20:2; Ps 21:26 [ET 22:26]). For Paul, whose mind was drenched in the language of the Septuagint, the word *ekklēsia* would have called to mind the assembly of God's elect. Paul uses *ekklēsia* to refer to the local Christian communities (1 Cor 16:1), as well as the Church universal (1 Cor 15:9; Gal 1:13; Phil 3:6). Paul describes the Church as the body of Christ, arguing that the diversity of roles and gifts are necessary just as a human body needs many different but complementary parts (Rom 12:4–5; 1 Cor 12:12–31). Echoing Old Testament imagery of God as the husband of Israel (Hosea 2:2, 14–23; Jer 2:2), Paul also depicts the Church as the bride of Christ (2 Cor 11:2–3; Eph 5:25–32) and as the temple of the Holy Spirit (1 Cor 3:16–17; Eph 2:19–22).

greetings [*chairein*]."[4] Paul changes the word "greetings" (*chairein*) to the related noun "grace" (*charis*) and adds the traditional Jewish greeting "peace." In so doing, Paul indicates from the very first line of the letter that this is no ordinary correspondence between friends. The love between Paul and these new converts springs from God's generosity.

Reflection and Application (1:1)

While preaching on the first verse of 1 Thessalonians, St. John Chrysostom discusses the extraordinary honor of being the church (*ekklēsia*) that is "in" God. Chrysostom was a native Greek-speaker who understood that the word *ekklēsia* was common in Paul's world: "For there were many assemblies [plural of *ekklēsia*]." To be an *ekklēsia* in God "is a great honor—nothing is equal to

4. See, e.g., the letter of the Jerusalem church in Acts 15: "The apostles and the presbyters, your brothers, to the brothers in Antioch, Syria, and Cilicia of Gentile origin: greetings [*chairein*]" (v. 23).

it!" Chrysostom also sees this description of the church in Thessalonica as a challenge to his own congregation, warning that those who live in sin reject God's embrace: "May it be, then, that this church also be so called. . . . [But] if someone is a servant of sin, he cannot be called 'in God.'"[5]

Thanksgiving (1:2–4)

> [2]**We give thanks to God always for all of you, remembering you in our prayers, unceasingly** [3]**calling to mind your work of faith and labor of love and endurance in hope of our Lord Jesus Christ, before our God and Father,** [4]**knowing, brothers loved by God, how you were chosen.**

OT: Deut 7:7–8; Ps 34:2
NT: 1 Cor 13:13; 2 Thess 1:3; 2:13
Catechism: theological virtues, 1812–19

After the greeting, Paul's Letters usually include a word of thanksgiving to God   **1:2** and a description of how he prays for the addressees. His letter to the Galatians omits the thanksgiving—it seems that Paul was in no mood to thank God for them. In contrast, here we see Paul overjoyed at the Spirit-empowered reception of the gospel by the Thessalonians. The thanksgiving section of this letter goes on through verse 10 and then starts again in 2:13, finally coming to a conclusion, arguably, at the end of chapter 3. As the letter progresses, we learn why Paul is so effusive in his thanksgiving to God. Though they are a very young community—perhaps only a few months old—they are already manifesting the joy of the Holy Spirit as they experience persecution (1:6).

How is it possible for Paul to **give thanks to God always** and to pray for the Thessalonians **unceasingly**? Though there is an element of hyperbole here, these words should not be dismissed as mere exaggeration. For Paul, prayer is not cordoned off into certain parts of the day or certain days of the week. One's whole life is to be lifted up to God in prayer through the Spirit (Rom 8:26; 12:1). He asks the Thessalonians to "rejoice always," "pray without ceasing," and give thanks in all circumstances (1 Thess 5:16–18). This is not to say that Paul recommends spending every moment reciting a prayer—as if that were possible. Rather, for Paul, prayer and life are coextensive. Every moment is to be caught up in praise to God. As Col 3:17 puts it, "Whatever you do, in word or in deed, do everything in the name of the Lord Jesus, giving thanks to God the Father through him."

5. *Homiliae in epistulam i ad Thessalonicenses* (PG 62:393 [my translation]).

The Life of Prayer

LIVING TRADITION

The Catechism notes that the unending prayer of which Paul speaks is strengthened by having certain times set aside for prayer.

> Prayer is the life of the new heart. It ought to animate us at every moment. But we tend to forget him who is our life and our all. This is why the Fathers of the spiritual life in the Deuteronomic and prophetic traditions insist that prayer is a remembrance of God often awakened by the memory of the heart: "We must remember God more often than we draw breath."[a] But we cannot pray "at all times" if we do not pray at specific times, consciously willing it. These are the special times of Christian prayer, both in intensity and duration.
>
> The Tradition of the Church proposes to the faithful certain rhythms of praying intended to nourish continual prayer. Some are daily, such as morning and evening prayer, grace before and after meals, the Liturgy of the Hours. Sundays, centered on the Eucharist, are kept holy primarily by prayer. The cycle of the liturgical year and its great feasts are also basic rhythms of the Christian's life of prayer. (2697–98)

a. St. Gregory of Nazianzus, *Orat. theo.*, 27, 1, 4: PG 36,16.

1:3   The opening thanksgivings in Paul's Letters serve a double purpose. They encourage the recipients by informing them of Paul's prayers on their behalf, but they also indicate the subjects that Paul is going to develop over the course of the letter. In this sense, the thanksgivings are almost like a little table of contents.[6] For example, Paul begins 1 Corinthians by thanking God for the spiritual gifts that have been given to the Corinthians (1:4–7). This becomes a major topic in the letter (chaps. 12–14). Philippians begins with thanksgiving for the Philippians' partnership in the gospel (1:3–5), a subject to which Paul returns repeatedly (2:25–30; 4:10–20). Here in 1 Thessalonians he thanks God for their **work of faith and labor of love and endurance in hope**. This is probably the first occurrence of the trio of faith, love, and hope in Christian literature, and it anticipates much of what Paul goes on to discuss.

What does Paul mean by "work of faith"? In a homily on this passage St. John Chrysostom offers a helpful explanation: "What is 'the work of faith'? That nothing turns you away from your constancy. . . . If you believe, suffer all things" without falling away.[7] The Thessalonians had responded to the gospel with faith, but since then they experienced hard times (1 Thess 1:6; 2:14; 3:3), and Paul was worried that their faith would be shaken (3:2–5). When Timothy returned from

---

6. Beverly Roberts Gaventa, *First and Second Thessalonians*, IBC (Louisville: John Knox, 1998), 14.
7. *Homiliae* (PG 62:394 [my translation]).

"Work" (*ergon*) in Paul

BIBLICAL BACKGROUND

The expression "work of faith" may sound strange to those accustomed to thinking of work and faith as opposites for Paul. In Galatians and Romans Paul does contrast "works of the law" to "faith of Christ," but he frequently uses the word *ergon* ("work") in a positive sense. In Galatians he goes on to describe the life of faith as "faith working through love" (5:6; see also 6:7–10, 15). Elsewhere he speaks of the work of Christian leaders like himself (1 Cor 3:13–15; 9:1; 16:10; Phil 1:22), declaring that work that is done well will receive a "wage" from God (1 Cor 3:14). Like Jesus, he teaches that God will repay everyone at the final judgment according to their works (Rom 2:6–7; 2 Cor 5:10).[a] He calls his churches to do obedient work (Rom 15:18), to excel in "the work of the Lord" (1 Cor 15:58), and he praises a coworker for doing "the work of Christ" (Phil 2:30). He promises that God will make it possible to "share abundantly in every good work" (2 Cor 9:8 NRSV), which in context refers to sharing money with others.[b] There are numerous other examples.[c] In this letter he asks the Thessalonians to hold their church leaders in high regard "on account of their work" (1 Thess 5:13), and in 2 Thessalonians he prays that God would strengthen them for "every good work [NABRE: "deed"]" (2:17; see also 1:11). Clearly, a simple work/faith antithesis is a caricature of Paul's theology. How can we determine what Paul means in each particular instance? I suggest using this diagnostic question: Is Paul speaking here of *work that is the result of God's grace empowering the believer*, as in 1 Thess 1:3, or is he speaking of *work that sets itself up against God's grace, imagining that God owes us something*, as in Rom 4:2–5?

a. For a good example of this in Jesus's teaching, see Matt 16:24–27; 25:31–46.
b. Though this passage refers to the collection for the poor of Jerusalem, 2 Cor 9:13 shows that Paul is concerned with giving to all who are in need.
c. See Eph 2:10; 4:12; Col 1:10; 1 Tim 2:10; 3:1; 5:10, 25; 6:18; 2 Tim 2:21. Paul also speaks of "work" in the sense of manual labor (1 Thess 4:11).

visiting them, Paul was overjoyed to learn that they continued to trust in God in their suffering (1:6; 3:6–10). Paul gives thanks to God that the Thessalonian Christians' faith continues to manifest itself in works, and he prays for the opportunity to visit them again and strengthen their trust in God even more (3:9–10).

The phrase "labor of love" in contemporary English refers to work done because of the pleasure derived from the task, such as meticulous detailing of a cherished old car. Paul's use of the phrase, however, could be paraphrased "acts of love." It refers to the deeds the Thessalonians have done because of the love they have been given by God. Timothy returned from Thessalonica with the happy news that they were manifesting love (1 Thess 3:6). It is likely that they have provided for one another financially (4:9–10). They have also endured in hope **of our Lord Jesus Christ** and his return in glory despite experiencing hardships (3:1–10; 4:13).

1:4   Paul's use of the word **brothers** (NRSV: "brothers and sisters") is so familiar that it would be easy to miss its significance. The most common meaning of the Greek word for "brother" (*adelphos*) was the same as the English word, but it could also be used to refer to more distant relations (1 Chron 23:21–22), fellow Hebrews (Exod 2:11), or fellow members of various other kinds of religious or political groups.[8] In the teaching of Jesus, the primacy of biological relations is challenged when he defines those who do the will of God as his mother, sisters, and brothers (Matt 12:49–50; Mark 3:34–35; Luke 8:20). When Paul calls Gentiles his "brothers," as here, it suggests that the bond between Christians transcends ethnic dividing lines.

The language of family is more important in 1 Thessalonians than in any other of Paul's Letters. The occurrence of the word "brothers" dwarfs its use in every other letter, occurring at an average of once almost every four verses. First Corinthians, which is often noted for its family language, mentions "brothers" only once every eleven verses. In 1 Thessalonians Paul also compares his relationship with them during their short time together to a nursing mother cherishing her dear children (2:7) and to a father with his sons (2:11). Being torn away from the Thessalonians has left Paul "orphaned" (see 2:17), but when they were together Paul was like a little child (2:7).[9] He also exhorts them to "brotherly love" (see 4:9–12). And of course God is called the Father and Jesus is his Son. This dense web of familial language reminds the Thessalonians that they have been "adopted"—as Paul would put it in later letters (see Rom 8:15, 23; Gal 4:5; Eph 1:5)—into the family of God.

Paul gives thanks because the Thessalonian Christians were **chosen** (*eklogē*) by God. The only other time that Paul uses the word *eklogē* is in Rom 9–11 while discussing how God chose Israel from all the nations. It is striking that he uses it here to describe a congregation that consisted of former pagans. This shows that God's election has extended beyond the boundaries of Israel to embrace the nations as well. Paul's language of the Thessalonians being both **loved** and

---

8. BDAG.

9. In 2:17 the NABRE translates the verb *aporphanizō* as "we were bereft" rather than "we were orphaned." There is an important †textual variant in 2:7. Paul may have described himself as "gentle" rather than as an infant. See the commentary on that verse for a discussion of the variant and of the surprising image of Paul as an infant.

chosen **by God** echoes Moses's explanation of Israel's election in the book of Deuteronomy:

> It was not because you [Israel] are more numerous than all the peoples that the LORD set his heart on you and *chose you*; for you are really the smallest of all peoples. It was because the LORD *loved you* and because of his fidelity to the oath he had sworn to your ancestors, that the LORD brought you out with a strong hand and redeemed you from the house of slavery, from the hand of Pharaoh, king of Egypt. (Deut 7:7–8 [italics added])

As Gordon Fee puts it, "The point, of course, is that Israel did nothing to deserve God's redemption from slavery and election as his people; it was God's doing altogether."[10] Just as divine love is the root cause of Israel's election and subsequent deliverance from Egypt in the exodus, so too it is divine love that has brought the Thessalonians into the family of God.

Reflection and Application (1:3–4)

This mention of faith, love, and hope is probably the earliest written occurrence of what later Christian tradition would identify as the three "theological virtues." This triad appears again in 5:8 and in Paul's subsequent letters (Rom 5:1–5; 1 Cor 13:8–13; Gal 5:5–6; Col 1:4–5). Faith, love, and hope are known as theological virtues because they are gifts from God that make it possible for "Christians to live in a relationship with the Holy Trinity" (Catechism 1812). Though Paul does not use the phrase "theological virtue," this is a deeply Pauline insight. Paul describes faith as a gift from the Spirit (Gal 5:22) that comes through the word of Christ (Rom 10:17). Hope comes by God's grace (2 Thess 2:16) through the Spirit (Gal 5:5). Love is poured into our hearts by the Holy Spirit (Rom 5:5; Gal 5:22) and compels us to live no longer for ourselves "but for him who for their sake died and was raised" (2 Cor 5:15).

Though faith, hope, and love are pure, undeserved gifts from God, it would be a mistake to conclude that they require no effort on our part. To think so would be to fail to recognize just how good these gifts are. When faith, love, and hope are received, they become truly ours. As Charles Cardinal Journet puts it, "God gives us, in Christ, the power to assent to him." Yet "it is my own assent. . . . At times it will have caused me real anguish, will have entailed victory over my passions—it is indeed my own. But it is due even more to God than

---

10. Gordon D. Fee, *The First and Second Letters to the Thessalonians*, NICNT (Grand Rapids: Eerdmans, 2009), 30.

to me, and the first thought that will come to my mind will be to say, 'Thanks be to you, my God, for having given me the power to answer your call; to you be the glory.'"[11]

Joy in Suffering (1:5–8)

[5]**For our gospel did not come to you in word alone, but also in power and in the holy Spirit and [with] much conviction. You know what sort of people we were [among] you for your sake. [6]And you became imitators of us and of the Lord, receiving the word in great affliction, with joy from the holy Spirit, [7]so that you became a model for all the believers in Macedonia and in Achaia. [8]For from you the word of the Lord has sounded forth not only in Macedonia and [in] Achaia, but in every place your faith in God has gone forth, so that we have no need to say anything.**

NT: Matt 16:21–28; 1 Cor 4:15; 11:1; Eph 5:1
Catechism: the Holy Spirit, 686–747

1:5 The thanksgiving that began in verse 2 continues in verse 5. Paul gives thanks to God because the Thessalonians were chosen by God, and in verse 5 Paul explains how he knows this. A paraphrase of verses 4–6 will help illuminate Paul's point:

> How do we know that God chose you? Because our preaching wasn't just talk. God enabled us to preach with power, by means of the Holy Spirit, and with confidence. We also know that God chose you because you became imitators of us and of the Lord by receiving the word in the midst of great affliction with joy from the Holy Spirit.

Paul believed that there were clear signs of divine assistance when he was working in Thessalonica. He did not come **in word alone**. God displayed **power** and filled the apostles with **conviction**.[12] It is possible that this "power" refers to God working through Paul's preaching (Gal 3:1–5), or it may refer to miracles that accompanied his words. Paul describes himself as a miracle-worker on other occasions, such as when he tells the Romans that it is his duty to "lead the

11. Charles Cardinal Journet, *The Meaning of Grace*, trans. A. V. Littledale (New York: P. J. Kenedy, 1962), 58–59.
12. The words "much conviction" might refer to the Thessalonians' conviction. See Abraham J. Malherbe's argument to the contrary in *The Letters to the Thessalonians: A New Translation with Introduction and Commentary*, AB 32B (New Haven: Yale University Press, 2000), 112–13.

Joy in Suffering according to St. Catherine of Siena

LIVING TRADITION

In 1:6 Paul briefly mentions the Thessalonians' joy in the midst of suffering as a sign that the Holy Spirit has enabled them to imitate Jesus. The startling image of Jesus being filled with joy on the cross is at the heart of St. Catherine of Siena's understanding of Christ's passion. Here are two excerpts from her letters that show how she draws especially on John's Gospel to explain Christ's suffering this way:

> He joyously shouts, "It is finished!" [John 19:30]. Yes, those seem to be sorrowful words, but they were words of joy to that soul aflame and consumed in the fire of divine charity, the soul of the incarnate Word, God's Son. It is as if the gentle Jesus wanted to say, "I have completely fulfilled what was written of me. Fulfilled too is my painful desire to redeem the human race. I am happy, exultant, that I have finished this suffering."[a]

> [Breaking into prayer while writing a letter] Oh fire, oh abyss of charity! You are a fire ever burning but not consuming. You are filled with gladness, with rejoicing, with gentleness. To the heart pierced by this arrow, all bitterness seems sweet, every heavy burden becomes light.[b]

a. *The Letters of St. Catherine of Siena*, vol. 1, trans. Suzanne Noffke, OP (Binghamton, NY: Medieval and Renaissance Texts and Studies, 1988), 88.
b. *Letters of St. Catherine of Siena*, 80.

Gentiles to obedience by word and deed, by the power of signs and wonders, by the power of the Spirit" (Rom 15:18–19; see also 2 Cor 12:12). Theodoret of Cyrus puts it this way: "We didn't just offer you instructive words. We demonstrated the truth of the words by performing wonders."[13]

The Thessalonians were gripped by the Holy Spirit, who empowered them **1:6** to become **imitators** of the apostles by accepting the gospel with joy, though they were suffering **great affliction** at the hands of other inhabitants of the city (2:14). For Paul, joy in the midst of suffering for the gospel is a clear sign that God is at work in a person (see 2 Cor 8:1–2). Through their joy in suffering the Thessalonians became imitators not only of the apostles but also of **the Lord** himself.[14] What does this mean? St. John Chrysostom notes that Paul must be referring to Jesus's willing self-emptying in his passion: "How were they imitators of the Lord? Because he also endured many sufferings but did not grieve. Rather,

13. *Interpretatio in xiv epistulas sancti Pauli* (PG 82:629 [my translation]).
14. On "imitation," see also 1 Cor 4:16; 11:1; Gal 4:12; Eph 5:1; Phil 3:17.

he rejoiced, for he came to this gladly. For our sakes he emptied himself [Phil 2:7]."[15] Paul does not retell here the full story of how Christ emptied himself for our sakes, but it is important to note that his words presuppose that the Thessalonians understand what he means. The new Christians in Thessalonica know that those who rejoice in suffering imitate Jesus, who "died for us" (1 Thess 5:10). This was part of the gospel message that they received when Paul was with them, as was the news that those who follow Jesus will also experience suffering (3:2–3).

1:7–8   The Thessalonians have not been Christians for long, but already the news of their joyful reception of the gospel has spread all over Greece and **in every place**. Even if we assume that Paul is exaggerating a bit in his exuberance—"*Everyone* is talking about it!"—we understand that the young Thessalonian church has made a big impression. They have become a **model for all the believers** in the region. The word translated as "believers" is one of Paul's fa-

vorite ways of describing members of the church. By choosing this translation, the NABRE highlights the importance of "believing" in the claims of the gospel. The word translated as "believe" is *pisteuō*; the corresponding noun is *pistis*. "Believe" is one possible translation of *pisteuō*, but *pisteuō* can also denote faith, trust, or faithfulness, among other things. There is a world of difference between mere belief—simply thinking that something is true—and faithfulness, which requires not just belief but faithful action as well. The only way to decide how these Greek words should be translated in a given case is to study their context. Paul sometimes uses *pistis* and related words to refer to belief or intellectual assent (Rom

Figure 3. *St. Catherine of Siena* by Giovanni Battista Tiepolo.

Public domain / WikiArt.org

10:9). There are many occasions, however, when Paul's *pistis* language is best translated with the word "trust." When we say we trust someone—say, a friend or a spouse—we mean that we rely on that person to be good to us.[16] To trust

---

15. *Homiliae* (PG 62:395 [my translation]).

16. When a bank extends someone credit—from *credo*, the Latin word that frequently translates *pisteuō* in the Vulgate—it does so because it has reason to trust that person to pay it back.

someone is to give oneself over to that person and (to one degree or another) make oneself vulnerable to him or her. A good example of *pistis* as trust appears in 1 Cor 10:13, where Paul uses the adjectival form *pistos* while warning the Corinthians not to fall into idolatry: "God is trustworthy [*pistos*]: he will not leave you to be tempted beyond your strength but with the testing he will make a way out so that you will be able to endure it" (my translation). Paul encourages the Corinthians to trust God to stand by them in their times of temptation. Here in 1 Thessalonians Paul describes the church as those who rely on God in times of suffering. Arguably, then, "the faithful" or "the trusting" would be a better translation here than "believers."

Reflection and Application (1:5–8)

For modern people, it is an insult to be called an imitator. We are frequently told how important it is to "be yourself." As Ralph Waldo Emerson puts it, "Insist on yourself; never imitate."[17] In striking contrast, Paul reminds the Thessalonian church how they learned to imitate him (1 Thess 1:6) and the churches in Judea (2:14). Did Paul expect the Thessalonians to be pleased when they heard this? Isn't this tantamount to calling them weak-minded followers with nothing to offer? How would the people in your local church respond if the pastor commended them for "imitating me"?

In order to understand Paul, we must grasp an important difference between his culture and ours. In Paul's day popular teachers frequently appealed to imitation as a path to growth in virtue. In contrast, since the late eighteenth century, Westerners have been increasingly convinced that everyone must find his or her own way. To discover your own unique path, we are told, you must search inside yourself rather than conforming to expectations imposed on you from the outside, whether from religion, family, or the wider society. To quote Emerson once again, "No law can be sacred to me but that of my nature. . . . The only right is what is after my constitution; the only wrong what is against it."[18] Or, as ads for cars, clothing, and beer sometimes put it, "Express yourself."

There are serious problems with the "be yourself" approach to life, one of which is a naïve individualism that imagines that we can live good lives on our own. The Thessalonian Christians were embarking on a new life of

17. Ralph Waldo Emerson, "Self-Reliance," in *Emerson's Essays on Manners, Self-Reliance, Compensation, Nature, Friendship* (New York: Longmans, 1915), 54.

18. Emerson, "Self-Reliance," 31. For an illuminating discussion of how the sentiments expressed by Emerson and other Romantics have become ubiquitous in the last fifty years, see Charles Taylor, *A Secular Age* (Cambridge, MA: Harvard University Press, 2009), 473–504.

worshiping the living God. Having only recently turned from a life of "lustful passion" (4:5), they needed to learn new habits to sustain a life of chastity (4:1–8), sobriety (5:1–8), and care for the weak (5:14), but they couldn't do this on their own. Like us, they needed examples to show them what it means to follow Jesus. This is what they found in Paul, Silvanus, and Timothy. Today we have many similar examples both among those we know personally and through the lives of the saints, a "great cloud of witnesses" (Heb 12:1) that has continued to grow.

The Living and True God (1:9–10)

⁹For they themselves openly declare about us what sort of reception we had among you, and how you turned to God from idols to serve the living and true God ¹⁰and to await his Son from heaven, whom he raised from [the] dead, Jesus, who delivers us from the coming wrath.

OT: Ezek 7:19; Zeph 1:15–18; Sir 5:6–7
NT: Matt 3:7; Luke 3:7; Rom 1:18–32
Catechism: the living God, 205

1:9–10 This short description of what people are saying about the Thessalonians is packed with important hints about the identity of the Thessalonian converts and about the gospel message that they received from Paul. The mention of turning away **from idols** suggests that the converts were Gentiles or non-Israelites. We don't know as much about religious life in ancient Thessalonica as we would like because the bustling modern city of Thessaloniki makes archaeological research difficult. We do know that Thessalonica was the home of many cults dedicated to a number of different deities, such as Isis, an Egyptian goddess and giver of immortality, or Dionysus, the Greek god of wine and fertility.[19] Among the deities that arguably would have caused the most trouble for the new Christians in Thessalonica were the Roman emperors themselves. When Augustus became emperor of Rome, he had his adopted father, Julius Caesar, declared divine. As Caesar's son, Augustus was called the son of a god. Thessalonica traditionally was loyal to Rome, and the city seems to have embraced worship of both deceased and living emperors. Coins from Thessalonica bear the image of Caesar and the word "God" (Greek *theos*). During Augustus's

19. Karl P. Donfried, "The Cults of Thessalonica and the Thessalonian Correspondence," *NTS* 31 (1985): 336–56.

Figure 4. *Divus* (Divine) Julius Caesar with ΘEOC inscription (obverse) and Octavian with ΘΕCCΑΛΟ-ΝΙΚΕΩΝ (reverse). Struck circa 28/27 BC in Thessalonica, Macedon.

Figure 5. *Divus* Julius Caesar with ΘEOC inscription (obverse). Struck circa AD 14 in Thessalonica, Macedon.

Figure 6. *Divus* Julius Caesar with ΘEOC inscription (obverse). Likely struck in Thessalonica, Macedon, between 27 BC and AD 14.

reign a temple was built in Thessalonica for the worship of the emperor. An inscription from the time refers to the appointment of a priest of "Emperor Caesar Augustus son of god."

Paul heightens the difference between Jewish monotheism and pagan worship by contrasting idols with **the living and true God**. In biblical and postbiblical traditions, the phrase "the living God" is used to express God's superiority to pagan deities, which are by implication dead or false gods. In Dan 14:5, King Cyrus asks Daniel why he refuses to worship Bel. Daniel responds, "Because I do not revere idols made with hands, but only the living God who made heaven and earth and has dominion over all flesh."[20] The phrase "the living God" also frequently connotes God's power to punish those who oppose Israel. For instance, before crossing into the promised land Joshua tells the Israelites, "By this you will know that there is a living God among you: he will certainly

20. See also 1 Sam 17:26, 36.

drive out before you the Canaanites and the Hittites and the Hivites and the Perizzites and the Girgashites and the Amorites and the Jebusites" (Josh 3:10 [my translation]).[21] The mention of **coming wrath** hints at something similar here. Paul warns that at an unknown time a day of judgment will arrive (1 Thess 5:1–5), calling to account all evildoers.

Paul's description of the one he calls God's **Son** in verse 10 shows that he had taught the Thessalonians that Jesus, a flesh-and-blood human being who had recently been killed in Judea, was God's Son (1:5–6; 2:14–15; 5:9–10). God raised Jesus from the dead, and Jesus now resides in heaven with God, where he acts jointly with God the Father on behalf of the Church (1:1; 3:11). The Thessalonians accepted this message, turned from idolatry, and now have the privilege of serving God while they await the return of Jesus from heaven. By reminding the Thessalonians of their shared belief, Paul prepares them for his further instruction on the fate of those who die before the Lord's return (4:13–18).

Reflection and Application (1:9–10)

It is difficult for many of us to know how to feel about Paul's insistence that God's "wrath" is coming. Paul mentions it almost in passing here, but he picks up and develops this theme repeatedly in the letters to the Thessalonians. How could a good God be the source of wrathful judgment? How is it possible to worship such a God? One way of thinking about this question is to imagine its opposite. What would it mean if God never brought judgment? What if God's final response to all human behavior was a shrug of the shoulders—or, worse, an affirmation that all the evil we have inflicted on one another is just fine? It is curious that we have become uncomfortable with divine wrath in an age in which humans have unleashed evils on one another unlike any the world had seen before. C. S. Lewis gets to the heart of the matter:

> When Christianity says that God loves man, it means that God *loves* man: not that He has some "disinterested," because really indifferent, concern for our welfare, but that, in awful and surprising truth, we are the objects of His love. You asked for a loving God: you have one. . . . Not a senile benevolence that drowsily wishes you to be happy in your own way, not the cold philanthropy of a conscientious magistrate, nor the care of a host who feels responsible for the comfort of his guests, but the consuming fire Himself, the Love that made the worlds, persistent

21. See also Deut 5:26; 2 Kings 19:4 // Isa 37:4.

as the artist's love for his work and despotic as a man's love for a dog, provident and venerable as a father's love for a child, jealous, inexorable, exacting as love between the sexes.[22]

If there is no divine wrath, it is hard to see how there could be divine love. The scandal of God's wrath is inherent to the gospel itself.

22. C. S. Lewis, *The Problem of Pain* (1940; repr., New York: HarperCollins, 2009), 39–40.

Paul's Behavior in Thessalonica

1 Thessalonians 2:1–8

In this section Paul continues to retell the story of his relationship with the Thessalonians.[1] In these verses and on into 2:9–12, Paul has much to say about what he, Silvanus, and Timothy were *not* like in Thessalonica, denying that they were greedy, deceptive, pushy, or sycophantic, among other things. Paul insists that he and his companions treated the Thessalonians like family. Scholars have not come to a consensus regarding why Paul spends so much time explaining what he did and did not do. There are two main explanations on the table. The first, which was dominant in modern scholarship until about thirty years ago, argues that Paul is defending himself against some unnamed detractor, an opponent from within the church or outside it.[2] The second view, which owes much to the work of Abraham Malherbe, reads 2:1–12 as †paraenesis, reminding the Thessalonians of how the apostles behaved and exhorting them to follow the apostolic example.[3] Which interpretation has the better argument? Though it certainly is possible that there were rumors around the city of Thessalonica that Paul was a charlatan, there are good reasons to doubt that Paul's principal concern is to defend himself against attacks. This passage is

---

1. The recounting of their relationship doesn't end until 3:10.

2. Some cite Acts 17:1–9 as evidence that the opponents were certain Jews in Thessalonica. Recent advocates of the view that Paul is defending himself include Jeffrey A. D. Weima, *1–2 Thessalonians*, BECNT (Grand Rapids: Baker Academic, 2014), 121–25.

3. Abraham J. Malherbe, "'Gentle as a Nurse': The Cynic Background to 1 Thessalonians 2," in *Paul and the Popular Philosophers* (Minneapolis: Fortress, 1989), 35–48; see also Malherbe's other works on 1 Thessalonians, including his commentary *The Letters to the Thessalonians: A New Translation with Introduction and Commentary*, AB 32B (New Haven: Yale University Press, 2000), 153–63.

quite similar to other first-century descriptions of how a good teacher should behave (see sidebar, "Dio Chrysostom," p. 53), and the rest of the letter gives no indication that Paul is on the defensive. On the contrary, Timothy reported that the Thessalonians continued to hold the apostles in high regard (3:6). Perhaps the strongest evidence that this section should be read as moral exhortation is the fact that most of the behaviors described in 2:1–12 resurface later in the letter when Paul discusses the areas in which the Thessalonians need to improve. He highlights the apostles' courage despite persecution (2:1–2), their attempt to please God and be found blameless (2:4, 6, 10), their avoidance of "impurity" (see 2:3), their hard work to avoid being a burden on others (2:9; see also 2:5), and their love for the Thessalonians (2:8) and gentle admonishment of them (2:7–8, 11–12). All of these issues come up again in the letter—often using the very same words—but in reference to the Thessalonians' own moral progress.[4] When reading 2:1–8 as well as 2:9–12, therefore, one ought not imagine Paul feeling hurt and defensive (see 2 Cor 11 for a good example of that). Instead, it is best to read this passage like the rest of the letter—that is, as an attempt to build up the Thessalonians' faith by strengthening his relationship with them and by giving them an example to imitate.

Preaching amid Opposition (2:1–2)

---

[1]**For you yourselves know, brothers, that our reception among you was not without effect.** [2]**Rather, after we had suffered and been insolently treated, as you know, in Philippi, we drew courage through our God to speak to you the gospel of God with much struggle.**

NT: Acts 16:11–17:10

Paul's mission to Thessalonica was among his most successful ventures, but   **2:1–2** it did not begin without difficulties. Before Paul arrived in Thessalonica he **suffered** and was **insolently treated** in nearby Philippi. Readers of Acts will think of how the chief magistrates of the city had Paul and Silas stripped, beaten, flogged, and thrown into prison for "advocating customs that are not lawful" (Acts 16:20–24). His difficulties continued in Thessalonica, where he faced **much struggle.** According to Acts 17:5–10, Paul was accused of

4. On enduring persecution, see 1:2–6; on pleasing God and being found blameless, see 3:13–4:1 and 5:23; on avoiding impurity, see 4:7; on working so as not to burden others, see 4:9–12; on love for others in the church, see 3:12; on the gentle admonishment of others in the church, see 5:14.

Gregory the Great on Enduring Conflict

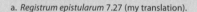

LIVING TRADITION

St. Gregory the Great cites 1 Thess 2:1 in a letter to Narses, a man enduring opposition because of his ministry. Gregory believed that Paul's suffering in Philippi was the reason his ministry bore fruit in Thessalonica.

I beg you during this time to call to mind something I believe you never forget: "That all who desire to live a pious life in Christ suffer persecution" [2 Tim 3:12]. . . . Let's listen to what the same teacher of the gentiles said to his disciples: "You yourselves know, brothers, that our coming to you was not in vain, but rather we suffered and were treated insolently" [1 Thess 2:1–2]. Look, dear boy, the holy preacher said his entrance would have been empty if he had not been shamefully mistreated. In your charity you wish to say good things, but you avoid enduring evil things. For this reason it is necessary that you prepare yourself more rigorously in the midst of adversities, so that adversity might all the more increase your desire for the love of God and your pursuit of good teaching.[a]

a. *Registrum epistularum* 7.27 (my translation).

treasonous behavior and was forced to flee Thessalonica during the night. In spite of these difficulties, Paul and his companions **drew courage through our God** and spoke boldly. Paul's point is not that they were unusually brave but that God was working in them to enable them to speak the gospel despite the difficulties they encountered.

God was at work in Paul to ensure that his time in Thessalonica **was not without effect**. The words "without effect" (*kenē*) could also be translated as "in vain" or "empty." On a number of occasions Paul speaks of his confidence that he is not laboring or running "in vain" (see especially 1 Cor 15:58; Gal 2:2; Phil 2:16). In 1 Thess 3:5 Paul reveals that he had been worried that the Thessalonians had fallen away and that his work had been "in vain" (*eis kenon*). This language echoes Isa 65:17–25, where God promises to create a new heavens and new earth, in which God's chosen "shall not toil in vain." Paul believed that this new creation had already broken into this world through the death and resurrection of Jesus, and that the efficacy of his preaching was due to the power of Christ. As he told the Corinthians, "Be firm, steadfast, always fully devoted to the work of the Lord, knowing that in the Lord your labor is not in vain" (1 Cor 15:58). His confidence was based not on his own speaking abilities or anything else of his, but on the Holy Spirit (1 Thess 1:5), who was at work.

The Character of Paul's Ministry (2:3–8)

> [3]Our exhortation was not from delusion or impure motives, nor did it work through deception. [4]But as we were judged worthy by God to be entrusted with the gospel, that is how we speak, not as trying to please human beings, but rather God, who judges our hearts. [5]Nor, indeed, did we ever appear with flattering speech, as you know, or with a pretext for greed—God is witness— [6]nor did we seek praise from human beings, either from you or from others, [7]although we were able to impose our weight as apostles of Christ. Rather, we were gentle among you, as a nursing mother cares for her children. [8]With such affection for you, we were determined to share with you not only the gospel of God, but our very selves as well, so dearly beloved had you become to us.

NT: Luke 22:24–30
Catechism: ministers are servants of all, 876
Lectionary: 1 Thess 2:2b–8; Memorial of Saint Augustine of Canterbury; Memorial of Saint Pius X

Paul denies that he preached out of **delusion, impure motives,** or **deception.**   **2:3–4**
The first word of the three, *planē*, probably refers to a mistaken belief (see Rom 1:27; 2 Thess 2:11). The third word, "deception" (*dolos*), refers to leading others into a mistaken belief. By combining "delusion" and "deception," Paul denies that he was deceived and also that he was deceiving. The word translated as "impure motives" is *akatharsia*, which means "impurity" or "uncleanliness." This word could refer to impure or immoral behavior in general, but in Paul's Letters *akatharsia* usually refers to sexual immorality (Rom 1:24; 2 Cor 12:21), including one instance later in this letter (1 Thess 4:7). Then as now, there were teachers who used their influence to coerce others into sexual relationships. Paul was confident that the Thessalonians would attest that he was not one of those teachers.

Instead of speaking deceitfully or with ulterior motives, they preached in a manner appropriate for those **judged worthy by God to be entrusted with the gospel.** One might compare this description to an employer who first tests a potential employee to see if she or he has what it takes to do the job and then continues to watch the new hire to ensure that good work is done. God has tested Paul and his companions and found them worthy of being "entrusted" with the gospel. Though they have received this trust, Paul is keenly aware that God continues to test his work. St. Basil the Great cites this verse along with Matt 6:1–2 to argue that Christians should do their work as if they were

---

The Second Vatican Council on How the Apostles Preached the Gospel

LIVING TRADITION

In its declaration on religious freedom, *Dignitatis Humanae* (Declaration on Human Freedom), the Council cited 1 Thess 2 as an example of how the apostles relied on the power of the word of God rather than using coercion or other methods that do not respect the dignity of human beings.

> Taught by the word and example of Christ, the Apostles followed the same way. From the very origins of the Church the disciples of Christ strove to convert men to faith in Christ as the Lord; not, however, by the use of coercion or of devices unworthy of the Gospel, but by the power, above all, of the word of God. (Cf. 1 Cor. 2:3–5; 1 Thess. 2:3–5.) (11)

---

standing before God: "We should not wish to put ourselves on display . . . but should instead act as if we are speaking for the glory of God in his presence."[5]

2:5–6   Paul denies that he used **flattering speech**. Aristotle defined a flatterer as someone who pleases others for the sake of self-advantage.[6] In Paul's own time, Dio Chrysostom complained about the abundance of flatterers among those who purported to be teachers (see sidebar, "Dio Chrysostom," p. 53). A **pretext for greed** goes hand in hand with flattery. The word "pretext" (*prophasis*) refers to an excuse for bad behavior, such as a preacher who pretends to have the listeners' best interests at heart, while really "preaching for money," as Theodoret of Cyrus puts it while commenting on this verse.[7] Paul denies that he was after their money, a claim that he can back up on the fact that he supported himself through manual labor. Similarly, Paul did not seek **praise** from people, either from the Thessalonians or from others. The word translated as "praise" (*doxa*) can refer to complimentary words, gifts, or special honors bestowed on someone important. St. John Chrysostom argues that apostles deserved "praise" beyond that of royal emissaries because they were sent by God, yet they thought it better to remain humble.[8]

In 2:5 Paul says that **God is witness** to his upright behavior in Thessalonica. In 2:10 he refers to both the Thessalonians and God as "witnesses." The word "witness" (*martys*) was common in legal or contractual settings referring to those who could testify to something, such as the requirement in Deut 19:15

---

5. *Regulae morales* 31.836 (my translation). See also *Regulae morales* 31.720.
6. *Nicomachean Ethics* 2.7.
7. *Interpretatio in xiv epistulas sancti Pauli* (PG 82:633 [my translation]).
8. *Homiliae in epistulam i ad Thessalonicenses* (PG 62:402).

Dio Chrysostom

The writings of the Greek rhetorician and philosopher Dio Chrysostom (AD 40–115) provide striking parallels to 1 Thess 2:3–8.[a] In this passage, he contrasts the reliable teacher to those who seek their own gain. The italicized words correspond to identical or related Greek words in Paul's self-description.

> To find a man who *speaks courageously* with *purity* and *guilelessness*, who does not pretend for the sake of *praise* or money, but out of goodwill and concern for others is ready, if necessary, to be mocked and to bear the disorder and confusion of the multitude—[to find such a man] is not easy but rather the good fortune of a city, so great is the scarcity of noble and free men, and such the abundance of *flatterers*, charlatans, and sophists. For my part, I seem not to have chosen this for myself, but by the will of some deity.[b]

There are many other similar examples in Dio Chrysostom's writings.[c] Like Paul, Dio is explaining how a teacher ought to behave, not defending himself from an attack.

a. Dio Chrysostom is not to be confused with St. John Chrysostom, the Christian orator who also was known as "golden mouth" (i.e., *chrysostom*).
b. *Orations* 32.11–12 (my translation).
c. See Malherbe, "'Gentle as a Nurse,'" 35–48.

that two or three witnesses are necessary to convict someone of a crime. In 1 Sam 12 the prophet Samuel looks back on his career leading Israel and calls God to witness to the fact that he was honest and upright as a leader. Samuel says, "The Lord is witness [*martys*] among you . . . that you have found nothing stolen in my hand" (LXX 1 Sam 12:5 [my translation]).[9] Similarly, Paul is confident that God will testify to his upright behavior with the Thessalonians. How can God be a witness? Did Paul expect God to testify on his behalf? Other references to God as witness in Scripture provide hints as to what Paul means. Naming God as a witness expresses the belief that God knows our actions and thoughts. As Wis 1:6 puts it, evil words will be punished because "God is the witness [*martys*] of the inmost self / and the sure observer of the heart / and the listener to the tongue" (see also LXX Mal 3:5; Jer 36:23 [ET 29:23]; 49:5 [ET 42:5]). By calling God as witness, then, one expresses confidence that God knows the truth, even if others do not.[10]

9. See also LXX Gen 31:44; 1 Sam 20:23; 20:42; Acts 5:32.
10. Matthew V. Novenson, "'God Is Witness': A Classical Rhetorical Idiom in Its Pauline Usage," *NovT* 52 (2010): 355–75.

2:7–8   As **apostles of Christ**, Paul and his companions had authority given to them by Jesus himself (1 Cor 9:1; 15:1–11). As bearers of this authority, Paul says that they **were able to impose our weight**, or, as we might put it, they could have "thrown their weight around," but they thought it better to be humble. In the Greek this phrase is connected to the preceding verse, where Paul denies that he sought glory from human beings. Then as now, authority figures often wore their power on their sleeves by seeking praise and by reminding those around them of their special status. Paul may also be referring to the way he, Silvanus, and Timothy worked hard so as not to place financial burdens on the Thessalonians. The word translated as "weight" is *baros*. Paul uses a related word a few verses later when he recalls how they worked "not to burden [*epibareō*] any of you" (1 Thess 2:9 [see also 2:5; 2 Thess 3:8]). Apostles had the right to expect financial assistance from the churches, a right that was based on a command of Jesus (see 1 Cor 9:1–18, especially v. 14). Paul, however, frequently chose not to accept financial assistance because, as he puts it in 1 Cor 9:12, "We endure all things rather than give hindrance to the gospel of Christ" (my translation). He gave up his right to payment in order to "offer the gospel free of charge" (1 Cor 9:18).

This is the earliest occurrence of the word "apostle" (*apostolos*) in a Christian text, and the only occurrence in the Thessalonian correspondence. Does the plural "apostles of Christ" indicate that Silvanus and Timothy were also considered apostles? The answer to this question depends in part on whether one thinks that the letter is from all three men or only from Paul. As noted in the commentary on 1 Thess 1:1, there is good reason to suppose that the Thessalonians would have read the letter as if it were from all three men, with Paul as the principal voice. Nevertheless, it is highly unlikely that Timothy was considered an apostle. In later letters of Paul, Timothy is not given the title "apostle" in the opening address (see 2 Cor 1:1). It is harder to judge in the case of Silvanus. At the conclusion of 1 Thessalonians Paul alone solemnly commands his audience to read the letter to "all the brothers" (5:27), which could indicate that they recognized that Paul had a unique authority.

Verse 7 contains a famous †textual variant. Some ancient manuscripts have "we were *infants* among you" rather than **we were gentle among you**. In Greek the difference between "we were infants" (*egenēthēmennēpioi*) and "we were gentle" (*egenēthēmenēpioi*) is only one letter, so it would have been easy for scribes to change one into the other unintentionally. Scholars are divided on the question of which of these is more likely to have been written by Paul. This may seem like a technical question of relevance only to scholars, but this one letter makes an enormous difference for how one reads the entire passage.

"Apostle" in the New Testament

The word "apostle" is used in a number of different ways in early Christian literature. The word comes from the Greek verb *apostellō* ("send") and can refer to anyone who is sent (John 13:16).[a] On other occasions the term is restricted to a group of twelve disciples (Matt 10:2; Mark 3:14; Rev 21:14) who were chosen by Jesus from among the larger group of disciples (Luke 6:13) and who became witnesses to Jesus's earthly ministry and resurrection (Acts 1:21–22). On still other occasions the term is applied to a wider group who were called by the risen Jesus to preach the gospel (Acts 14:4, 14). It is this last definition that applies to Paul. Paul's apostleship was disputed by some (1 Cor 9:1–2), perhaps in part because he apparently did not recognize the Twelve as having authority superior to his (Gal 1:1–2:10). It was important to Paul that his apostleship came not from human beings but rather, as he states to the Galatian churches, directly "through Jesus Christ and God the Father who raised him from the dead" (Gal 1:1).

a. Heb 3:1 refers to Jesus as an apostle in this sense.

The most reliable ancient manuscripts tend to support "infants." Despite this evidence, some find it hard to believe that Paul would have said, "We were infants among you, as a nursing mother cares for her children." That would be an abrupt shift of imagery, even by Paul's standards.[11] Those who think that Paul wrote "infants" respond by arguing that the NABRE and other translations have incorrectly punctuated this passage. Verses 2:1–8 feature a series of "not X but Y" contrasts.[12] Following this pattern, verses 5–8 should be punctuated like this:

Sentence 1: Nor, indeed, did we ever appear with flattering speech, as you know, or with a pretext for greed (God is witness), nor did we seek praise from human beings, either from you or from others (though we were able to impose our weight as apostles of Christ), but we became infants among you.

11. See the footnote in the NABRE: "Many excellent manuscripts read 'infants' (*nēpioi*), but 'gentle' (*ēpioi*) better suits the context here."

12. Verses 1–2 say that their reception *was not* in vain, *but rather* (*alla*) the apostles were emboldened to speak. Verses 3–4 say that their exhortation *was not* from impure motives, and so on, *but rather* (*alla*) they spoke as those entrusted by God. Verses 5–7 continue this pattern: the apostles *did not* use flattering speech, and so on, *but rather* (*alla*) they were like infants. The NABRE ignores this pattern in order to accommodate the poorly attested "gentle." For an extended argument, see Gordon D. Fee, *The First and Second Letters to the Thessalonians*, NICNT (Grand Rapids: Eerdmans, 2009), 65–72.

ΕΞΑΝΘΡωΠωΝΛΟΞΑ
ΟΥΤΕΑΦΥΜωΝΟΥΤΕ
ΑΠΑΛΛωΝΑΥΝΑΜΕΝΟΙ
ΕΝΒΑΡΕΙΕΙΝΑΙωϹΧΥΑ
ΠΟϹΤΟΛΟΙΑΛΛΑ**ΕΓΕΝ**ᴴ
ΘΗΜΕΝΝΗΠΙΟΙΕΝΜΕ
ϹωΫΜωΝωϹΕΑΝΤΡᵒ

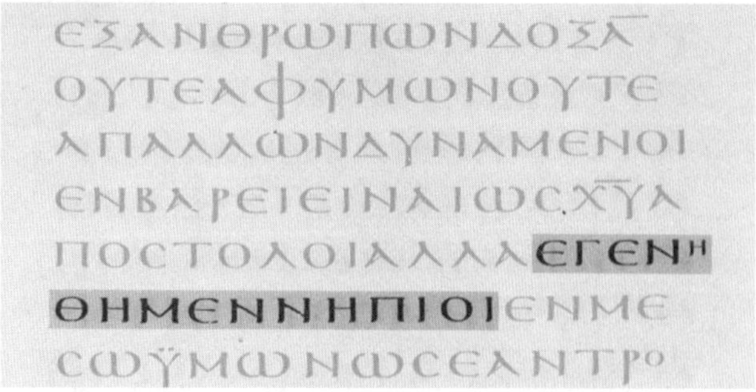

Figure 7. First Thessalonians 2:7 in Codex Vaticanus, which says (in highlight), "We became infants."

Sentence 2: Just as a nurse cares for her own children, so, in our deep longing for you, we were pleased to share with you not only the gospel of God but also our very selves, because you have become beloved to us. (my translation)

Paul doesn't say "we were infants like a nurse." Rather, the phrase "we became infants among you" completes the thought that began in verse 5. Then, in the second half of verse 7, Paul picks up a new image: the apostles were like a nurse cherishing her children. The shift from "infants" to nursing mother is somewhat abrupt, but this is not unusual for Paul (see Gal 4:19).

If Paul wrote "gentle," he would be explaining that he did not throw his weight around as an apostle, preferring instead to be kind to the Thessalonians. If, as I suggest, Paul wrote "infants," his point would be that he was humble and innocent.[13] Rather than making his weight felt in Thessalonica, Paul humbled himself and became like a child. The Church Father Origen saw a link between this verse and Jesus's teaching that those who want to be great must become like children. After discussing Matt 18:1–6 and Luke 9:48 ("For the one who is least among all of you is the one who is the greatest"), Origen writes, "He who humbles himself and 'becomes an infant in the midst' of all the faithful, though he be an apostle or bishop . . . is the 'little one' pointed out by Jesus."[14] In other words, by making himself small, Paul shows the path to greatness for all who would follow the crucified Messiah.

The image of apostles as children is followed by the even more surprising maternal image of apostles as nurses. The NABRE translates the end of verse 7 **as a nursing mother cares for her children**. The word *trophos* ("nursing mother") could refer to a nursing mother, but usually it referred to a woman who was

13. See the similar use of the related verb in 1 Cor 14:20: "In respect to evil be like infants [*nēpiazō*], but in your thinking be mature."

14. *Commentarium in evangelium Matthaei* 13.29 (my translation). See the use of "infant" (*nēpios*) to define the attitude of those who understand Jesus and will enter the kingdom in Matt 11:25; Luke 10:21. See also Matt 21:16.

Textual Criticism

BIBLICAL BACKGROUND

None of the original biblical manuscripts survive, from any book of the Bible. We possess many ancient copies of the books of the New Testament, but none of them are identical. The vast majority of the differences among these copies are minor, such as differences in spelling, but some introduce important questions about what the author originally wrote.[a] As a result, it is necessary to compare them in order to ascertain what the biblical author is most likely to have written. In addition to providing evidence of what the biblical author originally wrote, these manuscripts provide important insight into how biblical texts were interpreted in antiquity, because scribes sometimes changed the text to reflect what they thought it meant. Modern scholars have benefited from the discovery of many previously unknown manuscripts and from a refinement of our understanding of how the existing manuscripts relate to one another, but Christians have engaged in textual criticism of the Bible since antiquity.

Christians sometimes find textual criticism unsettling. How can Scripture be God's word if we're not sure which words belong in Scripture? In the liturgy the reading of the Bible is followed by the acclamation "the word of the Lord." This is a reminder that God is able to speak to the Church through imperfect translations based on various Greek, Hebrew, and Aramaic texts. After all, the originals no longer exist, and even if they did, few Christians would have the skill to understand them. The apostles cited the †Septuagint as Scripture, despite its differences from Hebrew texts, and the Vulgate has long had a privileged place in the Latin Church. In the same way, we hear "the word of the Lord" spoken in our own language in the liturgy.[b] Textual criticism of the Bible is an important task, but while our translations and text-critical work remain imperfect and we debate which manuscript has the superior reading, God will continue to speak to the Church through the Scriptures.

a. E.g., see the footnotes in any modern translation of the Bible at Luke 22:19–20.
b. For a detailed discussion of these matters, see *Divino Afflante Spiritu* (Inspired by the Holy Spirit) 12–14, and Paul Griffiths, "Which Are the Words of Scripture?," *TS* 72 (2011): 703–22.

hired to breastfeed or otherwise nourish a child.[15] Wet-nurses were common in the ancient world, and the children they nourished frequently remembered them fondly.[16] Indeed, though this image may seem bizarre to us, for those

15. LSJ; BDAG. In the Septuagint *trophos* translates a Hebrew word that means "one who gives suck."
16. Keith R. Bradley, "Wet-nursing at Rome," in *The Family in Ancient Rome: New Perspectives*, ed. Beryl Rawson (Ithaca, NY: Cornell University Press, 1986), 220; Beverly R. Gaventa, "Apostles

with firsthand experiences of wet-nurses, Paul's language would have painted a vivid picture of how he carried himself as an apostle. St. John Chrysostom used the image of the nurse to summarize all of 2:1–8: "As a nurse cares for her own children, so it is necessary for a teacher to be. The nurse does not flatter that she may obtain glory. She does not ask her little children for money. She is not burdensome or severe with them. Are not nurses even more kind than mothers?"[17]

The vividness of Paul's self-description is better understood in light of the alternate punctuation suggested above. Though the NABRE puts a period at the end of verse 7, in Greek it is likely that the sentence continues into verse 8 and provides further explanation of what Paul means by comparing himself to a nurse: "Just as a nurse cares for her own children, so, in our deep longing for you, we were pleased to share with you not only the gospel of God but also our very selves, because you have become beloved to us" (my translation). Paul gave his whole self to the Thessalonians, just as a nurse nourishes her children from her own body. He did not simply tell the Thessalonians about the gospel. He lived it by giving himself to them in imitation of Jesus, "who died for us, so that . . . we may live together with him" (1 Thess 5:10).

Reflection and Application (2:3–8)

These verses are an incisive description of common errors that have destroyed the credibility and effectiveness of many ministers. Greed, love of the limelight, and superciliousness have derailed many who wanted to serve the Church. Paul was already guarding against these dangers in the Church's earliest days, and two thousand years later we are all too aware that these problems have not gone away. Paul's description of leadership through patient, self-giving care, humility, and even vulnerability remains a powerful corrective to the human tendency to dominate others and work for personal gain. His teaching echoes that of his Lord, who had taught that one must become like a child in order to enter the kingdom (Matt 18:3) and that leaders in the Church must assume a lowly status, just as he did (Matt 20:24–28; Luke 22:24–27). While preaching on 1 Thess 2, St. Augustine makes a comment that gets to the heart of the matter: "There is

---

as Babes and Nurses in 1 Thessalonians 2:7," in *Faith and History: Essays in Honor of Paul W. Meyer*, ed. John T. Carroll, Charles H. Cosgrove, and E. Elizabeth Johnson (Atlanta: Scholars Press, 1990), 201.

17. *Homiliae* (PG 62:402 [my translation]). In Greek this is a series of rhetorical questions. The implied answer is obvious in Greek but not in English, so I have taken the liberty of translating loosely for clarity's sake.

The Catechism of Trent on Infants and Nurses

LIVING TRADITION

The preface of the Catechism of the Council of Trent draws on 1 Thess 2:7–8 to explain how priests must humbly and patiently adapt their teaching to the abilities of the people they serve:

> [When teaching] the natural ability, cultural background and particular circumstances of the people must be given attention, so that he who teaches may become all things to all people and be able to gain all to Christ (1 Cor 9:22). . . . Our zeal for the teaching of Christian doctrine should not be diminished because sometimes it must explain matters which seem humble and unimportant, and hence perhaps uninteresting to minds accustomed to the more sublime truths of religion. If the Wisdom of the eternal Father came down upon this earth in the lowliness of our flesh to teach us the way to the heavenly life, who is there whom the love of Christ does not compel to become 'little in the midst of his brethren, like a nurse caring for her children' (1 Thess 2:7)? St. Paul wished for the salvation of his neighbor so much that he desired to deliver "not only the Gospel of Jesus Christ to them, but even his own life for them," as he himself says (1 Thess 2:8).ᵃ

> a. *The Roman Catechism: Translated and Annotated in Accord with Vatican II and Post-Conciliar Documents and the New Code of Canon Law*, trans. Robert I. Bradley and Eugene Kevane (Boston: St. Paul Editions, 1985), 8–9 (translation slightly altered).

no greater proof of charity in Christ's church than when the very honor which seems so important on a human level is despised."[18]

Ultimately, however, a Christian's confidence rests not on the ability of authority figures to heed Paul's and Jesus's teaching, but on the faithfulness of God. Though the failures of ecclesiastical leaders are no small matter (Matt 18:6; 24:45–51; James 3:1), the weaknesses and failings of the Church's ministers serve to show forth the power of God, who works both through our obedience and in spite of our disobedience. As Paul puts it when describing his own ministry, "We hold this treasure in earthen vessels, that the surpassing power may be of God and not from us" (2 Cor 4:7).

18. *Sermons* 10.8. Cited in *Colossians, 1–2 Thessalonians, 1–2 Timothy, Titus, Philemon*, ed. Peter Gorday, ACCS 9 (Downers Grove, IL: InterVarsity, 2000), 65.

Continuing the Story
of the Apostles in Thessalonica

1 Thessalonians 2:9–20

Paul continues to remind the Thessalonians of their time together and give thanks to God for them. Many of the points made in chapter 1 are expanded upon here, as Paul continues to describe God's work in their midst, their reception of the word amid suffering, and their imitation of those who were in Christ before them.

Working Night and Day (2:9–12)

⁹You recall, brothers, our toil and drudgery. Working night and day in order not to burden any of you, we proclaimed to you the gospel of God. ¹⁰You are witnesses, and so is God, how devoutly and justly and blamelessly we behaved toward you believers. ¹¹As you know, we treated each one of you as a father treats his children, ¹²exhorting and encouraging you and insisting that you conduct yourselves as worthy of the God who calls you into his kingdom and glory.

NT: 2 Thess 3:6–9

2:9 Paul, Silvanus, and Timothy worked **night and day**, meaning that they worked not through the night but into it. Paul does not mention what sort of work they were doing, but later in the letter he admonishes the Thessalonians to work with their hands (4:11). The book of Acts describes Paul as a tentmaker (18:3),

The Catechism of Trent on Following Paul's Example with Money

LIVING
TRADITION

The Catechism of the Council of Trent holds up Paul as an example of generous frugality and hard work on behalf of the poor, admonishing priests to do whatever is necessary to help the needy:

> If one cannot help the needy with what he already has, then he should engage in some work in order to be able to do so. . . . This is what St. Paul himself did, and he exhorts others to imitate him. "You yourselves know," he says to the Thessalonians, "how you ought to imitate us" (2 Thess 3:7). "Aspire to live quietly, to mind your own affairs, and to work with your hands, as we charged you" (1 Thess 4:11). . . . This charity should be pursued even to the extent of some privation on our part. We should not want to be ourselves the object of others' charity. This frugality was characteristic of all the Apostles, but especially St. Paul. Thus he reminded the Thessalonians: "For you remember our labor and toil, brethren; we worked night and day, that we might not burden any of you, while we preached to you the gospel of God" (1 Thess 2:9).[a]

a. *The Roman Catechism: Translated and Annotated in Accord with Vatican II and Post-Conciliar Documents and the New Code of Canon Law*, trans. Robert I. Bradley and Eugene Kevane (Boston: St. Paul Editions, 1985), 435–36 (translation slightly altered).

a description that is consistent with what Paul says in his letters. Paul did not make a comfortable living and frequently found himself without enough food to eat and poorly clothed (1 Cor 4:11; 2 Cor 6:5; 11:27). Jesus had commanded that those who preach the gospel should receive a living (1 Cor 9:14). Though Paul could have accepted payment from the churches, he put himself through these hardships **in order not to burden any of you**. As he puts it in 1 Cor 9:12, "We endure all things rather than give hindrance to the gospel of Christ" (my translation). In 2 Thessalonians Paul gives the additional reason that he wanted to give the Thessalonians an example to imitate (3:7–9). Interestingly, Paul did accept money on numerous occasions from the church in Philippi (Phil 4:10–20; 2 Cor 11:9), and he describes the money they gave him as a sacrifice "pleasing to God" (Phil 4:18). Paul never explains why his policy varied from church to church. Presumably he believed that giving would benefit the Philippians (Phil 4:17), whereas other congregations would benefit more from receiving the gospel "free of charge" (1 Cor 9:18). Though he never explicitly connects his policy of forgoing payment to the example of Jesus, Paul tells the church in Philippi to follow the example of Jesus, who gave up his divine prerogatives and humbled himself to the point of death on a cross (Phil 2:1–13), and he asks the

Corinthians to give their money to needy Christians in Jerusalem, following the example of Jesus, who "became poor although he was rich, so that by his poverty you might become rich" (2 Cor 8:9). It is not hard to see Paul's renunciation of his apostolic prerogatives for the sake of others as his attempt to practice what he preached by imitating Jesus's own renunciation.

2:10   Paul is confident that God and the Thessalonian church would testify that Paul, Silvanus, and Timothy behaved **devoutly and justly and blamelessly**. The word for "devoutly" (*hosiōs*) could also be translated as "holy."[1] The words "holy and just" are a common pair in the Bible where they describe God's own character (Rev 16:5) as well as actions that are pleasing to God (Titus 1:8). The third word, "blamelessly" (*amemptōs*), refers to the absence of faults. In Phil 3:6 Paul says that when he was a Pharisee he was "blameless" under the law. Luke describes John the Baptist's parents as being "blameless" because they followed "all the commandments and ordinances of the Lord" (Luke 1:6). Paul uses this word two more times in this letter, praying that God would find the Thessalonians "blameless" when Jesus returns (3:13; 5:23; see also Phil 2:15).

2:11–12   After referring to the Thessalonians as brothers (1:4; 2:1) and describing himself as an infant and a nurse (2:7), Paul turns to paternal language, saying that **we treated each one of you as a father treats his children**. By comparing himself to a father **exhorting**, **encouraging**, and **insisting** with his children, Paul calls to mind both his authority and his compassion. The concept of fatherhood was a loaded one in the Roman Empire, carrying strong connotations of power. "Father" was sometimes used as the title of the gods and emperors, and in Roman law the *paterfamilias* sometimes had complete authority over his household, including adult children. Paul occasionally refers to himself as a father to remind others of his authority (1 Cor 4:14; 2 Cor 12:14). At the same time, Paul also applies the language of fatherhood to himself to emphasize his affection and care for his children in Christ (1 Cor 4:14–15; Philem 1:10). As John Chrysostom puts it while preaching on this passage, Paul, Silvanus, and Timothy spoke "not in a severe manner, but as fathers."[2]

Verse 12 provides a short summary of Paul's message. In Thessalonica Paul encouraged them, **conduct yourselves as worthy of . . . God**. The Greek text translated here as "conduct yourselves" literally says "walk," following a common Hebrew idiom. Scripture frequently uses the metaphor of walking to describe one's way of life (e.g., 2 Kings 20:3), and it is a favorite term of Paul's, appearing again twice in this letter (1 Thess 4:1, 12). The metaphor of walking reminds

---

1. Or rather with the archaic adverb "holily."
2. *Homiliae in epistulam i ad Thessalonicenses* (PG 62:406 [my translation]).

us that Paul called the Thessalonians to much more than a new set of ideas. By turning from idols to serve God (1:9), they have embarked on a new way of life.

Unlike the synoptic Gospels, Paul does not often speak of the "kingdom of God." Here, however, he says that God is calling them **into his kingdom and glory**. A newcomer to a country must learn the customs and laws of the land in order to thrive there. God was calling the Thessalonians into his kingdom and glory, so it was necessary for them to walk "worthily" (*axiōs*) of their new kingdom. Some ancient scribes found **the God who calls you** strange and changed it to "the God who *called* you." But Paul's use of the present tense describes a call that is ongoing, continually leading the Thessalonians to a new way of life (see also 1 Thess 2:12; 4:7; 5:23–24; 2 Thess 1:11).

Reflection and Application (2:9–12)

First Thessalonians is packed with the language of family, especially in chapter 2. Paul's description of being "orphaned" when he was separated from the Thessalonians (2:17) completes the complex web of familial language that includes the Thessalonians as brothers, and the apostles as infants and also as nurses caring for children. The apostles also compare themselves to a father exhorting his children. While writing this commentary, I taught a class on 1–2 Thessalonians to seminarians training to become Catholic priests. The seminarians were impressed with Paul's obvious affection for the Thessalonians as well as his zeal for their salvation. In particular, they gravitated to the language of fatherhood in 2:11. They aspire to become spiritual fathers and found in Paul a model. At the same time, more than one expressed bemusement at the infantile and maternal metaphors. How could an apostle be like a baby or a nursing mother?

It is undeniable that the familial language in this letter forms a kaleidoscope of quickly shifting images. Yet, each description portrays a different aspect of Paul, Silvanus, and Timothy's ministry to the Thessalonians that must not be ignored or explained away simply because it seems odd. When we imagine Paul as an infant, we imagine him as humble and guileless. The depiction of Paul as nurse calls to mind a flood of images: the loving chastisement of errant behavior, the teaching of basic skills, constant feeding and cleaning, and so on. By juxtaposing these descriptions with that of a father and a brother, Paul paints a nuanced portrait of apostolic ministry that is consonant with Jesus's command at the Last Supper that the apostles become like children and servants in imitation of him, who came as a servant (Luke 22:26–27).

Receiving the Word of God (2:13)

¹³And for this reason we too give thanks to God unceasingly, that, in receiving the word of God from hearing us, you received not a human word but, as it truly is, the word of God, which is now at work in you who believe.

OT: Isa 55:10–11
NT: Heb 4:12–13
Catechism: divine revelation, 81–82

2:13　Paul's Letters usually open with a word of thanksgiving to God and a description of how he prays for the addressees (see 1:3). In this letter, however, Paul takes up the thanksgiving a second time so he can continue retelling the story of how the Thessalonian converts received the gospel in the midst of persecution. He gives thanks that they received the apostles' teaching as **the word of God** rather than a merely **human word**. Though they received the message from Paul and his companions, the Thessalonians understood that the message did not originate with them. As Augustine puts it, "It is called the word of God . . . because a divine and not a human doctrine is handed down."[3] Paul's Letters show that he thought carefully about his responsibilities to the "word" that he proclaimed. As a carrier of God's word, Paul guarded the message as a precious object that did not belong to him. He saw himself as being entrusted with the word (2:4), as an ambassador from God to humanity (2 Cor 5:19–20) who needed to take care not to falsify the message (2 Cor 4:2) or use it for his own gain (2 Cor 2:17).

The NABRE interprets the relative clause **which is now at work in you who believe** to refer to God's word. According to this translation, the gospel message that Paul brought to Thessalonica is "living and effective" (Heb 4:12), continuing to work among the faithful. It is also possible, however, that the pronoun refers to God and should be translated as "*who* is now at work."[4] The difference between the two translations is not great. When the Thessalonians received the message of the gospel, they received God, who works within them to conform them to the message. In other words, to receive God's word is to receive God. In his commentary on the Song of Songs, St. Bernard (1090–1153) states this

---

3. *The Trinity*, trans. Stephen McKenna, FC 45 (Washington, DC: Catholic University of America Press, 1963), 478.

4. Note the Douay-Rheims Bible: "You received it not as the word of men, but (as it is indeed) the word of God, who worketh in you that have believed."

St. Bernard and St. Augustine on God's Self-Gift through Revelation

St. Bernard turned to Paul to explain that when one receives revelation, one receives God.

> Without doubt, the Son reveals the Father through the kiss [see Song 1:2], that is, through the Holy Spirit, as the Apostle testifies: "To us God revealed through his Spirit" [1 Cor 2:10]. In truth, it is by giving the Spirit through whom he reveals that he reveals himself. He reveals himself by giving himself, and he gives himself by revealing himself. Moreover, revelation, which is accomplished through the Holy Spirit, not only gives knowledge but also lights the fire of love, as Paul says: "The love of God has been poured into our hearts through the Holy Spirit, who has been given to us" [Rom 5:5].[a]

St. Augustine argued that Paul thanks God for the way the Thessalonians received the word of God because God was at work in the Thessalonians to respond in faith.

> Why does he give thanks here [in 1 Thess 2:13] to God? Certainly, it would be vain and meaningless if the person to whom he gives thanks for something is not the person who did it. But since this is not vain and meaningless, then certainly God, to whom he gives thanks for this work, is the one who brought it about that the Thessalonians, when they had received from the Apostle the word of the hearing of God, received it not as the word of men, but, as it truly is, the word of God.[b]

a. *Commentary on the Song of Songs* 8.5 (my translation).
b. *The Predestination of the Saints* 19.39, in *Four Anti-Pelagian Writings*, trans. John A. Mourant and William J. Collinge, FC 86 (Washington, DC: Catholic University of America Press), 266.

concisely: *dando revelat et revelando dat* ("He reveals himself by giving himself, and he gives himself by revealing himself").

Comparison to the Judean Churches (2:14–16)

[14]For you, brothers, have become imitators of the churches of God that are in Judea in Christ Jesus. For you suffer the same things from your compatriots as they did from the Jews, [15]who killed both the Lord Jesus and the prophets and persecuted us; they do not please God, and are opposed to everyone, [16]trying to prevent us from speaking to the Gentiles that they may be saved, thus constantly filling up the measure

of their sins. But the wrath of God has finally begun to come upon
them.

NT: Rom 9–11
Catechism: death of Jesus, 595–623

2:14   In chapter 1 Paul mentioned hardship endured by the Thessalonians. Here
he says a little more, noting that they have suffered at the hands of their
compatriots, a word that probably refers to other residents of Thessalonica.
Through this suffering they became **imitators of the churches of God that
are in Judea**, which themselves had experienced suffering because of other
residents of Judea. The language of imitation recalls Paul's thanksgiving that
the Thessalonians were imitators of the Lord and the apostles (1:6). Here the
Jewish Christians of Judea are held out as examples for the young Gentile
congregation. Paul does not explain the precise nature of the Thessalonians'
suffering. It is possible that they experienced persecution, or perhaps just the
inevitable estrangement from other residents of the city that followed from
their refusal to worship idols.[5]

2:15–16   In verses 15–16 Paul makes a lengthy digression in which he criticizes the
opponents of the churches in Judea, a group he labels **the Jews** (*hoi Ioudaioi*).
The criticism seems so harsh and sudden that some scholars argue that some
or all of 2:13–16 was added by a later scribe. There are no ancient manuscripts
lacking these lines, but it is argued that this condemnation of the Jewish people
better fits post–AD 70 anti-Jewish polemics than Paul's own thought.[6] If this
argument is correct, we would be forced to imagine a late first-century interpo-
lator who, as Markus Bockmuehl puts it, "successfully duped the entire textual
and interpretative tradition—and this despite the fact that he worked at least a
quarter-century after Paul, at which point other copies of the letter must have
existed."[7] If the text makes sense as it stands—and I suggest in the following
commentary that it does—then emendation is unnecessary.[8]

Paul charges "the Jews" with killing **the Lord Jesus and the prophets** and
hindering the evangelization of the nations. Of course, Paul is not blaming
all Jews for the death of Jesus any more than he is condemning all Gentiles in

5. See the discussion in John M. G. Barclay, "Conflict in Thessalonica," *CBQ* 55 (1993): 512–30.

6. For a defense of this view, see Birger A. Pearson, "1 Thessalonians 2:13–16: A Deutero-Pauline
Interpolation," *HTR* 64 (1971): 79–94; Earl J. Richard, *First and Second Thessalonians*, SP 11 (Collegeville,
MN: Liturgical Press, 1995), 17–19.

7. Markus Bockmuehl, "1 Thessalonians 2:14–16 and the Church in Jerusalem," *TynBul* 52 (2001):
1–31, here 7.

8. For a more complete argument, see Bockmuehl, "1 Thessalonians 2:14–16 and the Church in
Jerusalem."

verse 14.[9] After all, Paul and the other apostles were Jews (Gal 2:15), and the churches of Judea would have been predominantly Jewish as well (1 Thess 2:14). Two small corrections of the NABRE will help to clarify this point. First, the word *Ioudaioi*, which the NABRE translates as "Jews," can also refer to residents of the region of Judea or "Judeans." This sense of the word is in the foreground here because Paul is talking about those who have persecuted the churches "in Judea" (2:14). Second, the NABRE adds a comma at the end of verse 14 before the words "who killed . . . the Lord Jesus." This additional comma makes it sound as if Paul is blaming all Jews for Jesus's death. The Greek could be more satisfactorily rendered as follows: the churches of Judea suffered from "the Judeans who killed both the Lord Jesus and the prophets and persecuted us."[10] Paul is lambasting the residents of Judea who handed Jesus over for Roman execution, troubled the Judean churches, and opposed his mission. This is not to deny the broad, caricaturing nature of Paul's description here but rather to specify its necessary limits.

In charging the Judeans with killing the **prophets**, Paul is following a polemical tradition that goes back to the Old Testament. Prophets often identified their own generation with all who have opposed God's messengers throughout history and warned that God was about to bring retribution (e.g., 1 Kings 19:10; Jer 2:30). This same tradition appears in the Gospels. In the parable of the tenants, the chief priests and Pharisees are identified with those who killed all the prophets and Jesus (Matt 21:33–46 and parallels). In a passage very similar to 1 Thess 2:14–16, Jesus charges the scribes, Pharisees, and then "Jerusalem" with killing the prophets and warns that judgment is at hand, ironically telling them to "fill up" the measure of their ancestors (Matt 23:29–39). Like Paul's description of them **constantly filling up the measure of their sins**, this passage imagines sin building up like a debt until God finally collects what is due (see also Gen 15:13–16; 2 Macc 6:12–17).

Paul also alleges that the Judeans have **persecuted us** (i.e., the apostles). Paul was familiar with opposition to the apostles from both sides of the conflict, himself having formerly "persecuted the church of God" (Gal 1:13). His other letters attest to ongoing persecution of Christians by non-Christian Jews (Gal 4:29; 6:12). He mentions being whipped by fellow Jews (2 Cor 11:24), and prior to traveling to Judea he asks for others to pray that he would be delivered from "disobedient" Judeans (Rom 15:31). The mention of preventing **us from**

9. Bockmuehl, "1 Thessalonians 2:14–16 and the Church in Jerusalem," 11.
10. See Frank D. Gilliard, "The Problem of the Antisemitic Comma between 1 Thessalonians 2.14 and 15," *NTS* 35 (1989): 481–502.

speaking to the Gentiles could suggest that Paul has experienced opposition especially to his mission to the Gentiles (see Gal 6:12).[11]

The final sentence can be understood in a number of different ways: that the **wrath of God** has already come upon them (NRSV), or that the wrath of God is near or just beginning to be unleashed (NABRE). There had been a number of crises in recent history that Paul might have interpreted as signs of the beginnings of God's wrath on the Judeans who opposed his proclamation of the gospel.[12] In any case, the final unleashing of God's wrath would not occur until the day of the Lord (1 Thess 1:10; 5:1–9).

Reflection and Application (2:14–16)

In this passage Paul blames the Judeans for killing Jesus, but a moment's reflection shows that there is more to the story. For one thing, Jesus was "crucified under Pontius Pilate," as the Nicene-Constantinopolitan Creed puts it. Crucifixion was a Roman, not a Jewish, method of execution. Though the Gospels say that Jewish authorities handed Jesus over for crucifixion, not all Judeans were complicit, still less all Jews. The Second Vatican Council noted this and pointed out that Christ died freely in order that all people would be saved:

> True, the Jewish authorities and those who followed their lead pressed for the death of Christ; still, what happened in His passion cannot be charged against all the Jews, without distinction, then alive, nor against the Jews of today. . . . Furthermore, in her rejection of every persecution against any man, the Church, mindful of the patrimony she shares with the Jews and moved not by political reasons but by the Gospel's spiritual love, decries hatred, persecutions, displays of anti-Semitism, directed against Jews at any time and by anyone. Besides, as the Church has always held and holds now, Christ underwent His passion and death freely, because of the sins of men and out of infinite love, in order that all may reach salvation. It is, therefore, the burden of the Church's preaching to proclaim the cross of Christ as the sign of God's all-embracing love and as the fountain from which every grace flows. (*Nostra Aetate* [Declaration on the Relation of the Church to Non-Christian Religions] 4)

What, then, do we say about 1 Thess 2:14–16? These verses are best read as an outburst of righteous indignation at the opposition that the earliest Christians

---

11. The Greek for the phrase "persecuted us" could be translated as "drove us out." Some see here a reference to Paul's hasty exit from Thessalonica (see Acts 17:5–8).

12. Possibilities include the death of thousands of Jews in Jerusalem during Passover in AD 49 or the death of Herod Agrippa I in AD 44. See the discussion in Bockmuehl, "1 Thessalonians 2:14–16 and the Church in Jerusalem," 25–29.

received from some fellow Jews. But such expressions of judgment do not have the last word in Scripture. The Old Testament prophets, whom Paul imitates here, charge the people with killing the prophets and bringing wrath down on themselves, but they always offer the hope of restoration (e.g., compare Jer 2:30 with 31:1–40). Similarly, Paul did not rest with this word of condemnation. Indeed, again in *Nostra Aetate* 4, Vatican II turned to another passage of Paul's for explaining the Church's relationship to the Jewish people, Rom 9:

> The Church keeps ever in mind the words of the Apostle about his kinsmen: "theirs is the sonship and the glory and the covenants and the law and the worship and the promises; theirs are the fathers and from them is the Christ according to the flesh" (Rom 9:4–5), the Son of the Virgin Mary. She also recalls that the Apostles, the Church's main-stay and pillars, as well as most of the early disciples who proclaimed Christ's Gospel to the world, sprang from the Jewish people. . . . God holds the Jews most dear for the sake of their Fathers; He does not repent of the gifts He makes or of the calls He issues—such is the witness of the Apostle. In company with the Prophets and the same Apostle, the Church awaits that day, known to God alone, on which all peoples will address the Lord in a single voice and "serve him shoulder to shoulder" (Zeph 3:9).

Thwarted Attempts to Return (2:17–20)

---

¹⁷**Brothers, when we were bereft of you for a short time, in person, not in heart, we were all the more eager in our great desire to see you in person. ¹⁸We decided to go to you—I, Paul, not only once but more than once—yet Satan thwarted us. ¹⁹For what is our hope or joy or crown to boast of in the presence of our Lord Jesus at his coming if not you yourselves? ²⁰For you are our glory and joy.**

Catechism: Satan, 391–95

The striking familial language continues as Paul once again describes himself as a   2:17
little child longing for the Thessalonians as if they were his parents. The NABRE's **we were bereft of you** could be rendered more literally as "we were made orphans from you." As St. John Chrysostom, a native Greek-speaker, notes, "He does not say, 'separated from you,' or 'torn away from you,' or 'set apart from you,' or 'left behind from you,' but rather he says, 'orphaned from you.' He seeks language that is sufficient to show the pain of his soul."[13] This may indicate that Paul was

---

13. *Epistulae ad Olympiadem* 8.12 (my translation).

forcibly removed from their presence, and it certainly indicates that Paul felt real grief because he could not reestablish contact with them. It also implies that Paul needed them. It is not as if he dispensed wisdom and gained nothing in return. Indeed, one is struck above all by the vulnerability in Paul's self-description. He is an apostle who exhorts them as a father would his children, but he also is like a child and finds himself feeling like an orphan when he loses contact with them.

It was common for ancient letter writers to say that they remain united even as they are separated by distance, as Paul does when he says he is separated from them only **in person, not in heart**. Students who were learning to write letters were taught to say things like this. For instance, a handbook on how to write letters from the first century AD instructs students to say, "Even though I have been separated from you for a long time, I suffer this in body only. For I can never forget you."[14] Paul followed this polite convention on several occasions (1 Cor 5:3; Col 2:5; see 2 Cor 10:1–2), but it is clear these were not merely empty words for Paul. His sincere desire to see the Thessalonians and his concern for them leap off the page.

2:18   Since being separated from the Thessalonians, the apostles had tried to return to Thessalonica, but **Satan thwarted** their attempts. What does this mean? We discover in 3:1–2 that Paul was able to send Timothy to Thessalonica from Athens. We do not know why Timothy was able to return while Paul could not, nor do we know what convinced Paul that it was Satan who prevented him from returning to Thessalonica. What is clear is that Paul understands Satan to be a threat to the Thessalonian church. A few verses later he adds that he was worried that "the tempter" had convinced the Thessalonians to abandon their faith (3:5). Paul does not mention Satan often, but he regarded Satan as an enemy to be taken seriously. He taught that God's complete victory over Satan was assured (Rom 16:20) and that Satan's power was held in check by God (2 Cor 12:7). Nevertheless, Paul saw Satan as a real adversary with the power to tempt the faithful to sin (1 Cor 7:5), appearing as an angel of light (2 Cor 11:14) and working counterfeit miracles (2 Thess 2:9). Most strikingly, he refers to Satan as "the god of this age" with the power to blind people to the truth of the gospel (2 Cor 4:4).

2:19–20   When Jesus returns Paul expects the Thessalonian Christians to be his **crown**. When reading the word "crown," most people today will picture a metal hat that indicates the wearer's royal status, but Paul is most likely referring to leafy wreathes worn by victorious athletes. In 1 Cor 9:25 he compares the "perishable

---

14. Stanley K. Stowers, *Letter Writing in Greco-Roman Antiquity*, LEC 5 (Philadelphia: Westminster, 1986), 58.

crown" won by runners and other athletes with the "imperishable crown" for which he works in his ministry (my translation). In other words, athletes receive awards that wither away, but Paul competes for a crown that will endure forever. If Jesus returns and finds the Thessalonians standing faithfully (1 Thess 3:8), they will be like a crown of honor for Paul, proving that he had fought the good fight (2:2). Paul says something similar in 1 Cor 3:9–15, but there he uses the image of the wage due a worker instead of the crown of a victorious athlete. He builds up the Corinthian church and will receive a "wage" from God if the building is sound. Paul saw himself as entrusted with the task of calling the nations to serve God (Rom 15:15–21), and at the Lord's return, he hoped to present his churches blameless and unblemished to the Lord (1 Thess 3:12–13). Three hundred years later St. Basil the Great would cite this passage to encourage preachers in his day: "Those who preach the word should not slack off because of their own successes but should know that the improvement of the faithful is the distinct and special work of the office entrusted to them."[15]

Readers who are more familiar with Paul's negative uses of the word "boasting" (*kauchēsis*) may be taken aback by this description of a **boast** at the Lord's return. On other occasions Paul teaches that no one should boast because everything we have is a gift from God (1 Cor 4:7; see also Rom 3:27), and yet here he is looking forward to the day when he will boast in the presence of Jesus. The English word "boast" has an almost exclusively negative connotation. In contrast, the word Paul uses, *kauchēsis*, sometimes means "boasting" in the negative sense, but for Paul it can also mean the source of one's confidence or joy. We frequently find Paul claiming that his "boast" is based on Christ: "But may I never boast except in the cross of our Lord Jesus Christ, through which the world has been crucified to me, and I to the world" (Gal 6:14; see also Rom 5:11; 1 Cor 1:31; Phil 3:3). This confidence in Christ extended to confidence in the mission to which Paul was called. In his letter to the Romans he says that he has reason to boast in his ministry to the Gentiles because it is based on the power of God (15:15–21; see also 2 Thess 1:4). Though Paul does not make it explicit in 1 Thess 2:19–20, he has already said that the Thessalonians' faith, hope, and love are the work of God in them.

Reflection and Application (2:17–20)

Paul was desperate to return to the church in Thessalonica, but his attempts were repeatedly thwarted. One might expect him to conclude from his inability

15. *Regulae morales* 31.825 (my translation).

to return that it was not God's will for him to rejoin the Thessalonian church. Many Christians are quick to assume that whatever unfortunate events occur must be God's will for their lives. Paul, however, does not equate the way things are with the will of God. To be sure, he believes that God is able to tear down whatever barriers stand between him and the Thessalonians, and he prays that God will do this (3:11). Nevertheless, he does not consider his current inability to return to Thessalonica evidence that God does not want him to return. On the contrary, he interprets the obstacles that keep him in Achaia as diabolical opposition. Paul reminds us that Christians believe God is supreme, but that we do not need to see everything that happens as the direct result of God's will—indeed, we must not. Paul taught that creation is in bondage to decay (Rom 8:21–22) and that the god of this age—that is, Satan—is still at work (2 Cor 4:4). As the Catechism puts it, the world is in the power of the evil one, and as a result our life is a battle (409). Facile equations of the way things are with the will of God do not belong to a Christian view of reality.[16]

---

16. For a helpful discussion of this issue, see David Bentley Hart, *The Doors of the Sea: Where Was God in the Tsunami?* (Grand Rapids: Eerdmans, 2005).

Paul's Relief at the Return of Timothy

1 Thessalonians 3:1–13

While working in Athens, Paul sent Timothy back to Thessalonica to encourage the new church, lest their suffering and the devil's influence cause them to fall away. When Timothy returned with the good news that they endured in the faith, Paul was overwhelmed with relief, but he continued to pray that God would allow him to return to Thessalonica and that God would increase their love and so prepare them for the return of the Lord Jesus.

Timothy Returns to Thessalonica (3:1–5)

¹That is why, when we could bear it no longer, we decided to remain alone in Athens ²and sent Timothy, our brother and co-worker for God in the gospel of Christ, to strengthen and encourage you in your faith, ³so that no one be disturbed in these afflictions. For you yourselves know that we are destined for this. ⁴For even when we were among you, we used to warn you in advance that we would undergo affliction, just as has happened, as you know. ⁵For this reason, when I too could bear it no longer, I sent to learn about your faith, for fear that somehow the tempter had put you to the test and our toil might come to nothing.

NT: Mark 4:1–20

Paul continues retelling the story of his relationship with the Thessalonian church. Here he recounts how he sent Timothy in his stead to strengthen their faith. Paul was worried that they had been disturbed by the afflictions they were suffering (3:3). He also feared that Satan, whom he calls the tempter, had tempted them and brought Paul's work to nothing (3:5). Paul knew that suffering sometimes causes people to abandon their beliefs, and he assumed that Satan would be working to take advantage of this period of vulnerability, just as Satan had prevented him from returning to encourage the Thessalonians. Though Paul does not cite it, the parable of the sower (Mark 4:1–20 and parallels) is a good illustration of Paul's concern. It compares the preaching of the word to sowing seed. Some seed is eaten by birds before it can grow, which represents Satan stealing the word away. Other seed is sown on rocky ground, which represents those who receive the word with joy, but who quickly fall away in times of "tribulation or persecution" because they have no root. Paul was worried that the word would be snatched away from the Thessalonians before it could grow. After all, the Thessalonians were only recent followers of Jesus. Paul did not know what kind of "soil" they were.

3:1–2   Since Paul was unable to return, he **decided to remain . . . in Athens** and send **Timothy** to discover whether their faith was intact (3:5) and to **strengthen and encourage** them in their **faith** (3:2). He hoped that Timothy's presence and counsel would bolster their faith if it was wavering. This is a good example of how Paul's use of the word "faith" (*pistis*) is not limited to belief. It is not that Paul wondered if they had come to accept some new doctrine, but rather he wondered if they had remained faithful to the gospel in the midst of suffering.

3:3   When Paul was in Thessalonica he was careful to tell them ahead of time that **we are destined** for suffering. The Greek verb translated as "we are destined" could be rendered as "we are set up for." It's the same word Simeon uses when he tells Mary that the infant Jesus is "destined" for the falling and rising of many (Luke 2:34). Why would Paul tell the Thessalonians that God had appointed them to suffer? Jewish †apocalyptic writers frequently alluded to a time of great suffering that would precede God's decisive action in history (e.g., Dan 12:1). Paul believed that all who are in Christ would share in Christ's suffering as well as his resurrection. For Paul, the Thessalonians' reception of the gospel in the midst of suffering was clear evidence that the Holy Spirit was empowering them to become like Jesus (1 Thess 1:6). As he put it in his letter to the Thessalonians' neighbors in Philippi, God graciously allows Christians "not only to believe in [Christ], but also to suffer for him" because suffering leads to our salvation (Phil 1:28–29; see also 3:10–11; Rom 8:18).

3:4–5   The NABRE's translation **we used to warn you** correctly suggests that suffering was a central part of Paul's message. In their relatively short time together, Paul

Salvian the Presbyter (Early Fifth Century) on 1 Thessalonians 3:3

LIVING TRADITION

> Since the Apostle says that we are placed by God in this world to bear hardships, miseries and sorrows, what is strange about it if we who fight for the sake of sustaining all adversities should suffer all manner of evil? Many do not understand this and think that Christian men should receive these things [i.e., freedom from hardship] from God as tribute, as it were, for their faith.[a]

a. *The Writings of Salvian, the Presbyter*, trans. Jeremiah F. O'Sullivan, FC 3 (Washington, DC: Catholic University of America Press, 1947), 69–70.

taught them repeatedly that suffering is basic to the life of those in Christ. Yet, the word "warn" sounds too negative. A more wooden rendering of the Greek would be "we were telling you ahead of time." For Paul, faithful suffering was evidence that God was working to bring someone to salvation (2 Thess 1:3–12; Phil 1:28). It is not that Paul thought that suffering is good in itself, but rather he thought that God uses suffering to unite us with Christ so we will also share in his resurrection (Rom 5:3–5; Phil 3:10). Almost four centuries later, St. John Chrysostom would quote Paul's reminder to the Thessalonians that we are destined to suffer and quip, "And, as if we were destined for relaxation, we think it strange."[1]

What sort of "affliction" had the Thessalonians undergone? Paul does not specify the nature of their suffering—it was known well enough to them. Readers of Acts will think of how an angry mob attacked the house of one of the Thessalonian converts and dragged some of them before the city authorities, accusing them of what amounts to insurrection (Acts 17:5–9). It is almost inevitable that the Thessalonians would have experienced some personal turmoil. They had rejected the gods of their city and families as dead idols (1 Thess 1:9) and surely would have experienced the pain of strained or broken relationships and perhaps persecution. It is also likely that some of them had died (see commentary on 1 Thess 4:13–18).[2]

Timothy's Good News (3:6–10)

6But just now Timothy has returned to us from you, bringing us the good news of your faith and love, and that you always think kindly of us and

1. *Homiliae in epistulam i ad Thessalonicenses* (PG 62:410 [my translation]).
2. See introduction to 1 Thessalonians.

long to see us as we long to see you. ⁷Because of this, we have been reassured about you, brothers, in our every distress and affliction, through your faith. ⁸For we now live, if you stand firm in the Lord.

⁹What thanksgiving, then, can we render to God for you, for all the joy we feel on your account before our God? ¹⁰Night and day we pray beyond measure to see you in person and to remedy the deficiencies of your faith.

3:6 The story of Paul's relationship with the Thessalonians, which Paul has been telling since 1:2, finally comes to an end here as Paul describes the joy he experienced when Timothy returned with the good news that the Thessalonians had remained unshaken by their suffering. There are two main parts to Timothy's report as Paul describes it. First, Timothy reported that the Thessalonians continued in their **faith and love**. Their sufferings had not caused them to abandon their new life of loyalty to Christ and work on behalf of his kingdom (see 1:2–3). Paul spends most of the rest of the letter seeking to reinforce their faith, their love, and also their hope. The second part of Timothy's report was that the Thessalonians **always think kindly of us and long to see us as we long to see you**. In other words, the Thessalonians still hold Paul in high esteem and wish to deepen their relationship.

The talk of "longing" sounds rather overheated by our standards. To modern ears, this is the language of romance, not ecclesial correspondence. For Greek letter writers of Paul's day, however, it was conventional to speak of one's longing for the recipient. Indeed, 3:6–10 is filled with language that sounds effusive to us but that was standard in its own context. The mention of happy memories (3:6), the welfare of the other being a matter of life and death (3:8), and thanksgiving to God or gods (3:9)—all of this was common in letters between friends. This does not mean that 1 Thessalonians would have sounded stale or cliché when it was read aloud to the assembled Thessalonians—far from it. It bursts with arresting images and creativity. But Paul's description of his longing for the Thessalonians is quite conventional.

3:7–8 Paul is consoled in his **distress and affliction** because of the Thessalonians' enduring faith. His relief at hearing Timothy's good news is so great that he says **we now live, if you stand firm in the Lord**. St. John Chrysostom interprets this to mean that Paul's eternal life depends on the Thessalonians remaining steadfast: "What is equal to Paul, who thought the salvation of his neighbors was his own salvation, as a body toward its parts? . . . He has said not 'we rejoice' but rather 'we live,' referring to the life to come."³ On another occasion

---

3. *Homiliae* (PG 62:418 [my translation]).

Strong Emotions in Ancient Letters

Paul's expressions of intense longing were not uncommon among letter writers in his day. In this letter from the early second century AD, a woman named Taus tells her master that she "dies" because she cannot see him:

> Taus to Apollonius her lord, many greetings. First of all, I greet you, master, and I pray always for your health. I was in no small amount of agony, lord, to hear that you weren't feeling well, but thanks be to all the gods that they kept you free from harm. I appeal to you, lord, if it please you, also that you send for us. Otherwise, we die because we do not see you daily. Would that we were able to fly and come and make obeisance to you, for we are in agony not seeing you. So be reconciled with us and send for us.[a]

In addition to expressions of longing similar to Paul's, Taus prays "always" for her master's health and thanks the gods for keeping him from harm. This is similar to Paul's declarations of constant prayer for his churches and his thanks to God.

a. P.Giss. I 17 (my translation). Cited by Abraham J. Malherbe, *The Letters to the Thessalonians: A New Translation with Introduction and Commentary*, AB 32B (New York: Doubleday, 2000), 202.

Chrysostom cites this verse alongside Moses's prayer that God blot him out if God would not forgive his fellow Israelites (Exod 32:32).[4] Most modern commentators object that Paul is simply using hyperbole to express his relief.[5] As noted above, letters between friends frequently expressed this sort of sentiment, including the claim that the writer will die if he or she doesn't see the recipient (see sidebar, "Strong Emotions in Ancient Letters," above). At the same time, Paul did expect to be rewarded when Jesus returned, on the basis of the Thessalonian church (1 Thess 2:19–20), so Chrysostom's interpretation may not be too far off the mark. Paul needs the Thessalonians to "stand firm in the Lord" in order to fulfill his calling bring the gospel to the nations.

Since the beginning of the letter Paul has been retelling the story of his time **3:9** with the Thessalonians, their separation, his anxiety, the mission of Timothy, and finally Paul's great relief upon learning that they continue to stand firm "in the Lord." The story was punctuated with thanksgiving to God in 1:2 and 2:13. In 3:9–10 Paul finally brings the story and his thanksgiving to a close with this

4. *In sanctum Barlaam martyrem* (PG 50:676).
5. E.g., Béda Rigaux, *Saint Paul: Les Épitres aux Thessaloniciens*, EBib (Paris: Lecoffre, 1956), 480–81.

question: **What thanksgiving, then, can we render to God for you, for all the joy we feel on your account before our God?** This rhetorical question is similar to the English "How can I thank you?" Paul feels that it is appropriate for him to return thanks to God, but he knows that it is impossible for him to give thanks adequately for such a great gift. A similar question appears in Sir 7:28: "What can you give [your parents] for all they gave you?" One should honor one's parents by caring for them in their old age, but a child will never really repay her parents for all she has received. Similarly, Paul is searching for a way to thank God for this gift, even though he knows he never will.

The word translated as "render" (*antapodidōmi*) means "repay" or "pay back." To people today, it seems almost inappropriate to speak of paying God back with thanksgiving. We tend to imagine that payment and thanksgiving belong to completely separate categories, but in Paul's day it was not at all unusual to speak of repaying thanks to God or humans (see commentary on 2 Thess 1:3). The language of repaying thanks to God is found frequently in the Psalms. In LXX Psalm 115:3 (ET 116:12) the psalmist asks, "What shall I pay [*antapodidōmi*] to the Lord for all the things which he has paid [*antapodidōmi*] me?" (my translation). The Psalms frequently speak of vows to "repay" God with thanksgiving if God delivers one from distress.[6] In the psalm the temple is the ideal location to repay one's vows. Paul, however, sees himself already standing "before our God," in the presence of God in his current location.

3:10   In the NABRE, verse 10 is a new sentence, but in the Greek text Paul rambles on excitedly with the same sentence begun in verse 9. Though Timothy brought a good report, Paul still seems desperate to return to Thessalonica himself. He still feels that there are **deficiencies** in their faith that he needs to **remedy**. Though they have remained steadfast "in the Lord" (3:8) and Timothy was able to "strengthen" them in the faith (3:2), there is still progress to be made. At first glance it could seem as if Paul is contradicting himself here. If their faith is deficient, why is Paul elated? We tend to speak of faith as if it is something that one simply has or not, but faith language in the Bible is more complicated. One thinks of the distressed father who cried out to Jesus, "I believe. Help my unbelief!" (Mark 9:24 [my translation]). He was confident that Jesus could do what he promised, and yet the man knew that his faith was still lacking something. In 1 Thessalonians, Paul describes faith as something that can be built up and strengthened, or weakened and lost (3:2, 5). Faith is operative in works (1:3) and is closely associated with love (1:3; 3:6; 5:8). Faith must grow, as Paul reminds the Corinthian church (2 Cor 10:15). Thus, it is not a question

6. E.g., Pss 22:26; 50:14; 56:13; 61:6, 9; 66:13; 116:14.

of whether the Thessalonians had faith. They clearly did. But, as Chrysostom puts it while commenting on this verse, "They had not yet enjoyed the benefit of all his teaching, nor had they learned all that was necessary for them to learn."[7] Chapters 4 and 5 show us the main things that Paul probably had in mind.

Prayer for Reunification and Holiness (3:11–13)

[11]**Now may God himself, our Father, and our Lord Jesus direct our way to you, [12]and may the Lord make you increase and abound in love for one another and for all, just as we have for you, [13]so as to strengthen your hearts, to be blameless in holiness before our God and Father at the coming of our Lord Jesus with all his holy ones. [Amen.]**

OT: Zech 14:5
NT: Matt 25:31–46
Lectionary: 1 Thess 3:12–4:2; First Sunday of Advent (Year C)

Paul has finally finished retelling the story of his relationship with the Thessalonian church. He concludes this first section of the letter with a prayer that he would see them again and that they would be sanctified. In addition to concluding his account of prior events, this prayer also anticipates many of the main issues that Paul will raise in the following section devoted to explaining what kind of lives they should live (4:1–5:22). He prays that they increase in their love, which anticipates 4:9–12, and expresses concern for their preparedness for the return of Jesus, which anticipates 4:13–5:11. As noted in the introduction, these verses are an excellent summary of the letter as a whole, drawing together Paul's desire to see the Thessalonians again and his hope that they would grow in love and be ready for the return of the Lord.

The first part of the prayer is for **God himself, our Father, and our Lord** **3:11** **Jesus** to make it possible for Paul to return to Thessalonica. Though Satan has prevented Paul's reunification with the Thessalonians up to this point (2:18), Paul believes that God and Jesus can overcome this obstacle. Scholars disagree on the question of when Christians first came to see Jesus as fully divine. As a prayer to both Jesus and God in the oldest book of the New Testament, this verse has attracted a good deal of attention. Some have seen great significance in Paul's use of the Greek verb for **direct** in the singular, which in Greek presupposes a singular subject. What is more significant is that Paul addresses his prayer to

7. *Homiliae* (PG 62:419 [my translation]).

St. Athanasius and St. Ambrose on the Unity of the Father and the Son in 1 Thessalonians 3:11

LIVING TRADITION

St. Athanasius and St. Ambrose saw in Paul's prayer for the joint action of God and Jesus evidence of their unity.
Athanasius:

> For one and the same grace is from the Father and the Son, as the light of the sun and the sun's radiance is one, and the sun's illumination occurs through the radiance. In this way Paul prays for the Thessalonians, "Now may God himself our Father and the Lord Jesus Christ direct our way to you." He has guarded the unity of the Father and the Son. For he did not say, "May they direct," as if a double grace were given from one and the other. Instead, he prayed, "May he direct," to show that the Father gives this grace through the Son.[a]

Ambrose:

> The apostle said, "Now may God himself our Father and the Lord Jesus Christ direct our way to you." He mentions both the Father and the Son, but there is unity of directing because there is unity of power. For this reason in another place he says, "May our Lord Jesus Christ and God our Father, who loved us and gave us an eternal consolation and good hope in grace, console and strengthen your hearts" (2 Thess 3:16–17). What a great unity he reveals, so that there would be a unity of consolation.[b]

a. *Oratio III contra Arianos* 11.6 (my translation).
b. *De fide libri V* 2.10 (my translation).

both God the Father and Jesus and assumes that they will hear his prayer and answer. He sees Jesus and God as acting together in answering his request.

3:12   Paul does not often appeal to Jesus in prayer, but in verses 11–12 he does just that, addressing him as **the Lord** (see also 1 Cor 1:2; 16:22; 2 Cor 12:7–9). Paul prays that Jesus would cause a superabundance of love to well up in the Thessalonian converts, overflowing to love of one another and also **for all**. In 1 Thess 5:15 Paul says something similar, asking the Thessalonians always to "pursue the good, both for one another and for all" (my translation). In 4:10 he commends them for loving one another and also "all the brothers throughout Macedonia." The love that existed among the members of the local church was meant to overflow to those in Christ elsewhere as well as those outside the church (2 Cor 9:13; Gal 6:10).

3:13   Love for all people will transform the Thessalonians so that they will be **blameless in holiness** when Jesus returns and works are judged. We tend to think of "holiness" as our personal sanctity before God and love as something that turns our attention to others. In American Christianity, where we are tempted to divide Christianity up along the lines of the American political spectrum of "liberal" and "conservative," we sometimes associate "love" with liberal Christians and "holiness" with conservative Christians. So, a church that emphasizes "holiness" will stress things like freedom from sexual sin, whereas a church that emphasizes "love" will focus on welcoming outcasts into the community. Paul taught his churches to avoid sexual sin (1 Thess 4:3) and to accept others (Rom 15:7), but there is no split between holiness and love in his thought. On the contrary, in this prayer we see that holiness is expressed and achieved in love. Holiness conforms the Christian to Christ, who "loved" others and gave himself up for them (Gal 2:20). Paul prays that Jesus will find the Thessalonians sanctified through their love when he returns.

The prayer describes Jesus returning surrounded by **all his holy ones**. The word translated as "holy ones" (plural of *hagios*) is commonly translated as "saints." Despite the fact that every other occurrence of *hagios* in Paul's Letters describes humans, most commentators argue that "holy ones" refers to angels in this case.[8] Many ancient Jewish and Christian texts do describe the Lord's return in the company of angels. Zechariah 14:5 ("The LORD, my God, will come, and all his holy ones with him"), which Paul echoes here, is often read this way. Moreover, it is argued that Paul would be contradicting himself if he said here that the Lord returns in the company of the faithful, because in 1 Thess 4:16 Paul describes the faithful joining Jesus after his return. These are reasonable arguments, but the case for understanding "holy ones" as a reference to the faithful is stronger. Though the image of the Lord returning flanked by angels was traditional, so was the image of the Lord returning in the company of the people of God.[9] Indeed, Zech 14:5 itself may be referring to humans.[10] Most importantly, human "holy ones" makes much more sense in context. In this verse, Paul has just prayed that the Lord would strengthen them in holiness in preparation for the †parousia, so it is not surprising that when looking forward to that day he would refer to them as "the holy ones." The supposed contradiction with 1 Thess 4:16 disappears on closer examination. An early Christian text known as the *Didache* interpreted the Lord coming "with" all his saints as a reference to the resurrection of the dead (16:7), so that may be what

---

8. E.g., Abraham J. Malherbe, *The Letters to the Thessalonians: A New Translation with Introduction and Commentary*, AB 32B (New Haven: Yale University Press, 2000), 214.

9. 2 Thess 1:10; *Didache* 16:7; *Ascension of Isaiah* 4.14. See Rigaux, *Les Épitres aux Thessaloniciens*, 491.

10. *Didache* 16.7 (first or second century AD) interprets Zech 14:5 as a description of the resurrection of all Christians.

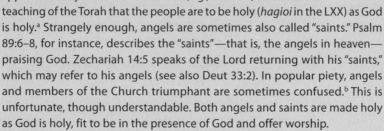

Humans and Angels as "Saints"

BIBLICAL BACKGROUND

In contemporary English the word "saint" is typically used by Catholics to refer only to members of the Church triumphant, men and women who lived lives of sanctity and now worship and intercede in heaven. In Scripture, however, members of the Church on earth are also called saints. Paul and other New Testament authors commonly refer to those in Christ as *hagioi*, which can be translated into English with either a word of Latin derivation ("saints") or of Old English ("holy ones"). This way of referring to the people of God appears already in the Old Testament (e.g., Ps 34:10) and recalls the teaching of the Torah that the people are to be holy (*hagioi* in the LXX) as God is holy.[a] Strangely enough, angels are sometimes also called "saints." Psalm 89:6–8, for instance, describes the "saints"—that is, the angels in heaven—praising God. Zechariah 14:5 speaks of the Lord returning with his "saints," which may refer to his angels (see also Deut 33:2). In popular piety, angels and members of the Church triumphant are sometimes confused.[b] This is unfortunate, though understandable. Both angels and saints are made holy as God is holy, fit to be in the presence of God and offer worship.

a. E.g., Lev 11:44–45; 19:2; 20:7; Num 15:40.
b. For an ancient example of martyrs being described as angels, see *Martyrdom of Polycarp* 2.3.

Paul had in mind. Paul describes the faithful meeting the Lord in the air after the resurrection (1 Thess 4:17), probably imagining that they will accompany him from that point on, returning "with him" to the earth for the last judgment (see commentary on 1 Thess 4:16–17).[11] According to 4:13–18, therefore, one may say that the Lord returns "to" the faithful but also that the Lord returns "with" the faithful.

Reflection and Application (3:11–13)

A frequent subject of debate among scholars of the New Testament and Christian origins is the question of when Jesus was first believed to be divine. First Thessalonians may be Paul's oldest surviving letter and also the earliest surviving Christian document. As such, it provides special insight into the beliefs of some of the earliest Christians. In these verses (3:11–13) Paul concludes the long first section of the letter with prayers that Jesus would increase the love of the Thessalonian church, and that Jesus and God would make it possible for

11. See also 1 Thess 4:14, which says that God will bring the faithful departed "with him."

Paul to return to them. Paul would not say this unless he believed that Jesus was indeed able to increase the Thessalonians' love, and that Jesus could work together with God the Father to eliminate the obstacles preventing Paul from traveling to Thessalonica.[12] It is also important to note that Paul does not explain to the Thessalonians how Jesus will accomplish these things. Though the Thessalonians were new believers and were confused about many things (as chap. 4 shows), they apparently already understood that Jesus was at work in their lives to increase their love.

If we back up and take stock of what the letter as a whole says about Jesus, we see that Paul taught that Jesus was a man who, like the prophets before him, was killed unjustly in Judea (2:14–15). Despite the fact that his execution was unjust, it had a larger purpose in God's plan. Jesus gave his life "for us" so that we might obtain salvation and live with him whether we are dead or alive (5:9–10). After he was killed, he rose from the dead and ascended into heaven (1:10; 4:14). The Church waits in hope of his coming, confident that he will save them from the wrath that will come in the final days (1:3, 10; 5:1–11) and in the hope that they will share in a resurrection like his and be with him always (4:13–18). Though this event remains in the future, Paul can already say that we live with Jesus (5:10) and that Jesus speaks through him (4:2). Paul also says that God gives us the Holy Spirit (4:8) and that God's "word" is at work among us to enable us to become holy and to be like Jesus by enduring persecution with joy (1:6). This process of sanctification has as its goal the moment when Jesus returns and those who are in him stand before him "blameless in holiness," perfected in love through the working of Jesus in our lives. This is not the developed trinitarian theology of later centuries, but from this earliest letter we see that Paul preached Jesus as a human who died and was raised and who works in our lives in concert with the Holy Spirit and God the Father.

---

12. See Chris Tilling, *Paul's Divine Christology*, WUNT 2/323 (Tübingen: Mohr Siebeck, 2012), 153–54.

Life Pleasing to God

1 Thessalonians 4:1–12

The chapter divisions in modern Bibles were not added until the thirteenth century, but on some occasions they rightly identify key turning points in the text. This is one of those occasions. From this point on in the letter, Paul turns to †paraenesis, encouraging and exhorting the new converts to please God with their lives (4:1). In 4:1–12, Paul discusses sexual purity and brotherly love. He had already told them some of these things when he was in Thessalonica (4:6, 11), but Timothy's report, though positive overall, led Paul to believe that there were certain problems that needed to be addressed (3:10). Paul carefully prepared his listeners for this section in chapter 2 when he described the apostles' own behavior. The apostles sought to please God (2:4), to be free from uncleanliness and greed (2:3), and to work so as not to burden others (2:8–9). Now Paul returns to all these same issues, telling the Thessalonians that they must do likewise. For Paul, the stakes were high: it was necessary to continue in this new way of life in order to be worthy of the kingdom of God.

Instructions on Pleasing God (4:1–2)

[1]Finally, brothers, we earnestly ask and exhort you in the Lord Jesus that, as you received from us how you should conduct yourselves to please God—and as you are conducting yourselves—you do so even more. [2]For you know what instructions we gave you through the Lord Jesus.

NT: 2 Cor 5:18–20

The NABRE's **Finally** makes it sound as if the letter were coming to a close. 4:1–2
The sense of the Greek is closer to "So then, as for the other matters . . ." Far
from wrapping the letter up, Paul has a number of pressing issues to address,
including sexual morality and the question of what happens to the faithful
after they have died. Though 1 Thessalonians remains friendly from start to
finish, in this section Paul adopts a more solemn tone, giving instructions
on vital matters and in some cases warning them of divine judgment should
they refuse to comply. The word translated as **instructions** (*parangelia*) is
often used in military and legal settings and could be translated as "commands" or "orders." These are not optional suggestions for their consideration
but rather a blueprint laying out the pattern of life that God requires. Paul
gives them these instructions **through the Lord Jesus**, meaning that the
ideas that follow in the section are not his personal preferences but instead
carry the authority of Jesus himself. As Theodoret of Cyrus explains, "Paul
makes the paraenesis [*parainesis*] worthy of belief by invoking the memory
of the Master."[1] Though Paul is giving commands from the Lord, he does
not describe God as an implacable taskmaster. Instead, Paul indicates at a
number of points in the letter that God will supply what the Thessalonians
need to keep God's commands (see especially 5:23–24). Paul thought that it
really was possible for them with God's help to live in a way that God would
find pleasing, just as he endeavored to please God in his own ministry (2:4;
see Rom 8:8–9).

Sanctity and Sexual Immorality (4:3–8)

---

[3]This is the will of God, your holiness: that you refrain from immorality,
[4]that each of you know how to acquire a wife for himself in holiness and
honor, [5]not in lustful passion as do the Gentiles who do not know God;
[6]not to take advantage of or exploit a brother in this matter, for the Lord
is an avenger in all these things, as we told you before and solemnly af-
firmed. [7]For God did not call us to impurity but to holiness. [8]Therefore,
whoever disregards this, disregards not a human being but God, who
[also] gives his holy Spirit to you.

NT: Acts 15:1–29
Catechism: the sixth commandment, 2331–400
Lectionary: 1 Thess 4:1–8; Memorial of Saint Augustine

---

1. *Interpretatio in xiv epistulas sancti Pauli* (PG 82:644 [my translation]).

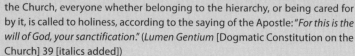

The Universal Call to Holiness

The Second Vatican Council cited 1 Thess 4:3 in support of its teaching that God calls all Christians to holiness, not just smaller groups of spiritual elites:

> The Church, whose mystery is being set forth by this Sacred Synod, is believed to be indefectibly holy. Indeed Christ, the Son of God, who with the Father and the Spirit is praised as "uniquely holy," loved the Church as His bride, delivering Himself up for her. He did this that He might sanctify her. He united her to Himself as His own body and brought it to perfection by the gift of the Holy Spirit for God's glory. Therefore in the Church, everyone whether belonging to the hierarchy, or being cared for by it, is called to holiness, according to the saying of the Apostle: "*For this is the will of God, your sanctification.*" (*Lumen Gentium* [Dogmatic Constitution on the Church] 39 [italics added])

This passage deserves careful attention because Catholics have sometimes thought that there are two tiers of Christians: those who are called to lives of radical holiness and those who do only the bare minimum. Such a distinction is completely foreign to Paul, who taught that God's sanctifying Spirit is at work in all the baptized. As St. John Paul II put it while commenting on Jesus's words to the rich young man (Matt 19:21), "This vocation to perfect love is not restricted to a small group of individuals. *The invitation,* 'go, sell your possessions and give the money to the poor', and the promise 'you will have treasure in heaven', *are meant for everyone*" (*Veritatis Splendor* [The Splendor of Truth] 18 [italics original]).

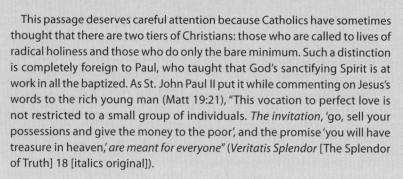

4:3   In this section Paul boldly proclaims the **will of God** for the Thessalonians, describing the way of life that God demands. First, he says that God desires their **holiness** (*hagiasmos*), a word that is very uncommon outside of Jewish and Christian literature. In the †Septuagint it refers to the consecration or sanctification of things set aside or purified to serve God (e.g., Amos 2:11; 2 Macc 14:36). In effect, Paul reminds the Thessalonians that they have become sacred vessels, recipients of God's Holy Spirit who must behave accordingly (1 Cor 6:19). Sanctification was not limited to sexuality for Paul, but in this passage it is defined as abstention from sexual **immorality** (*porneia*). Contrary to what the NABRE translation might suggest, the Greek word *porneia* refers specifically to sexual immorality, not all immorality. In classical Greek, *porneia* referred to prostitution, but by Paul's day Jewish writers used it to refer to almost any sexual relationship outside the relationship between a husband and a wife. The specific form of *porneia* that Paul has in mind here may be adultery (see below on v. 6), though scribes who made copies of the letter in antiquity understood Paul to be condemning every possible type of sexual immorality: from the fourth century on, Paul was quoted as saying "abstain from *all* fornication." It is possible that Timothy had informed Paul of specific instances of fornication, possibly of adultery between members of the church.[2]

After describing holiness in negative terms (avoid sexual immorality), Paul offers positive instructions: each of them must learn **how to acquire a wife for himself**. The phrase "acquire a wife for himself" is notoriously difficult to interpret.[3] The word translated as "wife" is *skeuos*, which means "vessel." What would it mean for the Thessalonians to learn how to acquire their own vessels? The NABRE interprets "vessel" as a metaphor for a wife. If this is correct, Paul would seem to be telling all the unmarried men to find wives. Though this interpretation was favored by some ancient Greek readers of Paul (St. Basil the Great, Theodore of Mopsuestia), there are serious difficulties with it. There is no clear evidence that the word *skeuos* was ever used in other Greek literature to refer to wives, despite the claims of some scholars to the contrary. First Peter 3:7 does refer to wives as "the weaker vessel," but the implication is that husbands are vessels too. A second difficulty with this interpretation is the unlikelihood of Paul telling all the Thessalonians that they must acquire a wife. Paul himself was not married, so it would have been odd to demand that all the Thessalonians, who were to become imitators of him (1 Thess 1:6), must get married (see 1 Cor 7:7–8).[4]

Another interpretation, one favored by many English translations (NRSV, NIV, CEB, ESV), understands "vessel" as a metaphor for human beings or their bodies. As Theodoret puts it, "Some interpret 'his own vessel' as 'spouse,' but I think 'vessel' means 'his own body.' For it is not only to those who have married he offers the legislation."[5] In other words, Paul would be telling all the Thessalonians, married and single, that they must learn to control themselves. Unlike "vessel" as wife, there is good evidence for "vessel" as a metaphor for human

4:4–5

2. See the careful attempt to ascertain the situation in Thessalonica in Nijay K. Gupta, "Mirror-Reading Moral Issues in Paul's Letters," *JSNT* 34 (2012): 361–81.

3. For detailed weighing of the options and a different conclusion from the one presented here, see Matthias Konradt, "Εἰδέναι ἕκαστον ὑμῶν τὸ ἑαυτοῦ σκεῦος κτᾶσθαι . . . Zu Paulus' sexualethischer Weisung in 1Thess 4,4f.," *ZNW* 92 (2001): 128–35.

4. Others propose "*live with* one's own wife." According to this interpretation, Paul was not telling the Thessalonians that they all needed to find a wife. He was telling them that they must live with their wives in "holiness and honor," without surrendering to lust. Unfortunately, however, this interpretation retains the translation "wife," which almost certainly is incorrect, as noted above.

5. *Interpretatio in xiv epistulas sancti Pauli* (PG 82:644 [my translation]).

beings. Indeed, Paul himself uses *skeuos* to refer to humans (Rom 9:21–23; 2 Cor 4:7–12). This interpretation has its own weaknesses, however. It is not clear what it would mean to "acquire" one's own body. Interpreters have taken *ktaomai* to mean "control," an interpretation for which there is little clear evidence. While "body" seems much more likely than "wife," it remains uncertain what it means to "learn to acquire" one's own body. St. John Chrysostom suggests that Paul said this because controlling one's body is difficult and requires repeated effort to learn; that is, one must learn to acquire self-control.[6] While not free of difficulties, this is perhaps the best explanation we have.

Why did Paul speak of "vessels" instead of stating what he meant more clearly? *Skeuos* ("vessel") is used frequently in the †Septuagint to refer to sacred vessels in the tabernacle or the temple, and it is also commonly used as a metaphor for people who are either used by God or used for evil. The metaphor of person as vessel emphasizes the different purposes that a person's life might have: a holy vessel for God or a profane vessel for ordinary things. For instance, 2 Timothy encourages becoming an honorable, pure, and holy vessel by avoiding sinful desires. The italicized words all have parallels in 1 Thess 4:3–8:

> In a large house there are *vessels* not only of gold and silver but also of wood and clay, some for *honorable use* and others for dishonorable use. If anyone *cleanses* himself from these things, he will be a *vessel* for *honorable use*, *consecrated*, useful to the master, ready for every good work. Flee youthful *desires* and pursue justice, faith, love, and peace, along with those who call on the Lord from *purity* of heart. (2 Tim 2:20–22 [my translation])

Regardless of one's opinion about the authorship of 2 Timothy, this passage provides a helpful parallel to 1 Thess 4:4–5. In both cases, the recipients are encouraged to act as holy vessels, pursuing purity and avoiding sinful desires. Paul contrasts the life to which God has called them, which is characterized by growth in holiness, honor, and the presence of the Holy Spirit, with lust, uncleanliness, and estrangement from God. They are to use their body in a way that is holy—that is, as vessels of God's Holy Spirit, like the sacred vessels used in the temple.

Verse 5 continues the sentence begun in 4:3. As holy vessels, the Thessalonians are to conduct themselves in holiness, not in **lustful passion**. The word translated as "lustful" (*epithymia*) could refer to good or bad desires, but here it describes "passion" (*pathos*) and probably refers to sexual urges. Warnings against passion do not appear in the Old Testament, but they were a common

---

6. *Homiliae in epistulam i ad Thessalonicenses* (PG 62:424).

topic of conversation among moral teachers in Paul's day, especially Stoic philosophers. One of the most influential philosophies of the first century, Stoicism taught that the passions were excessive impulses toward a particular thing that rob one of freedom.[7] Stoics taught that lust or desire (*epithymia*) was one of the four main types of passion, along with fear, pain, and pleasure. Similar warnings against the passions can be found in Paul's other letters and some early Christian writers.[8]

Readers today might well wonder what business Paul has telling the Thessalonians to control their passions. Modern people often see sexual urges and other emotions as more or less unchangeable and uncontrollable features of a person's makeup. In contrast, many people in Paul's day thought that passions could be mastered under the correct tutelage. For instance, the noncanonical book 4 Maccabees (first century AD) acknowledges that no one is able to eradicate their passions and desires, but "reason" provides a way not to be enslaved by them (3:2). Some ancient Jews argued that the Torah is the best antidote to the passions.[9] Paul taught that knowing God and receiving the Holy Spirit are what empower a person to overcome the passions (see 1 Thess 4:7–8). In his letter to the Galatians he would go on to name *enkrateia* ("self-control" or "self-mastery") as one of the fruits of the Spirit (Gal 5:23; see also Rom 1:26; Col 3:5). Similarly, in this letter Paul is confident that God will provide what is necessary for the Thessalonians to conquer their lusts.

Paul associates lustful passion with **the Gentiles who do not know God**. It was not uncommon for ancient Jews to link the Gentiles' false ideas about God with deviant sexual behavior (e.g., Wis 14:12; Rom 1:26). In this letter, Paul characterizes the Gentiles as those who worship idols, give in to their passions, and remain ignorant of the true and living God (1 Thess 1:9; 4:5). The people of Israel, on the other hand, were to be a "kingdom of priests, a holy nation" (Exod 19:6). Their holiness was meant to render them fit to commune with God (Num 15:40–41; Ps 51:11). The astonishing thing was that the Gentile Thessalonians had themselves become dwelling places of God's Spirit and, as such, were called to be "blameless in holiness" (1 Thess 3:13). Yet, as anyone acquainted with ancient philosophy can attest, Jews and Christians were not the only people in the Greco-Roman world who were concerned about sexual ethics. The first-century Stoic philosopher Musonius Rufus, for instance, condemned

---

7. E.g., Epictetus, *Discourses* 4.7.

8. E.g., Rom 1:24–26; *Didache* 1.4: "Abstain from fleshly and bodily desires" (my translation).

9. Paul's younger contemporary, Josephus, imagined Moses as someone who had mastered his passions (*Jewish Antiquities* 4.328).

all sexual activity outside of marriage, including sex between a man and his own female slaves, which was widely practiced.[10]

Given the presence of such "ethical pagans," why would Paul describe non-Jews as those who are controlled by their passions? There are two obvious reasons why Paul would talk this way in a letter to new converts. First, though ethical teaching was popular, acts of what Paul called *porneia* were widespread. Sex with married women was frowned upon because it trespassed on the honor of the cuckolded husband, but generally speaking, men were not discouraged from occasional sex with prostitutes or slaves. Thus, despite the presence of high-minded teachers like Musonius Rufus, it was not for nothing that the apostles instructed Gentile converts to "abstain from *porneia*" (see 1 Thess 4:3). Second, by speaking of the "Gentiles who do not know God" as some other mass of people, Paul reinforces the Thessalonians' sense of belonging to a new group. The Thessalonians were themselves Gentiles who had only recently turned to worship "the living God" (1:9). By speaking of "the Gentiles who do not know God" as some other group of people, Paul reinforces the Thessalonians' sense of belonging.

4:6   Since antiquity some interpreters, especially those who read the text in Latin, have thought that verse 6 marked the beginning of a new topic—namely, honesty in business dealings in the church. The words translated as **exploit** (*pleonekteō*) and **this matter** (*pragma*) are sometimes used to refer to greed with money. The Douay-Rheims Bible, which is based on the Vulgate, translates the clause as "And that no man overreach, nor circumvent his brother in business." Other ancient interpreters, such as John Chrysostom and Theodoret, take verse 6 to be a continuation of the discussion of chastity that began in verse 3, and there is good reason to believe that they were correct.[11] Verse 6 continues the sentence that began in verse 3 and repeats the language of holiness that pervades this discussion of sexuality. Exploiting **a brother** probably refers to harming a fellow member of the community by having sex with his wife, daughter, or slave. St. John Chrysostom offers a compelling explanation of why Paul would refer to fornication as the exploitation or robbery of a brother:

> God has assigned a wife to each man, and he has set boundaries to nature, namely, that intercourse is with one only. Therefore, transgressing with another is both robbery and "exploitation." Or rather, it is more grievous than any robbery, for

10. On Musonius Rufus and many other parallels between Paul and the philosophy of his day, see Abraham J. Malherbe, *The Letters to the Thessalonians: A New Translation with Introduction and Commentary*, AB 32B (New Haven: Yale University Press, 2000), 230.
11. Chrysostom, *Homiliae* (PG 62:424); Theodoret, *Interpretatio in xiv epistulas sancti Pauli* (PG 82:644).

we do not suffer so much when our possessions are carried away as when marriage is undermined.[12]

In other words, the man who sleeps with another man's wife exceeds the boundaries that God has set out for him and takes something that is not his. Modern readers can hardly fail to notice that Paul does not warn against defrauding a sister in these matters. The apostle appears to presuppose a patriarchal view of sex and family in which illicit sex with a woman is an offense primarily against the woman's husband or father. This very passage, however, contains ideas that would be used in the later tradition to begin moving toward the understanding that sexual sins are offenses primarily against the person directly involved and against God (see Reflection and Application on 4:3–8).

Paul stresses the gravity of committing fornication, reminding them that **the Lord is an avenger in all these things**. Most acts of *porneia* were legal under Roman law, adultery being the main exception. Nevertheless, those who commit these acts should expect to face divine judgment. The "Lord" who will execute justice is probably Jesus. *Kyrios* ("Lord") always refers to Jesus in 1 Thessalonians, and early Christians expected that Jesus "will come again in glory to judge the living and the dead," as the Nicene-Constantinopolitan Creed puts it (see, e.g., Acts 10:42; 2 Tim 4:1; 1 Pet 4:5). The word translated as "avenger" (*ekdikos*) refers here to one who ensures that justice (*dikē*) is done (see also 2 Thess 1:9). The image of Jesus as an avenger who will mete out just punishments on Christians who did not live holy lives is startling and stands in apparent tension with Paul's claim that the Thessalonian converts are God's chosen and beloved ones (1 Thess 1:4; 5:9). How could God choose them and then avenge their fornication? These two ideas run throughout Paul's Letters: God offers grace unconditionally (Rom 5:6–11), but God will also judge everyone according to their deeds (see 2 Cor 5:10; Rom 14:10). The Thessalonians have received the Holy Spirit, but they are expected to live holy lives (1 Thess 4:7). God empowers them to do this (1:6; 3:12–13), yet they must choose to live in holiness.

Verse 7 acts as a good summary of this section as a whole. In responding to God's call, the Thessalonians accepted the obligation to live in a particular way. Paul makes this point using the "not X but Y" form that he relies on so often in this letter: **God did not call us to impurity but to holiness**. God's call is a gift, but it also imposes obligations. To respond to the call requires the church to follow the way of life that God reveals. The antithesis between impurity (*akatharsia*) and holiness (*hagiasmos*) evokes both the moral and †cultic realms.

4:7–8

12. *Homiliae* (PG 62:424 [my translation]).

Morally, holiness describes a way of life ordered by love, and impurity refers to sin, especially sexual sin. These words also have a cultic sense, however; holiness refers to the realm of God, and impurity is what makes a person unfit to have access to God. The two fields of meaning, moral and cultic, are both in play in this passage. It is by living morally upright lives that the Thessalonians maintain their sanctity as recipients of God's Spirit. To give in to moral impurity would be to reject God's presence.

Unlike the NABRE, Paul does not use the same preposition in both halves of the antithesis. A better rendering would be "God did not call us to impurity but *in holiness*" or perhaps "through sanctification." That is, God's call has a sanctifying power on their lives. As 2 Thess 2:13 puts it, "God chose you as the firstfruits for salvation *through sanctification by the Spirit*" (italics added). God called the Thessalonians by giving the Holy Spirit to them (see commentary on the word of God in 1 Thess 2:13). This is why Paul sees the refusal to embrace sanctification as such a serious problem: it is tantamount to rejecting the Holy Spirit, a point that is reinforced in verse 8. Paul ends the section with another warning, repeating once again that the call to avoid fornication is not merely his personal preference but rather is God's command. Those who reject this command reject God, who **gives his holy Spirit to you**.

Reflection and Application (4:3–8)

In ancient Greece and Rome the social status of a woman determined whether it was moral or legal for a man to have sex with her.[13] Men were permitted to have sex with low-status women such as slaves, prostitutes, and courtesans. Such acts of *porneia* were seen as acceptable outlets for male sexual energy. Even if the man was married, sex with a low-status woman was not considered adultery (*moicheia*). Men also had complete authority over the bodies of their own slaves, whether male or female. Sex with free, respectable women, however, was considered adultery, in part because sex with them would dishonor their husbands or fathers. In other words, men were given great sexual license, provided the woman in question was low status and therefore sexually available. As Salvian, a fifth-century bishop, famously puts it while complaining about Roman culture, they are forever "forbidding adultery, building brothels."[14] While preaching on 1 Thessalonians, St. John Chrysostom staged a direct attack on all these assumptions, arguing that one's status before God

13. Kyle Harper, "*Porneia*: The Making of a Christian Sexual Norm," *JBL* 131 (2012): 363–83.
14. *On the Government of God* 7.22. Cited by Harper, "*Porneia*," 369.

is what matters, not one's social or marital status. Chrysostom compares the offense of sex with a list of possible women, descending in order of honor: a queen (*basilis*), a married slave, an unmarried slave, and a prostitute. The congregation listening to Chrysostom seems to have shared the widespread assumption that sex with a queen would be completely incomparable to sex with a prostitute because of their different levels of respectability. Though he expects the congregation to get angry, Chrysostom cites 1 Thess 4:8 to argue that no matter who the woman is, "the crime is the same" because in every case "you have committed the same crime against God." Even if one has sex with a prostitute and there is no husband to take offense, "nevertheless God avenges, for he avenges himself." Unfaithful men are punished "not by Roman laws but by God." He continues, "Listen carefully to what I say, for even if this message is difficult to bear, it must be said to set things right for the future. It is adultery not only when we corrupt a married woman. Even if the woman is available and free, it is adultery if we men are married. So what if she isn't married? You are!"[15]

Love and Work (4:9–12)

---

[9]On the subject of mutual charity you have no need for anyone to write you, for you yourselves have been taught by God to love one another. [10]Indeed, you do this for all the brothers throughout Macedonia. Nevertheless we urge you, brothers, to progress even more, [11]and to aspire to live a tranquil life, to mind your own affairs, and to work with your [own] hands, as we instructed you, [12]that you may conduct yourselves properly toward outsiders and not depend on anyone.

NT: 2 Thess 3:6–13
Lectionary: 1 Thess 4:9–11; Martyrdom of Saint John the Baptist

In 2:1–12 Paul described his affection for the Thessalonians, how he loved them and worked "night and day" to share the gospel with them without placing a financial burden on them. As noted in the comments on that section, Paul did this in part to offer an example to the Thessalonians of how they ought to behave. In this section Paul addresses the issue directly, exhorting the Thessalonians to grow in love and to live orderly lives that will allow them to conduct themselves becomingly with outsiders.

15. *Homiliae* (PG 62:425–26 [my translation]).

4:9–10   In this section Paul turns to the subject of *philadelphia*, a Greek word that the NABRE translates as **mutual charity** but that could be more woodenly translated as "brotherly love." This word ordinarily referred to the love between actual siblings.[16] Some ancient Jews, however, spoke of the "brotherly love" between fellow members of God's people (2 Macc 15:14). Paul uses the word in this sense, but he includes the Gentile members of the Thessalonian church, commending them for loving one another as brothers and sisters and urging them to do so **even more**. In contemporary English we tend to associate the word "love" with good feelings or romance. The love that Paul has in mind here, however, is constituted by actions (see 1 Thess 1:3, 7–8). It is something that the Thessalonians have "done." Strikingly, this love extended beyond the local congregation to include **all the brothers throughout Macedonia**. The language of family that permeates this letter extends also to those who are in Christ beyond the Thessalonian congregation. Paul is already cultivating a sense of the Church as "catholic," meaning "universal," including all who are in Christ regardless of their location. Paul doesn't say precisely how the Thessalonians were showing love for one another and other Christians across Macedonia. One possibility is that they were sharing their possessions. We know from 2 Cor 8:1–5 that the churches of Macedonia were quick to contribute to Paul's collection for the poor in Jerusalem. Though almsgiving did not exhaust the meaning of love for Paul (1 Cor 13:3), he considered it an expression of love (2 Cor 8:8, 24). The sharing of resources may also be part of what is behind the reluctance of some of the Thessalonians to work (see below on vv. 11–12).

The Thessalonians' acts of love are evidence that they are **taught by God**. The Greek translated as "taught by God" is one word, *theodidaktoi*, and it seems to be Paul's own coinage. One might ask why Paul goes on to write this section at all. If God is their teacher, why do they need Paul? Paul regularly assured readers that they did not need to hear about a particular topic, but he would then go on to talk about it anyway. This was (and is) a common rhetorical device called "paraleipsis," which allows the speaker to compliment the audience before making further requests (e.g., "You know better than most how important it is to tithe regularly"). More importantly, Paul is drawing on biblical promises of a coming age when God will become the teacher of all the people. For instance, the prophet Isaiah speaks of the time when "all your children shall be taught by the Lord" (54:13). Jeremiah promises a new covenant when God will write the law on the people's hearts (31:31–34), and Micah speaks of the

---

16. E.g., Plutarch, Paul's younger contemporary, wrote a treatise on the importance of *philadelphia*, by which he meant the love between actual siblings.

St. Augustine on Being "Taught by God"   LIVING TRADITION

Augustine draws on 1 Thess 4:9 to argue that God is a teacher who not only explains what must be done but also gives what is necessary for it to be done.

> Let grace be called "teaching" in the sense that God may be believed to infuse it more deeply and interiorly with ineffable sweetness, not only through those who plant and water externally, but also through himself, who gives the growth unseen so that he not only reveals truth but also imparts love. For thus God teaches them who have been called according to his purpose, simultaneously giving them what they need both to know what they must do and to do what they know. Thus the Apostle speaks to the Thessalonians, "Concerning brotherly love, you have no need that I write to you, for you yourselves are taught by God to love one another." And to show that they had been taught by God, he adds, "And indeed you do it for all the brothers in the whole of Macedonia," as if the surest proof that you have been taught by God is that you do what you were taught. This is how it is for all who are called according to his purpose, as it is written in the prophets, "They will be taught by God" (Isa 54:13).[a]

a. *The Grace of Christ and Original Sin* 1.13.14 (my translation).

Gentiles receiving the teaching of God instead of waging war (4:1–3).[17] Paul and other early Christians believed that texts such as these were describing the time they were living in when the Spirit was poured out even on the Gentiles. Thus, when Paul heard about the Thessalonian converts doing good deeds for the sake of Christians across Macedonia, he took it as confirmation that God was their teacher.

For Paul, there is no tension between being taught by him and taught by God, for he believes that he is God's chosen emissary to the Thessalonians. He goes on to ask them "to progress even more" (1 Thess 4:10), listing specific ways for them to do this. They are to **aspire to live a tranquil life**. The word translated as "aspire" (*philotimeomai*) means "to love honor" and frequently refers to the desire for public recognition that motivated extravagant gifts to one's city. The Thessalonian Christians, however, are to aspire to "live a tranquil life," or a "quiet" life. Instead of making it their ambition to draw attention to themselves they are to mind their own business, just as Paul has sought to please God rather than seeking glory from people (2:4–6). Paul also asks them **to work with your [own] hands**, a command that he had already given them when he

4:11–12

17. See also Deut 30; Ezek 36–37.

Manual Labor

Manual labor is described here as a means of loving fellow Christians and earning what one needs (see also 2 Thess 3). Ephesians 4:28 adds another argument in favor of manual labor: it allows one to produce something to give to the needy. This emphasis on labor in the Pauline tradition is paralleled by the early rabbis. The Mishnah records a saying of Rabban Gamaliel (who, according to Acts 22:3, was Paul's teacher) that the study of Torah combined with labor makes one forget sin, whereas Torah study on its own leads to iniquity.[a] In his instructions for monks, St. Basil the Great repeatedly cites Paul to argue that their prayers must not lead them to neglect manual labor.[b] Many religious orders share this concern. Benedictine monks, for instance, are known for the saying *ora et labora* ("pray and work"). In his commentary on 1 Thessalonians, St. Thomas Aquinas says that it is important to work with one's hands in order to avoid evil and to have something to share with the poor, citing Sir 33:28–29 and Ezek 16:49.[c] Even in the postindustrial age the Magisterium continues to stress the importance of manual labor and, along with it, all human labor. St. John Paul II's encyclical *Laborem Exercens* (On Human Work) appeals to the example of Christ himself, who worked with his hands (6), as does Pope Francis's encyclical *Laudato Si'* (On Care for Our Common Home):

> Jesus worked with his hands, in daily contact with the matter created by God, to which he gave form by his craftsmanship. It is striking that most of his life was dedicated to this task in a simple life which awakened no admiration at all: "Is not this the carpenter, the son of Mary?" (Mark 6:3). In this way he sanctified human labour and endowed it with a special significance for our development. As Saint John Paul II taught, "by enduring the toil of work in union with Christ crucified for us, man in a way collaborates with the Son of God for the redemption of humanity." (98)

a. *Mishnah Avot* 2:2.
b. *Asketikon: Longer Responses* 37, citing Acts 20:35; 2 Cor 11:27; Eph 4:28; 2 Thess 3:10.
c. *Super ad Thessalonicenses I reportatio* 4.1.90.

was in Thessalonica and that he had exemplified through his own labor. The purpose of this hardworking way of life was **that you may conduct yourselves properly toward outsiders and not depend on anyone**. Stated negatively, if some members of the church refused to work, they would make a poor witness to those outside the church, and if they were not wealthy, they would mooch off the goodwill of others.

Paul's emphasis on love is well known, but he speaks much less often on the importance of work. How do we explain the emphasis on this issue here?

One theory that has been popular in modern times is that some of the new converts had stopped working because they thought that the return of Jesus was imminent. One trouble with this theory is that Paul himself never links his teaching on the Lord's return with idleness. Another possibility is that the generosity of other Christians allowed them to stop working. Paul had already given the command to do manual labor when he was in Thessalonica (4:11), so perhaps he saw problems in this area beginning to develop. If Paul is the author of 2 Thessalonians, then it would seem that this problem grew worse after 1 Thessalonians was written. What is clear is that Paul sets out work and orderly living as a means of loving both those in the church and those outside of it (1 Thess 3:12) because it allows Christians to conduct themselves becomingly with outsiders and avoid sponging off of one another.

Reflection and Application (4:9–12)

In 4:9–12 Paul urges the Thessalonians to work with their hands and mind their own business in order to win the respect of non-Christians ("so that you may walk becomingly toward outsiders" [my translation]). This advice seems sensible enough: if some in the congregation were conspicuously lazy, it could bring the young church into disrepute (see also 1 Cor 10:32–33; Col 4:5). Yet Paul's concern for the congregation's reputation seems at first glance to contradict his own example of refusing to please people or seek praise from anyone (1 Thess 2:4, 6). Are Christians supposed to work to make good impressions on outsiders or not? This question becomes thornier when one considers the contrast that Paul draws between Christian and pagan ways of life. He celebrates the converts' renunciation of idols (1:9) and dismisses those outside the Church as children of darkness (5:5) and slaves of passion (4:3–8) destined for God's wrath (1:10; 5:1–11; see also 4:13). Even stronger contrasts appear in Paul's later letters, such as 1 Corinthians, which sets the message of Christ crucified in opposition to the wisdom and power of the world (1:18–2:16; see also Rom 12:2; 2 Cor 4:3–4). Is it possible to lead a countercultural life, disregarding the praise of others, while also working to establish a good reputation? Sharp debates in today's Church swirl around this question, with disagreements about whether the Church should be inward focused, withdrawing to ensure fidelity to a countercultural mandate, or outward focused, seeking to attract the wider world.

Origen (ca. 185–254) addresses this question while commenting on Rom 15:2 ("Let each of us please our neighbor for the good, for edification" [my translation]). Origen notes that the words "for the good, for edification" clarify in what sense the Christian should seek to please others: "For he is advising not that 'praise from people' (1 Thess 2:6) be sought but that edification be given to our neighbors by our deeds and words."[18] Origen then links these verses to the Sermon on the Mount, where Jesus teaches that good deeds should be done in secret—for God's eyes only (Matt 6:1–18)—but also instructs disciples to let others see their good works (Matt 5:16):

> As also in that place where the Savior says, "Let your light shine before people, and when they see your good works they praise your Father in heaven" (Matt 5:16). Through this he is certainly not exhorting the disciples to seek "praise from people." Rather, living righteously and honorably, they should edify those who see so that God may be praised.[19]

According to Origen, the motive driving one to make a good impression on others is of central importance. One might seek to impress others for one's own glory—which Paul and Jesus condemn—or for the good of others and the glorification of God.

---

18. Origen, *Commentary on the Epistle to the Romans* (according to Rufinus) 10.6 (my translation).
19. Origen, *Commentary on the Epistle to the Romans* 10.6 (my translation).

The Fate of Dead Christians and the Return of the Lord

1 Thessalonians 4:13–18

In this, the most famous portion of Paul's letters to the Thessalonians, Paul provides new teaching on the return of Jesus and the fate of dead Christians. When he was in Thessalonica, Paul told the new converts to wait for Jesus's return from the heavens to gather his people (1:10; 4:6, 14; 5:1–11). But when Timothy returned to check on them, he found them grieving the loss of some of their number. These unexpected deaths seem to have raised new, troubling questions for the Thessalonians. They may have assumed that they would all live to see the Lord's return, but now that some of them were dead, the remaining members worried that the deceased would be at some disadvantage when the Lord returned. In his response, Paul seeks to curb their grief and correct their understanding of the fate of the dead, quoting a word of the Lord declaring that the faithful departed will not miss out on the coming of Jesus and the gathering of his people. Though this passage presents some difficult puzzles, Paul's essential point is clear enough: those who die in Christ will rise first and will remain forever with him along with those who are alive at the time of his coming. In this way, all who belong to the Lord, whether living or dead, will always be together with the Lord.

The Fate of Those Who Have Died (4:13–18)

[13]We do not want you to be unaware, brothers, about those who have fallen asleep, so that you may not grieve like the rest, who have no hope.

[14]For if we believe that Jesus died and rose, so too will God, through Jesus, bring with him those who have fallen asleep. [15]Indeed, we tell you this, on the word of the Lord, that we who are alive, who are left until the coming of the Lord, will surely not precede those who have fallen asleep. [16]For the Lord himself, with a word of command, with the voice of an archangel and with the trumpet of God, will come down from heaven, and the dead in Christ will rise first. [17]Then we who are alive, who are left, will be caught up together with them in the clouds to meet the Lord in the air. Thus we shall always be with the Lord. [18]Therefore, console one another with these words.

OT: Dan 12:1–3
NT: 1 Cor 15; 2 Thess 1:5–10
Catechism: resurrection of the body, 988–1019
Lectionary: Commemoration of All the Faithful Departed

4:13   The words **We do not want you to be unaware** may signal that Paul is about to give them new information, unlike the majority of the letter, which is filled with reminders of what Paul had already said or done.[1] The Thessalonians already knew that Jesus died and rose (4:14), and they expected him to return in the near future (1:9–10; 5:1–2, 23). The area of confusion concerned the fate of those who died before Jesus's return. In the NABRE Paul refers to the deceased as **those who have fallen asleep**, a description of death that is common in the New Testament and among Greek-speakers more generally.[2] This description of departed Christians has prompted speculation over the centuries that after death the soul goes to sleep to be roused at the end of time, but there is little, if any, support for this view in Paul: sleep was a common euphemism for death found in Greek literature since the time of Homer. Similar to the modern idiom "passed away," it allows one to avoid stating bluntly that someone is dead. Even though "soul sleep" should be rejected as a literalistic misunderstanding of the idiom, it may be significant that three times in this short passage Paul refers to the dead as those who sleep, rather than simply saying they have died. The repeated language of sleep subtly reminds the Thessalonians that their loved ones are not permanently erased from existence but are only waiting to be roused

1. It is also possible that Paul had touched on this issue while in Thessalonica, but that the Thessalonians had not understood it. See Abraham J. Malherbe, *The Letters to the Thessalonians: A New Translation with Introduction and Commentary*, AB 32B (New Haven: Yale University Press, 2000), 284.
2. There is a variant here in the Greek manuscripts. What Paul wrote was probably the present-tense *koimōmenōn* ("those who sleep" [as printed in the text of Nestle-Aland[28] and followed by NIV and ESV]), not the perfect *kekoimēmenōn* ("those who have fallen asleep" [the variant translated by NABRE and NRSV]). The manuscript evidence for the present tense is stronger. Ancient copyists would have been inclined to change this to the perfect tense because it was a more common expression.

on the last day. Ancient Christians certainly understood biblical descriptions of the "sleep" of death this way and by the end of the second century AD began to refer to tombs as *koimētēria* ("sleeping places"), a word that eventually designated the places where many people were buried and that came into English as "cemetery."[3] For instance, a funerary inscription from second- or third-century Thessalonica refers to the tomb as "the place to sleep until the resurrection" (*to koimētērion heōs anastaseōs*).[4] A fourth-century inscription from Philippi says, "Lord, have mercy on us and raise us up, we who now sleep in the true faith."[5] St. John Chrysostom explains that in his day Christians called tombs "sleeping places" so that "you would learn that those who have perished and lie here have not died but sleep and lie at rest. . . . Since Christ, who died for the life of the world, has come, no longer is death called death, but slumber and sleep." He then cites 1 Thess 4:15 for support, along with other passages.[6]

Paul wants them to stop grieving **like the rest, who have no hope**. "The rest" probably refers to all who do not place their hope in Jesus. As in 4:5, Paul paints with a very broad brush, describing all who do not belong to Christ as those who have no hope when a loved one dies. In fact, people in Paul's day had a variety of different views about what happens after death and how one ought to grieve, just as they do today. Some continued to believe in the Hades of Greek myths, a dreary underworld where one might continue to exist in some form. Funerary inscriptions were frequently rather bleak, with phrases such as "No one is immortal" or "This is life"—that is, life inevitably ends in the grave. Others, however, were committed to a belief in the immortality of the soul and, like Paul, sought to curb excess grief. Famously, Socrates was supposed to have taught that the soul was immortal and, because of this, forbade expressions of grief at his death.[7] Paul's contemporary, the Roman philosopher Seneca the Younger, thought that a short period of grief was acceptable, but anything more was unnatural.[8] So, to be fair to "the rest," we must admit that there was a variety of beliefs about grief and hope. Why, then, would Paul, who knew more about how first-century people faced death than we do, say that everyone else is without hope? As in 4:3–5, he draws a sharp contrast between those who belong to Christ and those who do not. In a sense, pagans' varying attitudes toward death were insignificant. For him, Christ is the only ground for hope

3. Éric Rebillard, "*Koimetérion* et *Coemeterium*: Tombe, tombe sainte, nécropole," in *Mélanges de l'École française de Rome*, Antiquité 105/2 (Rome: l'École française de Rome, 1993), 975–1001.

4. *IG* X,2 1 440 (my translation).

5. *RIChrM* 234 (my translation).

6. *De coemeterio et de cruce* (PG 49:393–94 [my translation]).

7. Plato, *Phaedo* 117.

8. *Ad Marciam de consolatione* 7.1–2.

in the face of death (5:8–10). Paul is saying, not that there is no hope for the pagan world (see 1 Tim 2:3–4), only that they have no hope apart from Christ.[9]

Many ancient and modern interpreters have thought that when Paul says they should not "grieve like the rest" he means that Christians should not grieve at all. According to this view, Paul was prohibiting not just excess grief or grief without hope but *all* grief for the dead. The New Jerusalem Bible translates verse 13 to reflect this view ("Make sure that you do not grieve for them"), as does the Knox Bible ("You are not to lament over them"). Proponents of this view note that Paul uses a similar phrase in 4:5 to reject Gentile behavior completely:

- "not in lustful passion as do [*kathaper*] the Gentiles" (4:5)
- "so that you may not grieve like [*kathōs*] the rest" (4:13)

This parallel suggests that Paul wanted the church to reject grief for the dead just as they rejected unchastity. The idea of forbidding all grief for the dead may sound impossible—even cruel—but many Church Fathers understood Paul in this way. St. Cyprian cites this verse to show that "no one should be saddened by death."[10] In a letter to a bereaved mother, St. Jerome chides her for her grief and adds, "This I command through my apostle, that you not grieve for those who sleep, as do the Gentiles who have no hope."[11] St. John Chrysostom cites this passage in a homily and then asks the people, "But you, who expect a resurrection, why do you mourn? To mourn, then, is for those who do not have hope."[12] Similarly, the seventh-century Spanish bishop St. Braulio cites this verse to show that "the holy Apostle does not wish us to mourn for those who sleep."[13]

Some modern-day commentators argue that Paul's later letters show that he was not opposed to all grief. In Philippians he speaks of the grief he would have experienced if his coworker Epaphroditus had died (2:27), but this hardly demonstrates that he thought that grief was acceptable. In 2 Corinthians he distinguishes between godly grief and worldly grief (7:8–12) and describes himself as "sorrowful yet always rejoicing" (see 2:1–11; 6:10), but the context has nothing to do with grief for the dead. Moreover, he makes no distinction between good and bad grief in 1 Thessalonians.

---

9. M. Eugene Boring, *I & II Thessalonians*, NTL (Louisville: Westminster John Knox, 2015), 160.

10. *Ad Quirinum* 3.58 (my translation). See also *De mortalitate* 21.

11. *Epistulae* 39.3 (my translation).

12. *Homiliae* (PG 62:431 [my translation]).

13. *Iberian Fathers*, vol. 2, *Braulio of Saragossa, Fructuosus of Braga*, trans. Claude W. Barlow, FC 63 (Washington, DC: Catholic University of America Press, 1969), 47.

Grief for the Dead in Christian Antiquity

Some ancient Christians believed that their faith in the resurrection of the dead required them to refrain from grieving for loved ones who died. Funerary inscriptions offer glimpses into the struggle of ordinary Christians to put this belief into practice. One funerary inscription from third-century Macedonia instructs the wife and children of the deceased to "stop crying" and "refrain from excessive lament" because it was their loved one's "destiny" to die.[a] A fourth-century inscription erected by a Sicilian couple on the occasion of their baby daughter's death concludes with these words:

> While her parents bewailed her death at every moment, the voice of [God's] majesty was heard at night, forbidding them to lament for the dead child. Her body was buried in its tomb in front of the doors of the shrine of the martyrs.[b]

To modern sensibilities it seems monstrous to forbid bereaved parents to grieve. Yet, their struggle to conquer grief and the child's burial in front of a shrine of the martyrs was a powerful reminder of the ancient and modern belief that Christ has conquered death.

a. *ICG* 3013 (my translation).

b. Translation from Peter Brown, *The Cult of the Saints: Its Rise and Function in Latin Christianity* (Chicago: University of Chicago Press, 1981), 69. Cited by John M. G. Barclay, "'That You May Not Grieve, like the Rest Who Have No Hope' (1 Thess 4.13): Death and Early Christian Identity," in *Pauline Churches and Diaspora Jews*, WUNT 275 (Tübingen: Mohr Siebeck, 2011), 217–35.

Despite the considerable support for the view that Paul opposed all grief for dead Christians, few today would seriously consider this a real possibility. St. Ambrose (339–97) wrestled with this issue after the death of his brother. After admitting that Paul's teaching in 1 Thess 4 asks him to restrain his sorrow, he goes on to defend his tears:

> But we have not committed a serious fault by our weeping. Not every display of sorrow is a sign either of a lack of trust in God or of weakness in ourselves. Natural grief is one thing, sorrow which comes from lack of hope is another. . . . Whenever a patriarch was buried, his people wept profusely. Tears are, therefore, indicators of devotedness, not inciters of grief. Hence, I frankly allow that I, too, have wept, but the Lord also wept [John 11:35].[14]

14. *Funeral Orations by Saint Gregory Nazianzen and Saint Ambrose*, trans. Leo P. McCauley et al., FC 22 (Washington, DC: Catholic University of America Press, 1953), 165.

Jesus's own example, along with the overwhelming evidence of experience and the other biblical examples to which Ambrose appeals, provides a powerful counterweight to the view that all grief is forbidden. Regardless of the debate regarding 1 Thess 4:13, godly people will go on lamenting the dead (Acts 8:2), just as Jesus did for Lazarus (John 11:33–35).[15]

4:14   Paul begins his instruction with a point that he and the Thessalonians already hold in common: **For if we believe that Jesus died and rose** . . . The NABRE's translation "if we believe" could suggest that Paul is holding out a hypothetical possibility. A better translation would be "*Since* we believe that Jesus died and rose" (NRSV). Jesus's death and resurrection were essential to Paul's preaching, and Paul expected the Thessalonians to understand this much already (see 1:10). Most scholars suspect that Paul is quoting an early Christian creedal statement that preceded even him. The phrase is terse, pared down to essentials, and it includes features that do not match Paul's usual way of speaking. Paul rarely refers to his Lord as "Jesus," usually preferring "Jesus Christ" or "Christ Jesus." Even more strikingly, apart from this verse Paul never says Jesus "rose" (*anestē*), usually preferring to say that Jesus was raised (*egeirō*) from death by God. Like those who knew Christ before he did, Paul is confident that Jesus died and rose again and uses this basic confession to instruct the Thessalonians on other points.

In the second half of verse 14, Paul applies the essential belief in Jesus's death and resurrection to the question facing the Thessalonians. Since Jesus died and rose, **so too will God, through Jesus, bring with him those who have fallen asleep**. In later letters, Paul links Jesus's death and resurrection with the future resurrection of the dead in Christ (1 Cor 15; 2 Cor 4:14). One might expect Paul to say that since Jesus died and rose, God will *raise* those who have fallen asleep. Instead, he says, "God will *bring* [*agō*] . . . those who have fallen asleep" (italics added). Of course Paul thinks that the dead in Christ will rise from the dead, and he says so in verse 16. Why, then, would Paul link Jesus's resurrection to God's "bringing" or "leading" the dead? The Thessalonians do not seem to have doubted that dead Christians would rise again, but they still worried that the dead would be at some sort of disadvantage when Christ returned. Paul assures them that God would indeed gather them up on the last day.[16] The description of God "bringing" or "leading" his people to salvation also recalls numerous biblical promises. The prophets frequently describe God leading (*agō*) the people to salvation (LXX Isa 42:16; 48:21; 49:10; 63:11–14; Jer 38:8

---

15. See Rebekah Ann Eklund, *Jesus Wept: The Significance of Jesus' Laments in the New Testament*, LNTS (London: Bloomsbury, 2015).

16. See the related verb *anagō* ("lead, bring up"), which is used to describe resurrection in Rom 10:7; Heb 13:20. See also LXX 1 Sam 2:6; Ps 29:4 (ET 30:4).

Resurrection from the Dead according to Paul

BIBLICAL BACKGROUND

It would not be an exaggeration to say that resurrection is the key to Paul's theology. Like some other Jews in the first century, Paul thought that God would raise the dead at the end of history (Dan 12; 2 Macc 7). Paul and other early Christians believed that this end-time event had already begun because Jesus had risen from the dead. Jesus's resurrection was seen not as an isolated event but as the first resurrection, which guaranteed that all of God's people would be raised (see 1 Cor 15:12–13). For Paul, the two events—Christ's resurrection and the resurrection of those who belong to Christ—are parts of an indissoluble whole.

Resurrection is at the very heart of Paul's understanding of what God has done for humanity through Christ. In the present life, Christians already experience the power of the resurrection by dying to sin and walking "in newness of life" through baptism (Rom 6:1–4). Paul taught that death was unable to separate the faithful from Christ (Rom 8:35–39; 1 Thess 5:10), and he spoke occasionally of hoping to be with Christ after death (Phil 1:23; 2 Cor 5:8). Unlike many modern Christians, however, he did not pin his hopes on "going to heaven" after death. Instead, he taught his churches to look forward to the resurrection of the dead, as he does in 1 Thess 4:13–18. Belief in resurrection of the body affirms the goodness of the material world, but Paul is well aware that resurrection bodies could not be mere reconstituted versions of our current bodies. Our bodies are built to flourish for a short while and then die. Resurrection bodies, Paul says, are imperishable, built for eternal communion with God (1 Cor 15:35–57; Phil 3:21).

[ET 31:8]; Ezek 20:10). For instance, in Isa 43 God promises to gather all the exiled people of Israel, leading them home:

> But now, thus says the LORD,
>> who created you, Jacob, and formed you, Israel:
> Do not fear, for I have redeemed you;
>> I have called you by name: you are mine.
> When you pass through waters, I will be with you;
>> through rivers, you shall not be swept away.
> When you walk through fire, you shall not be burned,
>> nor will flames consume you.
> For I, the LORD, am your God,
>> the Holy One of Israel, your savior. . . .

> Fear not, for I am with you;
>> from the east I will bring back [Greek *agō*] your offspring,
>> from the west I will gather you.
> I will say to the north: Give them up!
>> and to the south: Do not hold them!
> Bring back my sons from afar,
>> and my daughters from the ends of the earth:
> All who are called by my name
>> I created for my glory;
>> I formed them, made them.
> Lead out [Greek *exagō*] the people, blind though they have eyes,
>> deaf though they have ears. (vv. 1–3, 5–8)

Whether Paul was thinking of passages like this or not, his point is that the faithful can trust God to gather up their deceased loved ones and bring them together with Jesus when he returns.

The phrase "through Jesus" is somewhat ambiguous in the Greek. It could be taken to modify "those who have fallen asleep." The NIV follows this interpretation and translates "those who have fallen asleep *in him*" (italics added). Paul's usual way of saying this would be "in Christ," not "through Jesus," and this would be an odd use of the preposition *dia* ("through"). It is more likely that "through Jesus" describes how God will bring the dead, which is the NABRE's interpretation. God is the one who accomplishes this gathering, whereas Jesus is the agent through whom it is done. This sort of cooperation between God and Jesus is a recurring pattern in Paul.[17] Creation is *from* God, but all things exist *through* Jesus (1 Cor 8:6), and the same is true of the new creation (1 Cor 15:21; Col 1:15–20).

4:15   Verse 14 argued on the basis of traditional belief in Jesus's resurrection, which the Thessalonians already shared. Verse 15 continues the argument on the basis of new information, a **word of the Lord**. Here as elsewhere in the letter "the Lord" is probably Jesus. The following verses do not correspond exactly to anything in the Gospels. What is the source of this "word of the Lord"? There are two main possibilities: (1) Paul could be summarizing a traditional teaching of Jesus that doesn't sound like anything in the Gospels because it wasn't written down or because Paul does not cite it word for word (see Matt 24:29–33, 40–41). (2) The saying could have come through a Christian prophet who spoke "by the word of the Lord" just as some Old Testament prophets (e.g., 1 Kings

17. Gordon D. Fee, *The First and Second Letters to the Thessalonians*, NICNT (Grand Rapids: Eerdmans, 2009), 171.

106

13:2) and John the Seer had done (e.g., Rev 1:9–20). It is difficult to decide between these possibilities. Fortunately, however, it makes little difference to our understanding of what Paul says. Another question about this "word of the Lord" confronts us: Which part of what follows is from Jesus, and which part is Paul's commentary? There are no quotation marks in Paul's text to help us decide. Many commentators argue that verse 15 is Paul's application of the message to the Thessalonians' situation and that the actual word of the Lord is found in verses 16–17. This latter portion contains non-Pauline vocabulary and sounds like a generic description of the †parousia, whereas 4:15 focuses on the Thessalonians' worry that the dead would be at some disadvantage.

Verse 15 introduces the word of the Lord by drawing out the point that Paul wants the Thessalonians to take away from it. Paul emphatically denies that **we who are alive, who are left until the coming of the Lord** will be in a better position than those who have died. His language is emphatic: the living **will surely not** (*ou mē*) **precede** those who have died. As noted above, the Thessalonians seem to have believed in the resurrection of the dead, but they worried that those who were not alive when the Lord returned would miss out on Jesus's triumphant return in some way. Some first-century Jews believed that those who remained alive until the end of time would be better off. The noncanonical text *4 Ezra* (late first century AD) states that those who remain until the end are more blessed than those who have died because they will be protected during the trials of the last days (13.24). It is, however, doubtful that the Thessalonian congregation would have known about inside debates of Jewish †apocalyptic expectation. Perhaps Paul's description of the triumphant return of Jesus (1 Thess 1:9–10) impressed them so much that they assumed that those who died before it occurred would lose out. Their anxiety—like our anxieties—does not need to have been sophisticated or even sensible.

The word that Paul uses to describe the "coming" of the Lord is *parousia*, a word that could refer to any ordinary arrival or coming (e.g., 2 Cor 7:6) but was often used to describe the momentous arrival of a god or human dignitary. The New Testament uses the word in the latter sense to refer to the return of Jesus in glory (e.g., Matt 24:3, 27; James 5:7–8; 2 Pet 3:4; 1 John 2:28). For Paul, the *parousia* is synonymous with "the day of the Lord," the time when Jesus will return to consummate the victory won in his resurrection and to gather his people (1 Thess 2:19; 3:13; 5:23). First and Second Thessalonians describe this day as a global event when the wicked will be punished and God will test the worthiness of his people (2 Thess 1:5–2:2). *Parousia* became a technical term in Christian piety, used without explanation to refer to Jesus's return. For instance, a fifth- or sixth-century funerary inscription from Macedonia marks the grave of a church lector and concludes by saying that he "awaits . . . the *parousia*," with no further explanation.[18] The Vulgate translates *parousia* with *adventus*, which is why the liturgical season especially focused on the *parousia* is called "advent."

When Paul says, "we who are alive, who are left until the coming of the Lord," it sounds as if he expects to be alive when Jesus returns. He had apparently also given the Thessalonians the impression that they would live to see that day as well—otherwise it is hard to imagine why they would have found the death of some of their number so unsettling. Porphyry, a third-century opponent of Christianity, thought that this proved Paul to be a fraud: "Paul's lie becomes quite clear when he says: 'We who are alive.' For it is three hundred years since he said this and no one anywhere has been snatched away from their bodies— either Paul or anyone else. May the confused rambling of Paul remain silent for it agitates in confusion."[19] Some retort that the "we" of verse 15 refers generically to all Christians who happen to be alive at that time. As Chrysostom puts it, "When he said 'we,' he did not speak of himself, for he was not to remain until the resurrection. Rather, he speaks of the faithful."[20] Much has been written about this question and about the question of whether Paul's †eschatological expectation developed from this early letter to later letters where he expects to be with Christ after he dies (2 Cor 5:6–10; Phil 1:20–24). Yet, Paul himself tells us what he thought about the timing of the parousia in the next section of this letter: it will come unexpectedly. By his own admission, then, Paul did not know when it was to occur. When he wrote 1 Thessalonians, he seems to have assumed that he would live to see it, but even then he emphasized his conviction that the Lord would return at an unknown time.

4:16–18   Paul continues the explanation of the fate of the dead by citing the word of the Lord. These verses are filled with evocative imagery drawn from Jewish tradition. In modern times some have attempted to use these verses to construct a detailed map of end-time events, but, as Beverly Gaventa has noted, "this passage has more in common with poetry than with blueprints."[21] Paul felt free to use vivid †apocalyptic images drawn from the prophet Daniel and elsewhere, but in comparison to some ancient Jewish thinkers he was uninterested in defining exactly how these events would occur. He also varies his descriptions of the last things, emphasizing different things depending on what the audience

18. *IG* X,2 2 151 (my translation).
19. Robert M. Berchman, *Porphyry against the Christians*, SPNPT 1 (Leiden: Brill, 2005), 211.
20. *Homiliae* (PG 62:436 [my translation]).
21. Beverly Roberts Gaventa, *First and Second Thessalonians*, IBC (Louisville: Westminster John Knox, 1998), 66.

needs to hear, like a good teacher who knows better than to try to squeeze every important point into an introductory lecture. For instance, this passage omits any mention of Christ's defeat of evil (see 1 Cor 15:24–25), as well as details mentioned elsewhere in this very letter, such as Christ's evaluation of people's deeds (1 Thess 2:19; 3:13). In these lines he focuses on only one thing: when the Lord returns, the dead in Christ will rise from the dead first, and then the living will join them, and all will be with Christ forever.

The return of the Lord from heaven is heralded by **a word of command, with the voice of an archangel and with the trumpet of God**. Jewish and Christian texts frequently describe angels as heralds of the last judgment. Archangels or "chief" angels do not appear in the Old Testament, but the book of Daniel describes the angel Michael as the "great prince," and the Judaism of Paul's day showed increasing interest in angelic hierarchies. Jude 1:9 and Rev 12:7, for instance, name Michael as the chief angel. In the Old Testament, trumpet blasts mark God's presence (Exod 19:19; Ps 47:6; Hosea 5:8). They also call troops to battle (Judg 6:34) and mark the beginning of feasts (Num 10:10). Prophets such as Hosea and Zechariah use trumpet imagery to describe the time when God will come to put things right. Joel 2:1 is similar to our passage: "Blow the horn in Zion, / sound the alarm on my holy mountain! / Let all the inhabitants of the land tremble, / for the day of the LORD is coming!" In texts closer in time to Paul, trumpets often presage the resurrection or judgment.[22] Matthew 24 says that, when the Son of Man returns on the clouds of heaven, "he will send out his angels with a trumpet blast, and they will gather his elect from the four winds, from one end of the heavens to the other" (v. 31). For a Jew like Paul, the combination of the voice of the archangel and the trumpet of God would indicate the return of the Lord and the last judgment.

Three events follow the trumpet's blast: (1) Jesus will descend from heaven; (2) the dead in Christ will rise; and (3) the living and the newly resurrected dead will be snatched up together in the air, where they will greet Jesus. The sequence of these events is important because it shows that the dead will not miss out in any way. Contrary to what the Thessalonians seem to have thought, their friends who have died will experience the return of the Lord in all its splendor. Paul concludes by emphasizing this central point one more time: **we shall always be with the Lord**. The return of Christ and the resurrection of the dead are familiar to modern Christians from the Nicene Creed, but the third event listed—the snatching up of the living and the newly resurrected in the air—is more difficult to understand. The verb translated **caught up** (*harpazō*) usually

---

22. E.g., 1 Cor 15:52; *Greek Apocalypse of Ezra* 4.36; *Testament of Abraham* 12.10.

describes the violent, sudden snatching away of something, and sometimes it is used to describe miraculous changes of location, such as God's sudden taking of Philip (Acts 8:39) and Paul's own experience of being caught up into "Paradise" (2 Cor 12:1–5). In the next passage (1 Thess 5:1–11) Paul compares the Lord's return to a thief suddenly appearing at night, so the sense of something sudden and swift is entirely appropriate.

In his concern to emphasize that believers will always be with Christ, Paul doesn't say what happens after those who are in Christ go to meet him in the air, other than to affirm that "we shall always be with the Lord." Do they remain in the air, ascend to heaven, or return to earth? Many scholars say that Paul implies a return to earth, noting that people sometimes went out from a city to **meet** (*apantēsis*) a visiting dignitary before accompanying him back into the city. Josephus describes one such event and explains that the purpose of the meeting (*apantēsis*) was to honor the dignitary and show him that he was welcome.[23] St. John Chrysostom explains this verse similarly, though he thinks that such meetings are designed to show honor to those who are permitted to go forth to meet the dignitary as he arrives:

> When a king processes into a city, the honorable people go forth to meet [*apantēsis*] him, while the condemned stay within the city awaiting the judge. Or when an affectionate father arrives, his children—and those worthy to be his children— are taken out in a chariot to greet and kiss him, but members of the household who have offended wait within. We are carried on the chariot of the Father. For the Father received Jesus in the clouds (Acts 1:9), and "we will be caught up in the clouds" (1 Thess 4:17). You see how great the honor is? We greet him as he descends and—most fortunate of all—in this way we will be with him.[24]

Chrysostom assumes that Christ will descend to earth and interprets the meeting in the air as the first step in the last judgment: Christians join their Lord while the condemned await judgment. This may very well be what Paul had in mind, but he doesn't say one way or the other, because he was instructing the church on a different matter—namely, that the dead are at no disadvantage on the last day.

The Vulgate translates *harpazō* with *rapio*, which is why the "snatching up" of Christians has come to be known as a "rapture." In the last two hundred years some people—especially American evangelicals—have interpreted this "rapture" to mean that all Christians will suddenly be taken to heaven while the rest of the world is left behind, wondering at the disappearance of their

23. *Jewish Antiquities* 13.101.
24. *Homiliae* (PG 62:440 [my translation]).

Christian friends. This scenario belongs to a larger †eschatological framework known as premillennial dispensationalism, a theological innovation usually traced to a nineteenth-century Irish Protestant, John Nelson Darby. Perhaps it would have remained one among many discarded eschatological speculations, but Darby's theology found its way into a series of enormously popular books, from the Scofield Reference Bible in 1909 to Tim LaHaye and Jerry Jenkins's *Left Behind* series. As a result, premillennial dispensationalism has become the default eschatology of many American Christians. The problems with this theology are many, including a tendency to weave bits from different passages across the Bible into a larger framework that has nothing to do with the concerns of the biblical authors. Unfortunately, however, biblical scholars and theologians tend to ignore rapture theology as fundamentalist tripe beneath their notice, and in their silence confusion flourishes. The principal error in the treatment of 1 Thessalonians is in failing to recognize that this passage is about the final return and decisive victory of God, an event that early Christians called "the coming of the Lord" (4:15). Paul's description of the living being "raptured" refers to the moment on the last day when the living will join the dead to be with Christ forever. Instead of describing the disappearance of Christians from the world, this passage looks forward to the day when Jesus will "come again in glory to judge the living and the dead," as the Nicene Creed puts it.

Paul presupposes a traditional biblical †cosmology in this passage. Christ descends from above, which suggests that heaven is "up" above us. The faithful are brought to meet him as he descends, joining him **in the air**, which was often thought to be the realm of spirits (see Eph 2:2). Apocalyptic texts sometimes describe clouds as heavenly modes of transport (Dan 7:13; Matt 26:64), and the phrase **in the clouds** probably functions similarly. The faithful are taken up by means of clouds, just as Acts describes a cloud taking Jesus in his ascension (1:9). Scholars disagree about the extent to which the ancients took these descriptions literally. Did Paul think that God was in the sky and people could ride on clouds? Today, N. T. Wright is perhaps the foremost defender of the view that Paul and other ancient Jews knew very well that this language was not strictly literal but rather was intended to describe what would otherwise be indescribable. Wright compares biblical descriptions of Christ's return to the attempt to describe color to a person born blind. It would be necessary "to 'translate' your experience of colour into a different context: sound, for instance, or touch. You might describe bright red as a hard, loud colour."[25] According

---

25. N. T. Wright, *Paul for Everyone: Galatians and Thessalonians* (Louisville: Westminster John Knox, 2002), 123.

to Wright, Paul is doing something similar here. Paul didn't think that Jesus is "physically above us at the moment" or that Christians would literally ascend vertically.[26] He is attempting to describe the life of the world to come, and "the only possible language is that of pictures."[27] It should be frankly admitted, however, that the biblical authors did not share our scientific understanding of the cosmos. Paul himself is not particularly interested in cosmological details and is capable of describing them differently as the occasion demands. His concern is to comfort the Thessalonians with the certainty of the resurrection and their eternal presence with the Lord.

Reflection and Application (4:13–18)

People who have lost loved ones do not stop grieving simply because they learn new information. Why, then, does Paul address the Thessalonians' grief by correcting their ignorance? Eugene Boring notes that modern readers would expect a more personal response: "I'm so sorry to hear about the death of so-and-so."[28] Indeed, in our cultural context a more personal expression of comfort would probably need to accompany the instruction for it to be accepted. Nevertheless, we should not underestimate the pastoral wisdom of Paul's response. For Paul, there is no division between "pastoral" and "dogmatic" theology, because he assumes that the truth *is* pastoral. This truth reorders the lives of Christians around the hope of their salvation. The truth of the resurrection is not to be said once and then tucked away as a piece of trivia; rather, it is to be ruminated on, repeated by Christians to one another (4:18). For this reason it is easy to see why Catholic tradition speaks not only of corporal works of mercy, such as feeding the hungry, but also of spiritual works of mercy, which include instructing the ignorant. Paul performed a work of mercy for the Thessalonians, sharing with them not mere information but rather a new way of understanding their lives in light of their final ends. The dead in Christ are not gone but remain Christ's and will be raised from the dead.

26. Wright, *Paul for Everyone*, 125.
27. Wright, *Paul for Everyone*, 124.
28. Boring, *I & II Thessalonians*, 161.

The Day of the Lord

1 Thessalonians 5:1–11

After assuring the Thessalonians that the dead will not be at a disadvantage when Jesus returns (4:13–18), Paul goes on to address the question of how the living should prepare themselves for this event, admonishing them to continue in faith, love, and hope. Though he warns that the day of the Lord will come suddenly and without warning, he assures the new converts in Thessalonica that God has destined them for salvation.

The Suddenness of the Day of the Lord (5:1–3)

¹Concerning times and seasons, brothers, you have no need for anything to be written to you. ²For you yourselves know very well that the day of the Lord will come like a thief at night. ³When people are saying, "Peace and security," then sudden disaster comes upon them, like labor pains upon a pregnant woman, and they will not escape.

NT: Matt 24; Mark 13
Lectionary: 1 Thess 5:1–6, 9–11; Memorial of Saint Gregory the Great

The opening words of this chapter indicate a shift to a new topic: the **times** 5:1–2 **and seasons,** a phrase that early Christians used to refer to the timing of the final consummation of God's plan (see Acts 1:7). Paul had apparently already taught them that **the day of the Lord will come** when they do not expect it, and he denies that they need **anything to be written** about it. Nevertheless, he goes ahead and discusses the issue anyway in order to deepen and reinforce what they already know (see 1 Thess 4:9). The phrase "day of the Lord" refers to the same event as the "†parousia" of the preceding section. The varying descriptions are indicative of Paul's varying emphases: there it was comfort, here it is judgment. The expression "day of the Lord" and related expressions such as "that day" occur often in the prophets to describe the time when God will come to punish people for their wickedness and deliver the people of God from their oppressors. As the prophet Obadiah warns, "Near is the day of the LORD / against all the nations! / As you have done, so will it be done to you, / your conduct will come back upon your own head" (v. 15).[1] For Paul, the "Lord" is Jesus, and the "day of the Lord" is his return to judge the nations (2 Thess 1:7–8).

5:3   Paul compares the sudden coming of the day of the Lord to the nighttime invasion by a burglar and to the sudden onset of childbirth. The former image is intuitive; we are at our most vulnerable when asleep, oblivious to what is going on around us. The only way to prepare for such an event would be to stay awake and watch. Childbirth, however, no longer obviously evokes **sudden disaster** from which there is no escape. In our age of scheduled inductions and caesarean sections, childbirth frequently occurs right on schedule. But absent these interventions labor can begin at any point over a frustratingly wide span of time, and of course childbirth is painful and the rate of mortality is higher in the absence of modern medicine (see Isa 13:8; Jer 6:24). Paul's point is that the calamitous day of the Lord cannot be predicted ahead of time. What we **know very well** about the times and seasons (1 Thess 5:1–2) is that we don't know much at all! The day of the Lord will come at a time we do not expect.

When the day of the Lord comes, people will be obliviously speaking of **peace and security**, assuming that life will go on as it always has. This image is similar to Jesus's parable of the rich fool who plans to build bigger barns to hold his growing wealth, pathetically ignorant of his own imminent demise (Luke 12:13–21). The self-assured and comfortable luxuriate in safety and prosperity, oblivious of imminent destruction and total loss. Readers have long recognized the similarity between this passage and the Old Testament prophets' condemnations of those who cry, "Peace, peace!" when there is no peace (e.g., Jer 6:13–15; 8:11; Ezek 13:10). More recently, some scholars have argued that "peace and security" was a Roman slogan that Paul cites in order to challenge the empire's pretensions to bring stability to the world.[2] The word "peace" is

---

1. See also Isa 13:6; Joel 1:15; 2:1; Zeph 1:14.
2. See especially Jeffrey A. D. Weima, *1–2 Thessalonians*, BECNT (Grand Rapids: Baker Academic, 2014), 348–51. See also the cautious remarks of Joel R. White, "'Peace and Security' (1 Thessalonians 5.3): Is It Really a Roman Slogan?," *NTS* 59 (2013): 382–95.

Jesus Tradition in Paul's Teaching

BIBLICAL BACKGROUND

Paul is famous for emphasizing the direct revelation that he received from Christ, especially in his letter to the Galatians (see especially 1:1–2:9). On other occasions, however, Paul is happy to cite traditions that were handed over to him by those who were in Christ before him (e.g., 1 Cor 15:3–11). In 1 Thess 5:1–11 Paul does not indicate that he is drawing on earlier tradition, but it seems likely that he was. His warnings about the unknown time of the Lord's return include a number of intriguing parallels with the teaching of Jesus as known from the synoptic Gospels.[a] Some of these parallels could be coincidences, but others, such as the warning that Jesus would return like a thief at night, were part of a common tradition:

> The day of the Lord will come like a thief at night. (1 Thess 5:2)

> Be sure of this: if the master of the house had known the hour of night when the thief was coming, he would have stayed awake and not let his house be broken into. So too, you also must be prepared, for at an hour you do not expect, the Son of Man will come. (Matt 24:43–44 [see also Luke 12:39–40; 2 Pet 3:10; Rev 3:3])

> Sudden [*aiphnidios*] disaster comes upon [*ephistēmi*] them . . . and they will not escape [*ekpheugō*]. (1 Thess 5:3)

> Beware that your hearts do not become drowsy from carousing and drunkenness and the anxieties of daily life, and that day [fall on (*ephistēmi*) you suddenly (*aiphnidios*) as] a trap. For that day will assault everyone who lives on the face of the earth. Be vigilant at all times and pray that you have the strength to escape [*ekpheugō*] the tribulations that are imminent and to stand before the Son of Man. (Luke 21:34–36 [NABRE altered to show similarities])

> Let us not sleep [*katheudō*] as the rest do, but let us stay alert [*grēgoreuō*] and sober. (1 Thess 5:6)

> Watch [*grēgoreuō*)], therefore; you do not know when the lord of the house is coming, whether in the evening, or at midnight, or at cockcrow, or in the morning. May he not come suddenly and find you sleeping [*katheudō*]. (Mark 13:35–36 [see also the parable of the faithful or unfaithful slave: Matt 24:45–51; Luke 12:42–46])

a. See the analysis of these parallels in Christopher Tuckett, *From the Sayings to the Gospels*, WUNT 328 (Tübingen: Mohr Siebeck, 2014), 324–33.

indeed very common in imperial propaganda. To take one example among many, the *Res gestae divi Augusti*, the funerary inscription commemorating the deeds of Augustus in AD 13, brags about how Augustus "restored to a state of

Figure 8. Octavian. Struck 28 BC in Ephesus. Obverse depicts Octavius with the inscription "IMP-CAESAR-DIVI-F-COS-VI-LIBERTATIS-P-R-VINDEX" ("Emperor Caesar, son of the Divine [Julius], Consul for the sixth time, Defender of the Freedom of the Roman People"). Reverse depicts Pax with the inscription "PAX" (peace).

peace [*eirēnē*]" the provinces of the Gauls, the Spains, and Germany (26.2–3). Regardless of whether Paul intended to mock the empire, his main point is that the day of the Lord will shatter the foolish self-assurance of those who put their trust in present comfort. Unlike Luke 12:13–21 and the prophets, Paul's point is not to persuade his audience away from a path of destruction but rather to encourage them with the news that they have already left it (see 1 Thess 5:4).

Children of the Day (5:4–11)

⁴**But you, brothers, are not in darkness, for that day to overtake you like a thief. ⁵For all of you are children of the light and children of the day. We are not of the night or of darkness. ⁶Therefore, let us not sleep as the rest do, but let us stay alert and sober. ⁷Those who sleep go to sleep at night, and those who are drunk get drunk at night. ⁸But since we are of the day, let us be sober, putting on the breastplate of faith and love and the helmet that is hope for salvation. ⁹For God did not destine us for wrath, but to gain salvation through our Lord Jesus Christ, ¹⁰who died for us, so that whether we are awake or asleep we may live together with him. ¹¹Therefore, encourage one another and build one another up, as indeed you do.**

OT: Isa 59:17
NT: Matt 25:1–12; Eph 6:13–17

In the preceding verses Paul described how the day of the Lord will be expe-   5:4–5
rienced by those who trust in the security of this life. Now Paul assures the
Thessalonians that they should look forward to the day of the Lord with hope,
confident that God has destined them to gain salvation. Though the day of the
Lord will indeed arrive like a thief at night, people will experience this event
differently depending on their own preparation for it. The Thessalonians are
children of the light and children of the day, but all the rest of humanity
belongs to the darkness. In this dichotomy, night is associated with sleeping,
drunkenness, and the experience of God's wrath when the unexpected day
comes. In contrast, the day is associated with the Lord's presence, watchfulness,
sobriety, and the hope of salvation.

The division between light and darkness is common in ancient Judaism and
in other cultures as well, possessing an intuitive appeal. Eugene Boring rightly
notes that "humanity for most of its history had lived in a world without the
instant availability of artificial light. The sun was the source of life and light;
darkness was deep, dangerous, and all-permeating."[3] It is not surprising that
many would think of good and evil in terms of this contrast. A well-known
recent example is Elie Wiesel's *Night*, a book that uses language of night and
dark to describe the devastation of the author's experience in a Nazi concentration camp.[4] In ancient Jewish and Christian texts, the day and the light are
associated with God's presence (John 1:1–18; 1 Tim 6:16; Rev 21:23), knowledge
of the truth (John 1:9; Eph 1:18), moral behavior (Matt 5:14–16), and the day
of judgment when God will bring to light what people have done (1 Cor 3:13;
4:5; Heb 10:25). Night and darkness are linked to the opposites of these things:
the absence of God's presence (Matt 8:12), opposition to God (Luke 22:53),
ignorance of the truth (Eph 4:18), and immoral behavior that seeks to avoid
detection (John 3:20; Eph 5:11). One of the Dead Sea Scrolls known as the War
Scroll uses language similar to 1 Thess 5, speaking of the coming day when
there will be a battle between the "children of light" and "children of darkness."

In designating the Thessalonians "children of the light and children of the
day," Paul means that they should joyfully look forward to "the day of the Lord."
The day of the Lord is, in a sense, *their* time, the coming of their master and the
fulfillment of their hope. This gives the image of the "thief in the night" a different application in this letter from what it has in the Gospels, where it stands as
a warning to the Church. According to Paul, Christians will not experience the
Lord's sudden appearance as a horrifying home invasion, because those who

---

3. M. Eugene Boring, *I & II Thessalonians*, NTL (Louisville: Westminster John Knox, 2015), 181.
4. Elie Wiesel, *Night* (London: Penguin, 2008).

Origen on Night Signifying Evil

LIVING TRADITION

In his commentary on the Gospel of John, Origen pauses to reflect on the unforgettable, short statement following Judas's departure from Jesus: "and it was night" (John 13:30):

> But if we must also examine the statement, "And it was night," so that it has not been interjected in vain by the Evangelist, we must say that the perceptible night at that time was symbolical, being an image of the night that was in Judas' soul when Satan, the darkness that lies over the abyss, entered him. "For God called the darkness night," of which night, indeed, Paul says we are not children, nor of darkness, when he says, "Therefore, brothers we are not of the night, nor of darkness," and, "But let us who are of the day be sober" [1 Thess 5:4–8]. There was no night, therefore, but brightest day, for those who allowed their feet to be washed by Jesus, who were cleansed and allowed the filth on the feet of their soul to be cast aside. And there was no night par excellence in the one who reclined on Jesus' breast, for Jesus loved him, and destroyed all darkness with his love. Nor was there night in Peter when he confessed, "You are the Christ, the Son of the living God," when the heavenly Father revealed it to him, but there was night in him too at the moment of his denial. And in the present instance, moreover, when Judas received the morsel [and] went out immediately, night was present in him at the time he went out, for the man whose name is "Sunrise" was not present with him because he left "the sun of justice" behind when he went out. And Judas, who was filled with darkness, pursued Jesus; but the darkness and the one who had taken it up did not apprehend the light that was pursued.[a]

a. *Commentary on the Gospel according to John Books 13–32*, trans. Ronald E. Heine, FC 89 (Washington, DC: Catholic University of America Press, 1993), 400–401.

know him are always preparing for that day through lives of prayer and hope. In this way they always live "in the day." St. Cyprian of Carthage expresses this well in his commentary on the Our Father: "To the sons of light, even in the night there is day. For when is he without light who has light in his heart? Or when does he not have sun and day, to whom Christ is Sun and Day?"[5]

One might accuse Paul of making things simpler than they actually are by dividing humanity into "people of the day" and "people of the night." Christians are aware of areas of darkness in their own lives, and it is obvious that truth (and therefore "light") can be found outside the Church. Paul might counter that this objection fails to take seriously God's call on Christians' lives: they have received God's Holy Spirit, a fact that makes it legitimate to speak of a

5. "The Lord's Prayer," in *Treatises*, trans. Roy J. Deferrari, FC 36 (Washington, DC: Catholic University of America Press, 1958), 159–60.

crucial difference between them and others. Moreover, Paul may have had pastoral reasons for using a simple dichotomy between insiders and outsiders. The Thessalonians' conversion had triggered major disruption in their lives, including opposition from their fellow citizens. It would be comforting to them to see the world framed in simple terms, assuring them that they had found the source of hope.[6] It is also important not to press this difference more than Paul does. Paul was not so naïve as to assume that there are two essential kinds of people—good and bad (see below on v. 6). He knew all too well that it was possible for the Thessalonians to fall away (3:5; 4:8).

In verse 6 Paul shifts from reminders and encouragement to exhortation. In   **5:6–7** order for them to be children of the day, it was necessary for the Thessalonians to live accordingly, remaining **alert and sober**, rather than sleeping and getting drunk. Though the biblical tradition is very positive about wine (Ps 104:14–15), it routinely condemns drunkenness (e.g., Rom 13:13; Eph 5:18; though see John 2:10). Paul's point here, however, is not to condemn drinking any more than it is to condemn sleeping. Instead, he is continuing to develop the metaphors of night and day. "Night" is the realm of those who do not know God, and sleeping and drunkenness are characteristic nighttime activities. As Paul puts it in verse 7, **Those who sleep go to sleep at night, and those who are drunk get drunk at night**. This refers to a way of life that is immoral and oblivious to the coming of the Lord. Opposed to this is the life of the "day," which refers both to the coming "day of the Lord" and to the moral life that is expected of those who wait for it.

Christians belong to the day and should therefore **be sober**, which refers not   **5:8** to abstention from alcohol but to alert readiness for the Lord's coming. Without discarding the day/night imagery, Paul at this point draws in another cluster of metaphors, linking sobriety to **putting on the breastplate of faith and love and the helmet that is hope for salvation**. Roman breastplates and helmets would have been familiar sights to Paul and the Thessalonians, but the main inspiration for this image was Scripture. Isaiah 59:17 says that God "put on justice as a breastplate and put the helmet of salvation on his head" (my translation). Paul places this divine armor on the church, and he adapts it to match the triad with which he began the letter, changing "justice and salvation" to "faith and love and the . . . hope for salvation." The image of armor suggests that those who have received faith, love, and hope will be well prepared to endure difficulties to come. As St. Cyril of Alexandria puts it, "the soldier of Christ" who "fights not with breastplate of bright iron" but "in the armor of God, faith, hope, and

---

6. John M. G. Barclay, "Conflict in Thessalonica," *CBQ* 55 (1993): 517–20.

love" will be "vigorous and unbreakable in spirit, with a heart not easily shaken, but, rather, firm and unswerving."[7] Are the Thessalonians already wearing this armor, or does he want them to put it on, as in the better-known exhortation of Ephesians: "Put on the armor of God" (6:11)? In the Greek it is not clear whether the "putting on" has already happened or if they are to be sober by continuing to wear the armor.[8] Theologically, however, Paul's answer would be both. They are already protected by faith, love, and hope (1 Thess 1:3), but they must put them on again and again to continue and grow (3:12; 5:11).

5:9   God has destined the Thessalonians not for **wrath** but for **salvation**. The "wrath" refers to the sudden appearance of the day of the Lord, the time when evil will be defeated. Paul is confident that this day will not be a day of wrath for Christians, because it is God's plan to rescue them (see 1:10). In modern English, "salvation" has come to refer largely to the remission of sins, but the Greek word *sōtēria* referred to any sort of salvation, political, bodily, or otherwise.[9] For Paul, salvation refers to much more than forgiveness of sins—an idea that isn't even mentioned in 1 Thessalonians. In this letter, the hoped-for salvation is that one will be found blameless on the day of the Lord and be joined with him forever.

The Thessalonians' hope of salvation is based on God's plan: **God did not destine us for wrath**. Throughout the letter Paul stresses God's prior initiative in bringing the Thessalonians to salvation (e.g., 1:4). This "destining" does not mean that their fate is predetermined. The Thessalonians are still free to choose good or evil, which is why Paul bothers to write to them in the first place. But God has appointed them for salvation. It is God's plan that they should attain it, and this plan is the basis of their hope.

After "God did not destine us for wrath," one might have expected Paul to finish the sentence with the parallel expression "but God destined us for salvation." Instead, he writes, "to *gain* salvation." This phrase, which could be more woodenly translated as "for the obtaining of salvation," troubles some commentators because it could be taken to suggest that salvation belongs to Christians as their own possession, perhaps implying that they earned it themselves.[10] This worry is unnecessary. For Paul, the salvation of Christians on the day of the Lord is something that God does through Jesus, but this does not exclude human

---

7. *Festal Letters 1–12*, trans. Philip R. Amidon, FC 118 (Washington, DC: Catholic University of America Press, 2009), 197.

8. The grammatical question hinges on the relationship of the aorist participle "putting on" to the present-tense main verb "let us be sober." See the discussion in Weima, *1–2 Thessalonians*, 362.

9. *Oxford English Dictionary*, 2nd ed. (1989), s.v. "salvation," 1.a.

10. E.g., Weima, *1–2 Thessalonians*, 367.

participation. The essence of this salvation is that when the Lord returns he will find Christians "blameless in holiness" (3:13; 5:23). As Theodoret of Cyrus puts it while commenting on this verse, God "called us not to punish us but so that he might deem us worthy of salvation."[11] Through Christ, it is God's plan to mold the Thessalonians in faith, love, and hope so that they will be found holy on the day of the Lord.

In comparison to Paul's other letters, 1 Thessalonians does not put much   **5:10–11** emphasis on Jesus's death, but here Paul describes Jesus as the one who effects salvation by dying **for us**. The conviction that Jesus died for other people was widespread in early Christianity (e.g., Mark 10:45; 1 Tim 2:6). Sometimes it was explicitly said that Jesus's death was for sins, as in 1 Cor 15:3 ("Christ died for our sins in accordance with the scriptures"). In 1 Thess 5:10 Paul says that Jesus died "for us" **so that whether we are awake or asleep we may live together with him**. That is, because of Christ's death, both the living (those who are awake) and the dead (those who are asleep) will live together with Christ (see 4:14). Then, picking up the call to encourage one another from 4:18, Paul again challenges them to use what he has written to encourage one another, adding that they should **build one another up** with this message.

Reflection and Application (5:4–11)

Hope, one New Testament scholar recently suggested, is the central idea in 1 Thessalonians.[12] The word Paul uses, *elpis*, like its English translation, can mean many things. A hope can be a mere wish or desire for something, like hoping for good weather. Hopes can turn out to be ill founded, like the hope of the Protestant evangelist Harold Camping, who taught that Jesus would return on May 21, 2011, or the false hope of those who have been tricked into trusting rich people who seek only to take advantage of them (Sir 13:1–7). "Hope" can describe mere optimism, the expectation that things are generally going to go well. More cynically, some have suggested that hope is the indefinite deferral of happiness: we hope in order to console ourselves with lies that make life more bearable. As the English poet Alexander Pope famously puts it, "Hope springs eternal in the human breast: / Man never is, but always to be blest."[13]

For Paul, hope does not mean expecting life to go well. He tells the Thessalonians to expect just the opposite: they should expect trials (1 Thess 3:3).

11. *Interpretatio in xiv epistulas sancti Pauli* (PG 82:652 [my translation]).
12. Nijay K. Gupta, *1–2 Thessalonians*, NCC (Eugene, OR: Cascade, 2016), 1.
13. Alexander Pope, *Essay on Man*. See the discussion of this poem and the overall argument of Terry Eagleton, *Hope without Optimism* (New Haven: Yale University Press, 2015), 42.

Hope, for Paul, was not a mere emotion or sunny outlook, nor was it reducible to information about the future. The hope of which Paul speaks in 1 Thessalonians is a God-given habit of mind that produces joy in the midst of suffering. It is characterized by endurance or patience (1:3), providing confidence that God has conquered death through Christ (4:13; 5:8). In other words, for Paul, hope looks forward to a glorious future, but also it offers a changed life in the present (see Rom 5:2–5). From this perspective, it is easy to see why later tradition called hope a "theological virtue." It is "theological" in the sense that it is a gift from God and helps the recipient to know God. It is a "virtue" because it is not simply an idea or emotion but rather a firm disposition that changes one's entire outlook on life. The medieval Irish hymn "Be Thou My Vision" expresses this perfectly with a line that echoes 1 Thess 5:10: "Waking or sleeping, Thy presence my light." Knowing God reframes how we view reality, giving us "light." Hope brings a new way of life, one that is lived in light of our final end.[14]

14. On all of these points, see Pope Benedict XVI's encyclical on hope, *Spe Salvi* (Saved in Hope).

Final Admonitions

1 Thessalonians 5:12–28

Paul concludes, as he usually does, with a series of final exhortations. Paul talks about how to treat leaders and enemies within the church, encourages unceasing prayer, and prays for the complete sanctification of all within the congregation. This section is packed with traditional Christian teachings (e.g., "See that no one returns evil for evil") that Paul has adapted for this particular occasion. A lazy reader might be tempted to skim over this material, but the letter's conclusion summarizes many of the letter's key points, and it contains some of its most memorable and influential lines.

Regard for Authorities in the Lord (5:12–13)

¹²We ask you, brothers, to respect those who are laboring among you and who are over you in the Lord and who admonish you, ¹³and to show esteem for them with special love on account of their work. Be at peace among yourselves.

NT: Gal 6:6; 1 Tim 5:17–22
Catechism: the body of Christ, 1267–70

Up until this point in the letter no mention has been made of ecclesial authori- 5:12–13
ties other than the apostles themselves, but here we learn that certain unnamed members have a special responsibility to care for the congregation. Though three tasks are mentioned (laboring, exercising authority, admonishing), in

Blessed John Henry Newman on the Development of Doctrine

In his *Essay on the Development of Christian Doctrine*, Newman remarks on the impossibility of finding a point in the ancient Church when doctrine stopped growing.

> If we turn our attention to the beginnings of apostolical teaching after His ascension, we shall find ourselves unable to fix an historical point at which the growth of doctrine ceased, and the rule of faith was once for all settled. Not on the day of Pentecost, for St. Peter had still to learn at Joppa about the baptism of Cornelius; not at Joppa and Caesarea, for St. Paul had to write his Epistles; not on the death of the last Apostle, for St. Ignatius had to establish the doctrine of Episcopacy; not then, nor for many years after, for the Canon of the New Testament was still undetermined. Not in the Creed, which is no collection of definitions, but a summary of certain *credenda*, an incomplete summary, and, like the Lord's Prayer or the Decalogue, a mere sample of divine truths, especially of the more elementary. No one doctrine can be named which starts *omnibus numeris* at first, and gains nothing for the investigations of faith and the attacks of heresy. The Church went forth from the world in haste, as the Israelites from Egypt "with their dough before it was leavened, their kneading troughs being bound up in the clothes upon their shoulders."[a]

a. *An Essay on the Development of Christian Doctrine* (London: James Toovey, 1845), 107–8.

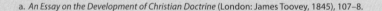

the Greek it is clear that Paul is talking about one group of people rather than three. At this point in Paul's ministry it is unlikely that Greek-speaking Christians used the titles *episkopoi* ("bishops"), *presbyteroi* ("elders"), or *diakonoi* ("deacons"), which is probably why we do not find them in this passage. Later New Testament texts do use these terms but do not distinguish between bishops and elders (Acts 20:17, 28; Phil 1:1; Titus 1:6–7).[1] By the beginning of the second century, the three ordained offices are clearly distinguished in the letters of St. Ignatius of Antioch, but bishops and elders are not given the designation "priest" (*hiereus*) until later than that (see sidebar, "St. Ignatius of Antioch on Respect for Leaders," p. 126). Nevertheless, this passage is evidence that from the earliest days of Christianity there were leaders in local churches. In later centuries, readers of 1 Thessalonians understandably took Paul to be talking about respect for ordained clergy. John Chrysostom, for instance, assumes that

1. See the discussion of Titus 1:6–7 in George T. Montague, *First and Second Timothy, Titus*, CCSS (Grand Rapids: Baker Academic, 2008), 219–20. Montague notes that St. Jerome (*Letters* 146.1) also acknowledged that the offices of bishop and elder are one and the same in the New Testament.

this passage is about respect for local priests, and Thomas Aquinas takes it to refer to deference to Church authorities.[2]

These leaders' responsibilities include "admonishing" the rest of the church, a word that could refer to moral exhortation (see 5:14), as well as other instruction. These unnamed leaders are also **laboring** and doing **work** for the sake of the church, words that Paul uses to describe his own manual labor (e.g., 2:9) as well as the work of those who preach the gospel (e.g., 1 Cor 15:10). In addition to teaching and moral exhortation, the leaders' work might include mundane administration in support of the community's life, such as the distribution of resources to those in need. Another possible task of leaders who could read probably included reading this letter aloud to the gathered church (1 Thess 5:27).

The leaders are also said to be set **over you** (*proistēmi*) **in the Lord**. The word *proistēmi* commonly refers to people who have an official responsibility to manage or help others, such as court officials, pagan priests, or legal guardians. In 1 Timothy it refers to the "presiding" role of presbyters (5:17) and the "managing" of households (3:4–5, 12).[3] Since the early twentieth century some have argued that *proistēmi* could mean "care for" or "show interest in" rather than "rule over," hence the NIV's translation, "care for you in the Lord." Due to ongoing disputes about the nature of authority in the Church, scholars have subjected this phrase to extra scrutiny, and there is a marked tendency in some recent commentaries to prefer interpretations that downplay these leaders' authority as much as possible in hope of demonstrating that the Church was egalitarian at this early stage.[4] But the evidence of *proistēmi* being used to refer to simple "caring" is not strong.[5] When it does refer to caring or providing, it is the caring expected of someone in an official capacity.[6] There is no doubt that these leaders "cared for" the congregation, as the NIV suggests, but they also wielded a measure of authority as teachers. Paul did not share the modern wish for a church without authority.[7]

---

2. John Chrysostom, *Homiliae in epistulam i ad Thessalonicenses* (PG 62:455); Thomas Aquinas, *Super ad Thessalonicenses I reportatio* 5.1.124.

3. It also appears in Rom 12:8, where its meaning is not clear.

4. E.g., Abraham J. Malherbe, *The Letters to the Thessalonians: A New Translation with Introduction and Commentary*, AB 32B (New Haven: Yale University Press, 2000), 311–13.

5. Already in 1928 Adolf von Harnack ("Κόπος [κοπιᾶν, οἱ κοπιῶντες] im frühchristlichen Sprachgebrauch," *ZNW* 27 [1928]: 1–10, here 10) noted that the "laborers" here were a group of people with the office of caring for and admonishing the congregation.

6. For instance, BDAG cites Josephus, *Jewish Antiquities* 14.196, and *Letter of Aristeas* 1.182 as evidence of "care for," but in both cases the caring is done ex officio, by rulers and court officers respectively. Compare to LSJ and *The Brill Dictionary of Ancient Greek*. See the discussion in Béda Rigaux, *Saint Paul: Les Épitres aux Thessaloniciens*, EBib (Paris: Lecoffre, 1956), 577–78.

7. See Benjamin L. White, "The Traditional and Ecclesiastical Paul of 1 Corinthians," *CBQ* 79 (2017): 651–69.

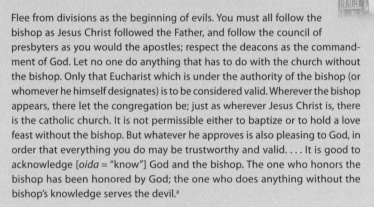

St. Ignatius of Antioch on Respect for Leaders

LIVING TRADITION

In the early second century, Ignatius, bishop of Antioch, was taken to Rome to be martyred. While on the way, he wrote a series of letters to various churches. His letter to the church in Smyrna sheds light on Paul's use of the word "know" (*oida*) in 1 Thess 5:12 and attests to an emerging emphasis on episcopal authority:

> Flee from divisions as the beginning of evils. You must all follow the bishop as Jesus Christ followed the Father, and follow the council of presbyters as you would the apostles; respect the deacons as the commandment of God. Let no one do anything that has to do with the church without the bishop. Only that Eucharist which is under the authority of the bishop (or whomever he himself designates) is to be considered valid. Wherever the bishop appears, there let the congregation be; just as wherever Jesus Christ is, there is the catholic church. It is not permissible either to baptize or to hold a love feast without the bishop. But whatever he approves is also pleasing to God, in order that everything you do may be trustworthy and valid. . . . It is good to acknowledge [*oida* = "know"] God and the bishop. The one who honors the bishop has been honored by God; the one who does anything without the bishop's knowledge serves the devil.[a]

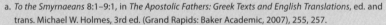

a. *To the Smyrnaeans* 8:1–9:1, in *The Apostolic Fathers: Greek Texts and English Translations*, ed. and trans. Michael W. Holmes, 3rd ed. (Grand Rapids: Baker Academic, 2007), 255, 257.

How did Paul expect the congregation to treat its leaders? Unlike some other early Christians, he does not ask the congregation to obey its leaders (see Heb 13:17). Instead, he asks them to "know" (*oida*) their leaders, a word that the NABRE translates as **respect**. What does this mean? The Thessalonian church was small and had existed only for a short time, so it could hardly mean that they should "get to know" their leaders. Paul sometimes uses the language of knowing to indicate respect (e.g., 1 Cor 16:18), but these passages use a different Greek word. Fortunately, Ignatius of Antioch provides us with a close parallel to what Paul says here, using "know" to refer to honoring God and the bishop (see sidebar, "St. Ignatius of Antioch on Respect for Leaders," above). "Knowing" in this case would mean something like "acknowledging" them with appropriate honor or respect (see 2 Thess 1:8). Theodoret of Cyrus, an ancient Greek interpreter of Paul, summarizes this passage accordingly: "It is right for all of you to consider your teachers worthy of honor."[8]

8. *Interpretatio in xiv epistulas sancti Pauli* (PG 82:653 [my translation]).

Paul also asks the congregation to esteem these leaders. Unfortunately, the NABRE translation of this verse (**show esteem for them with special love on account of their work**) leaves much to be desired: what exactly is "special love?" The NRSV is more satisfactory: "Esteem them very highly in love because of their work." Paul wants the congregation to hold these leaders in high regard because their efforts make the life of the Thessalonian church possible. St. John Chrysostom compares this love to the affection that one should have for the person who introduced you to your spouse; the gratitude is in proportion to the importance of the work.[9] Paul also asks the congregation to be **at peace among yourselves**. This does not necessarily imply that he thought there was a problem, but Paul would have known very well that disputes could easily arise in the future. Some of the most reliable ancient manuscripts read, "Be at peace among *them*." If this is what Paul wrote, then the point would be to forestall conflict with the leaders of the congregation.

Short Exhortations (5:14–22)

[14]**We urge you, brothers, admonish the idle, cheer the fainthearted, support the weak, be patient with all.** [15]**See that no one returns evil for evil; rather, always seek what is good [both] for each other and for all.** [16]**Rejoice always.** [17]**Pray without ceasing.** [18]**In all circumstances give thanks, for this is the will of God for you in Christ Jesus.** [19]**Do not quench the Spirit.** [20]**Do not despise prophetic utterances.** [21]**Test everything; retain what is good.** [22]**Refrain from every kind of evil.**

Lectionary: 1 Thess 5:16–24; Third Sunday of Advent (Year C)

As the letter draws to a close, Paul gives a series of final, rapid-fire instructions.   **5:14** Some interpreters since John Chrysostom have thought that in verse 14 Paul is giving special instructions to the leaders. He just described leaders as those "who admonish you" (5:12), and here he says, **We urge you, brothers, admonish the idle**. Though Paul surely expected the leaders to be prominent among those admonishing, these instructions are probably addressed to the whole church. There is no signal in the text that would indicate a restricted audience, and the exhortations that follow in 5:15–22 certainly apply to everyone. St. Caesarius of Arles rightly concludes that in this passage the "Apostle also preaches not

9. *Homiliae* (PG 62:455).

only to the clergy but to the laity."[10] The word translated as "idle" (*ataktos*) usually means "disorderly," and is often used to describe unorganized troops. The NABRE, following an old custom among English translations, overinterprets this word, assuming that it refers to a specific kind of disorder: refusal to work. Lazy disorder is clearly a problem in 2 Thessalonians (3:6–10), and in the present letter Paul does remind the congregation of the importance of work (4:11), but it is not obvious that this is what Paul is talking about here. A more cautious approach is to leave open the possibility that Paul is concerned about other sorts of disorder as well. Paul wants the congregation to reach out to the disorderly, **the fainthearted**, and **the weak**. Paul's concern for these groups makes a great deal of sense given what we already know about the congregation from chapter 4. We know that there were Christians in Thessalonica who were struggling to refrain from fornication (4:3–8), and that some of them were grieving the loss of some of their number (4:13–18). It is certain, therefore, that there was plenty of disorder and faintheartedness to admonish and encourage.

5:15   The members of the Thessalonian congregation are to correct and encourage one another, but it is inevitable that they will sometimes wrong one another, unintentionally or otherwise. When this happens, they must refuse to repay **evil for evil**. The Old Testament command of "eye for eye" (e.g., Exod 21:23–24) was designed to limit retaliation by forbidding disproportionate acts of revenge, and in the other Old Testament and noncanonical Jewish texts it is sometimes said that it would be better not to seek vengeance at all (Prov 20:22). Paul teaches that it was not enough simply to refuse to get revenge. One must go a step further and **always seek what is good** for others in the Church **and for all** people outside the Church as well. This command goes beyond passivity or nonretaliation to actively pursue the benefit of others. John Chrysostom calls this way of life "the greater philosophy, not only to refrain from repaying evil with evil, but to repay evil with good."[11] Exhortations to love of enemies became common in early Christianity and are best known from the Sermon on the Mount.[12]

5:16–18   The conclusion of the letter recalls its beginning. The letter begins with Paul, Silvanus, and Timothy's claim to "give thanks to God always for all of you, remembering you in our prayers, unceasingly" (1:2). They rejoice that the Thessalonians have endured persecution with the joy of the Holy Spirit. Now, at the letter's end, Paul asks the grieving congregation to **rejoice**, **pray**, and **give thanks** at all times. Is it possible to pray and give thanks at all times? Paul uses

10. *Saint Caesarius of Arles: Sermons, vol. 1 (1–80)*, trans. Mary Magdeleine Mueller, FC 31 (Washington, DC: Catholic University of America Press, 1956), 349.
11. *Homiliae* (PG 62:457 [my translation]).
12. See Matt 5:38–48; Luke 6:27–36; Rom 12:17; 1 Pet 3:9; Polycarp, *To the Philippians* 2.2.

The Necessity of Forgiveness and Love of Enemies

Paul, without further explanation, asks the Thessalonians to return evil with good. Two main rationales for refusing vengeance appear elsewhere in the Pauline Letters and in the broader biblical tradition. The first is that vengeance belongs to God alone (Prov 20:22; 24:29). Humans are not able to deal out judgment with fairness and must leave this to the true judge. As Paul puts it in Romans, "Beloved, do not look for revenge but leave room for the wrath; for it is written, 'Vengeance is mine, I will repay, says the Lord'" (12:19, citing Deut 32:35). The second rationale is summed up in Eph 4:32: "Be kind to one another, compassionate, forgiving one another as God has forgiven you in Christ." In other words, God's people ought to show others the same mercy that God showed them. The Our Father links God's offer of forgiveness to our forgiveness of others (Matt 6:12, 14; see also Mark 11:25), and the parable of the unforgiving servant (Matt 18:23–35) makes the same point very clear: those who have been forgiven must extend the same forgiveness to others or else face divine judgment. Since God is merciful, God's people must love their enemies (Luke 6:35–36). In the second century, Polycarp told the church in Philippi that God would raise them from the dead if they "love what Jesus loved" by forgiving and refusing to repay "evil for evil" (*To the Philippians* 2.2–3). In the second century, *Acts of John* 81 says that one must not repay evil for evil.

> For though we have done much evil toward God and no good, God gave us not vengeance but repentance. Though we were ignorant of his name he did not neglect us but had mercy on us. Though we blasphemed he did not [punish] but had pity. And when we disbelieved him he did not bear a grudge. . . . He did not repay us but gave us repentance and abstinence from evil and exhorted us to come to him. (my translation)

three parallel phrases describing the perpetual nature of these activities: **always** (*pantote*), **without ceasing** (*adialeiptōs*), **In all circumstances** (*en panti*). The first and third suggest not unceasing activity but praise that is offered in all kinds of circumstances. The word *adialeiptōs* does suggest nonstop behavior, though there could be an element of exaggeration here (see the use of the same word to describe prayer in 1 Macc 12:11). Even so, prayer that is more or less unceasing is a tall order (see Reflection and Application on 5:14–22).

For Paul, a life of thanksgiving and prayer did not mean walking around with the light feeling that accompanies good times, or plastering a smile over inner turmoil. Instead, he trusted that the Holy Spirit would enable Christians to give thanks to God regardless of the circumstances. Paul's letter to the Philippians provides a good example of him putting his own teaching into practice. Writing from prison and expecting to be killed, he gives thanks to God (1:3–14) and asks the Philippians to do the same (4:4–6), not because he expects things to go well, but because he believes Christ will be exalted by his death or his life (1:20–21).

Reading 1 Thess 5:16–18 in a modern Bible, one could get the impression that Paul has turned from the question of how church members should treat one another to talk about individual piety. The original text was not divided into verses, however. The call to "rejoice" follows immediately after the preceding command to seek the good for all. Though standard English does not distinguish between the second-person singular and plural, the words "rejoice," "pray," and "give thanks" are plural imperatives in Greek. They are commands addressed to the entire congregation. This passage concludes with a solemn explanation: **for this is the will of God for you** [plural] **in Christ Jesus**.

5:19–22   **Do not quench the Spirit**, Paul warns. The word translated as "quench" is often used of fire, and of course the Spirit was associated with fire (e.g., Acts 2:3). Quenching the Spirit would mean "putting out" the fire of God's presence. How could humans do such a thing? Paul does not think that people are able to harm God, but he does think that they can "quench" the Spirit's work in the community's life by opposing the Spirit's gifts. One example of quenching the Spirit—perhaps the one that Paul was most concerned about—is the despising of **prophetic utterances**. In the Old Testament, the Spirit of God inspired prophets to convict the people of sin, warn them of coming judgment, and comfort them with words of coming restoration. Jesus was widely recognized as a prophet (e.g., Mark 8:28), and the book of Acts teaches that after Jesus's ascension the Holy Spirit gave prophetic gifts to the Church (e.g., Acts 2:14–18). In a later letter, Paul teaches that the gift of prophecy is for the "building up, encouragement, and solace" of the Church (1 Cor 14:3), though Paul takes it to be self-evident that not all Christians have this gift (1 Cor 12:29). Paul encourages the Thessalonians to use their prophetic gifts but also to subject supposed prophetic messages to critical scrutiny. They are not to **despise** prophecies, but to **Test everything; retain what is good**, and **Refrain from every kind of evil**. If a brother or sister claimed to speak prophetically, the congregation was not to assume the validity of such speech but instead to test the message in light of what they knew to be good and evil (see 1 Cor 14:29; 1 John 4:1). The prophet's message needed to accord with the truth that had already been revealed (see commentary on 2 Thess 2:2). In later centuries this passage became the blueprint for how the Magisterium should deal with movements that emerge in the Church: the bishops must take care not to quench the Spirit by discouraging such movements, but they must be tested so that the good can be retained.[13]

The warning against quenching the Spirit (v. 19) should not be taken to refer only to the acceptance of prophecies (v. 20). Patristic commentators generally interpreted verse 19 as encouragement to fan the flame of the Spirit more generally, and with good reason: verses 19 and 20 are not linked grammatically, and the significance of the Spirit for Paul extends far beyond charismatic gifts. For Paul, the Spirit enables Christians to become more like Christ (1:6). Any behavior that works in the opposite direction would be an effort toward quenching the Spirit. For instance, in 4:3–8 Paul warned that through sexual immorality the Church could become "impure" and reject the Holy Spirit. Athanasius and John Chrysostom interpret this passage to be saying that people could quench the Spirit through unholy deeds.[14] Gregory of Nazianzus links keeping the flame of the Spirit alive with being reconciled to God.[15] According to Thomas Aquinas, one could quench the Spirit simply by stopping someone from performing a generous deed.[16]

Reflection and Application (5:14–22)

Over the centuries, many readers have wrestled with Paul's instruction to "pray without ceasing" (5:17; see also Eph 6:18; Col 4:2; Luke 18:1). The nineteenth-century Russian text *The Way of a Pilgrim* begins when a mendicant attends the liturgy and hears 1 Thess 5:17:

> I heard the following words: "Pray without ceasing." This verse especially fixed itself in my mind, and I began to wonder how one could pray unceasingly, since each man must occupy himself with other matters as well, in order to make a living. . . . I thought about this for some time but was unable to understand it.[17]

He continues to wrestle with this for the remainder of the book, eventually learning continual "interior prayer" by reciting the "Jesus prayer" ("Lord Jesus Christ, have mercy on me!") without ceasing. St. Augustine admits that it is impossible to pray unceasingly if we restrict ourselves to formalized prayers

---

13. Fifth Lateran Council 4; *Lumen Gentium* 12; Catechism 801.
14. Athanasius, *Festal Letters* 3.4, citing Wis 1:5; John Chrysostom, *Homiliae* (PG 62:461).
15. *Orations* 29.21.
16. *Super ad Thessalonicenses I reportatio* 5.2.133.
17. *The Way of a Pilgrim; and, The Pilgrim Continues His Way*, trans. Olga Savin (Boston: Shambhala, 2001), 1.

that involve "bending the knee, prostrating the body, or lifting up our hands." But there is, Augustine claims, "another inward kind of prayer without ceasing, which is the desire of the heart." If you long for God, you do not cease to pray, for "the continuance of your longing is the continuance of your prayer."[18] In other words, all of life can be done for God's sake, recognizing that all good things are God's gifts, and become in this way prayer and thanksgiving. Moreover, according to Augustine, God speaks back by shaping our desires, uniting our will to his.[19]

In his commentary on 1 Thessalonians, Thomas Aquinas gives his own answer to this question by drawing on the opinions of many who preceded him. He says that it is possible to pray without ceasing in three ways. First, we do so by praying at the appointed times during the day. Second, following Augustine, Thomas says that we pray when we desire God and God's will. Third, drawing on the biblical idea that gifts for the poor are gifts for God (e.g., Phil 4:18), Thomas teaches that almsgiving sets off a cascade of prayer that continues unceasingly, because "the one who receives your gift prays for you even while you are asleep."[20]

Prayer for Complete Sanctification (5:23–25)

[23]**May the God of peace himself make you perfectly holy and may you entirely, spirit, soul, and body, be preserved blameless for the coming of our Lord Jesus Christ. [24]The one who calls you is faithful, and he will also accomplish it. [25]Brothers, pray for us [too].**

OT: Lev 19:1–2; Isa 6:1–7
NT: Matt 5:48
Catechism: grace, 1996–2005

5:23–24   As in a number of his other letters, Paul begins to conclude with a prayer for peace, often referring to God as **the God of peace**. It is striking that Paul would associate God with peace so soon after mocking those who erroneously think that there is peace (5:3). The implication is that not everything called "peace" deserves the name. The peace offered by the Roman Empire, obtained by violence, is fleeting and will be revealed as a sham on the day of the Lord (5:1–3).

18. *Exposition on the Book of Psalms* 38.13 (*NPNF¹* 8:107).
19. *Epistolae* 130.8.17. See Paul J. Griffiths, "Pray without Ceasing," *Christian Reflection: A Series in Faith and Ethics* (Waco: The Center for Christian Ethics at Baylor University, 2009): 11–17.
20. *Super ad Thessalonicenses I reportatio* 5.2.130 (my translation). Thomas attributes these words to the *Vitae Patrum*.

In contrast, the peace that Paul prays for is from God and is certain because it rests on God's own faithfulness (5:24). This peace involves the renewal of creation and the total sanctification of those who belong to Christ.

Like the prayer in 3:11–13, this prayer summarizes many of the key ideas in the letter: the importance of the holiness of the Thessalonians, the coming of Jesus, and God's faithfulness to them as they wait for this day. The prayer consists of two parallel parts that repeatedly stress the importance of complete holiness. First, Paul prays that God would sanctify the Thessalonian congregation **perfectly**, or completely. They are already **holy** because they are recipients of the Holy Spirit (4:3–8), yet they need to progress to attain complete holiness (3:11–13; 4:3). Second, Paul prays that they would be **preserved** by God in sanctity, being kept **blameless** when Jesus returns. As in 3:11–13, Paul is presupposing a final judgment, assuming that when the Lord returns he will evaluate everyone's deeds. But this judgment is not something to be feared but instead is to be anticipated in hope, because God will faithfully make the church ready for this day.[21]

The prayer states that "the God of peace himself" will do the sanctifying, and verse 24 assures the Thessalonians that the **one who calls you is faithful, and he will also accomplish it**. How could Paul be so confident that God would do this work for them after claiming earlier in the letter that they must learn to behave in way that is pleasing to God (e.g., 4:1–8)? It is often difficult for modern readers to grasp, but Paul saw no contradiction between saying that people must strive to be holy and saying that holiness is God's gift. Paul states this in a pithy way in Phil 2:12–13: "Work out your salvation with fear and trembling, for God is the one working in you" (my translation). God's faithfulness provides hope because believers know that their fate does not rest in their own excellence. At the same time, God's gift is the sanctification of believers, and for that sanctification to be real it must be lived. For this reason St. Basil the Great was right to cite 1 Thess 5:24 and then add, "provided we keep His commandments by the grace of Christ in the Holy Spirit."[22]

Paul's prayer is for complete sanctification, touching every part of a Christian's life. Their holiness must be complete, extending to **spirit, soul, and body**. Some, such as St. Irenaeus and Origen, have interpreted the mention of spirit, soul, and body to mean that humans are made up of three different parts, but

---

21. See Pope Benedict XVI, *Spe Salvi* 43.
22. *Saint Basil: Ascetical Works*, trans. M. Monica Wagner, FC 9 (Washington, DC: Catholic University of America Press, 1962), 68.

this is an overinterpretation.[23] There is no hint in Paul's other letters that he saw humans as being divided into three parts. Paul's point here is very similar to the †Shema: one must love God "with all your heart, and soul, and strength" (Deut 6:5 [my translation]). This means loving God with your entire being, not that people are made up of three parts. The mention of the body is, however, a good reminder that salvation is not an escape from the body and material creation but rather the sanctification and redemption of it.

The Thessalonians are already holy inasmuch as they have received the Holy Spirit and are called to live in sanctity and purity (4:3–8). Nevertheless, Paul sees the coming presence of the Lord as the decisive moment when complete sanctity will be required. His thinking here is not unlike Isaiah's vision of God in the temple. The fiery seraphim hail God as "holy, holy, holy," and Isaiah panics, realizing that he is a sinner unfit to be in God's presence: "Woe is me, I am doomed! For I am a man of unclean lips, living among a people of unclean lips, and my eyes have seen the King, the LORD of hosts!" (6:5). In response, one of the seraphim takes an ember from the altar and touches Isaiah's mouth, saying, "Now that this has touched your lips, your wickedness is removed, your sin purged" (6:7). Similarly, Paul prays for the Thessalonians' complete sanctification in preparation for the presence of Jesus, knowing that it is not possible to dwell with God, the all-holy One, while remaining in sin and impurity.

In his commentary on this passage, Thomas Aquinas suggests that Paul prays that they will be kept "blameless" instead of "without sin" because only Christ can be sinless. Blamelessness, Thomas says, "may describe those who may commit venial sins, but nevertheless do not commit grave sins by which their neighbors would be led to sin."[24] Thomas then cites Luke 1:6, which speaks of Zechariah and Elizabeth living "blamelessly" according to God's commands. Thomas is certainly correct that the word "blameless" (*amemptōs*) was not used to mean utter perfection. Shortly after being called blameless, Zechariah was chastised by the angel Gabriel for his lack of faith in God's promise (Luke 1:18–20). Paul himself says that prior to being called by Jesus he was "blameless" in the righteousness of the Torah (Phil 3:6), and Paul is the first to admit that he was not without sin in those days. The word translated as "blameless" (*amemptōs*) appears frequently on pagan inscriptions, where it suggests not utter perfection but a life lived well in service of the city.[25] Thomas's sugges-

---

23. E.g., Irenaeus, *Against Heresies* 5.6.1; Origen, *Commentary on the Epistle to the Romans* 1.10.2. In his commentary on 1–2 Thessalonians, Thomas Aquinas labels this view "condemned in church teaching" (*Super ad Thessalonicenses I reportatio* 5.2.137). See also Catechism 367.

24. *Super ad Thessalonicenses I reportatio* 5.2.137 (my translation).

25. BDAG.

St. Augustine on the Mutual Prayer of the Bishop and the People

LIVING TRADITION

In a sermon St. Augustine explains why he needs the congregation to pray for him.

Let us always look forward with longing toward our everlasting joy; let us always pray for fortitude in our temporal labors and trials; let us offer prayers for one another; let my prayers be offered for you, and yours for me. And, brethren, do not think that you need my prayers, but that I have no need of yours. We have mutual need of one another's prayers, for those reciprocal prayers are enkindled by charity and—like a sacrifice offered on the altar of piety—are fragrant, and pleasing to the Lord. If the Apostles used to ask for prayers on their own behalf, how much the more does it behoove me to do so? For I am far from being their equal, although I long to follow their footsteps as closely as possible; but I have neither the wisdom to know nor the rashness to say what progress I have made. Those men, with all their greatness, were anxious to have prayers offered by the Church in their behalf. They used to say: "We are your glory, as you also will be ours, in the day of the Lord Jesus Christ." They used to pray mutually for one another in anticipation of the day of our Lord Jesus Christ; for on that day there will be glory, but until that day there will be weakness. Let us pray in weakness, that we may rejoice in glory.[a]

a. *Commentary on the Lord's Sermon on the Mount with Seventeen Related Sermons*, trans. Denis J. Kavanagh, FC 11 (Washington, DC: Catholic University of America Press, 1951), 354–55.

tion is, therefore, a good reminder that human "blamelessness" cannot mean complete sinlessness in this life.

Just after praying for the Thessalonians, Paul asks that they pray for him, as **5:25** he does of the recipients in most of his letters (Rom 15:30–33; 2 Cor 1:11; Phil 1:19; Philem 1:22). He does not indicate what he wants them to pray for, though a careful reader of the letter would be likely to pray for Paul's sanctification (1 Thess 5:23) and that God would make it possible for him to visit Thessalonica again (2:18; 3:10–11). Since Paul is the authority figure in the relationship, asking for their prayer also contains an implicit lesson, as Theodoret of Cyrus recognizes: "He asks them to pray, not only so he will have the help of their prayer, but also so he may teach them how to behave."[26] By asking for their prayer, he shows that he too needs to progress on the path of sanctification (Phil 3:12–14) and that their intercession is significant.

26. *Interpretatio in xiv epistulas sancti Pauli* (PG 82:656 [my translation]).

Conclusion (5:26–28)

---

[26]Greet all the brothers with a holy kiss. [27]I adjure you by the Lord that this letter be read to all the brothers. [28]The grace of our Lord Jesus Christ be with you.

5:26   Paul frequently ends his letters by instructing the church members to greet one another with a **holy kiss** (Rom 16:16; 1 Cor 16:20; 2 Cor 13:12). The holy kiss was also practiced beyond Paul's churches (1 Pet 5:14), and by the mid-second century it had become a fixed point in the liturgy.[27] In the Greco-Roman world, kisses were exchanged between lovers and family members, but also in a wide range of other settings that would seem odd to most modern Westerners, at least in the English-speaking world. Kisses could be a way of creating or strengthening relationships, like a more robust alternative to our habit of shaking hands. For instance, the Roman historians Tacitus and Suetonius mention emperors kissing troops to ingratiate themselves to mutinous soldiers.[28] Judas Iscariot's kiss, which the Church Fathers often contrast with the holy kiss, profanes the intimacy of a friendly kiss, which is what makes it so memorably cruel. John Chrysostom interprets the holy kiss as Paul's way of uniting the members of the Church: "Having united them with his [†]paraenesis, he naturally commands them also to be joined through the holy kiss. For this kiss unites and gives birth to one body."[29] Together with the prevalence of familial language in 1 Thessalonians, the holy kiss was a way of uniting the new converts as a family along with Christians in other cities. Paul usually asks churches to greet "one another" with a holy kiss, but here he asks them to greet **all the brothers** in this way. If there were any doubt about whether some of the erring members of the congregation should receive the holy kiss, stating the command this way would ensure that no one is left out. It is also possible that Paul wants them to greet one another and Christians from elsewhere in Macedonia with a holy kiss. The Thessalonian congregation was not an isolated community; it was part of a wider body that included Christian neighbors in Philippi (1:7–8).

5:27   Since the letter is from Paul, Silvanus, and Timothy, most of it is written in the first-person plural, but in a few places Paul uses the singular (2:18; 3:5),

---

27. Justin Martyr, *First Apology* 65–67. The same practice is well attested in other Church Fathers.
28. Tacitus, *Histories* 1.36.12; Suetonius, *Vitellius* 7.3.7; cited by Michael Philip Penn, *Kissing Christians: Ritual and Community in the Late Ancient Church* (Philadelphia: University of Philadelphia Press, 2005), 28.
29. *In epistulam i ad Corinthios* (PG 61:376 [my translation]).

which is a clue that he has been the principal author all along. Here it is likely that Paul took the pen from the †amanuensis to write the conclusion in his own hand, as he does in other letters (e.g., 1 Cor 16:21; Gal 6:11; 2 Thess 3:17). He issues a warning: **I adjure you by the Lord that this letter be read to all the brothers**. When American courtrooms ask a witness to place a hand on a Bible and swear to tell the truth, they are implicitly calling God to witness and to compel the witness to tell the truth. Similarly, to adjure (*enorkizō*) someone by God or another power was to attempt to place that person under an oath before God. In Mark's Gospel, demons attempt to place Jesus under oath (*horkizō*) by God not to torture them (5:7), and in Acts certain exorcists unsuccessfully attempt to use the formula "I adjure you by the Jesus whom Paul preaches" to cast out evil spirits (19:13). In the centuries that followed, Christian funerary inscriptions sometimes adjure visitors by God, Jesus, or other beings not to disturb the grave. Paul's language here is surprisingly solemn.

Why was this solemn adjuration necessary? It shows that Paul considered the letter absolutely vital for them to hear. It was not enough for some of them to read it and share the gist of the message. They all needed to hear these words read aloud. The letter probably would have been delivered in the first place to the leaders, and Paul wants to ensure that it is shared with all, including those who would have been unable to read it for themselves. Also, although there is no indication that Paul knew that he was writing Scripture when he composed this letter, this verse shows that the letter was always intended for an ecclesial setting. Its natural habitat is not the scholar's study or the individual Christian's private reading but rather the congregation, before "all the brothers." Reading and studying in these other settings is essential, but the setting that is most closely analogous to its original one is ecclesial.

All of Paul's Letters end with a benediction. Instead of a simple "farewell," **5:28** Paul offers one more prayer, stressing yet again the fundamental importance of God's generosity: **The grace of our Lord Jesus Christ be with you** (see commentary on 1 Thess 1:1). "Grace" or "gift" (*charis*) becomes a major topic in Paul's later letters when he feels that some Christian teachers are attacking God's generosity (see especially Galatians). But even before those events Paul puts a special emphasis on God's grace, going so far as to invent an idiosyncratic way of opening and closing letters with invocations of God's grace.

Thanksgiving for Endurance in the Midst of Suffering

2 Thessalonians 1:1–12

Not long after writing 1 Thessalonians, Paul learned that the church's struggles were far from over.[1] The Thessalonians continued to be confused about the timing of the Lord's return, some were directly flouting Paul's instructions about the importance of work, and on top of all this they were experiencing significant opposition from outside the church. This short letter was written to respond to these crises and to encourage the Thessalonians to remain faithful.

In the letter's opening, Paul and his associates give thanks for the Thessalonians' endurance in the midst of difficult times. Paul also comforts them with the reminder that when Jesus returns he will comfort the afflicted and punish their oppressors, and he reminds them of his prayers that God will deem the young congregation worthy of the kingdom of God.

Letter Opening (1:1–2)

---

[1]Paul, Silvanus, and Timothy to the church of the Thessalonians in God our Father and the Lord Jesus Christ: [2]grace to you and peace from God [our] Father and the Lord Jesus Christ.

NT: 1 Thess 1:1

1. Paul's authorship of 2 Thessalonians is debated. See the discussion of authorship and circumstances of the letter's composition in the introduction. In the commentary I occasionally consider how a passage would be interpreted if Paul were not the author.

The opening address is almost identical to the opening of 1 Thessalonians.[2] Once   **1:1**
again the letter is said to be from **Paul, Silvanus, and Timothy**. Are Silvanus
and Timothy real coauthors of this letter, or were they simply present with Paul
when he dictated the letter?[3] Like 1 Thessalonians, 2 Thessalonians occasionally
lapses into the first-person singular, indicating that Paul is the main author.
In 2:5 the author asks the Thessalonians to remember what "I told you," and
3:17 concludes the letter by emphasizing that Paul himself has penned the final
greeting with his own hand. Nevertheless, the fact that Silvanus and Timothy
are listed in the opening suggests that the letter is to be read as if it came from
all three men, and it is reasonable to suppose that they participated in the
letter's composition. As noted in the comments on 1 Thess 1:1, Paul's Letters
often mention coworkers who are present with him without mentioning them
as coauthors. Silvanus and Timothy were present during the initial mission to
Macedonia, and they join Paul in revisiting the Thessalonians through this letter.

Only in the letters to the Thessalonians does Paul refer to himself simply by
his name. In his other surviving letters he gives more elaborate self-descriptions
such as "Paul, an apostle of Christ Jesus by the will of God" (2 Cor 1:1). Paul's
more fulsome descriptions of himself in his letter openings sometimes indicate
that his authority or teaching has been called into question, as in the letters to
Corinth and Galatia.[4] In Galatians, for instance, he identifies himself as "Paul, an
apostle not from human beings nor through a human being but through Jesus
Christ and God the Father who raised him from the dead" (1:1). Paul thereby
reasserts the divine origin of his teaching against those who had come to Galatia after him teaching "a different gospel" (1:6). The simple self-description in
the Thessalonian letters could suggest that Paul did not feel that his authority
was under attack. Paul also had a good relationship with the Thessalonians'
Macedonian neighbors, the Philippians, so it is interesting to note that his self-
description in that letter too is relatively simple: "Paul and Timothy, slaves of
Christ Jesus" (Phil 1:1).

The only significant difference between the openings of the two Thessalonian   **1:2**
letters appears in the greeting; in the second letter Paul specifies that **grace** and
peace come from **God** as well as **the Lord Jesus Christ**.[5] The phrase "grace to

---

2. See introduction on the similarities between the two letters.

3. See commentary on 1 Thess 1:1.

4. See also Rom 1:1–7, where the length of Paul's self-introduction is worthy of the emperor Com-
modus. See Dio Cassius, *Roman History* 73.15.5.

5. 1 Thess 1:1 simply states "grace to you and peace." The NABRE brackets "our" in 2 Thess 1:2 because it is missing from some important ancient manuscripts. See the arguments in favor of its original
absence in Gordon D. Fee, *The First and Second Letters to the Thessalonians*, NICNT (Grand Rapids:
Eerdmans, 2009), 244.

you and peace from God [our] Father and the Lord Jesus Christ" is familiar from Paul's other letters, but it is important not to rush past it and miss its surprising content. Grace and peace are described as coming from a single source, God and Jesus, who together form the joint object of the preposition **from** (*apo*). God and Jesus are distinguishable, and yet Paul assumes that they work in concert in granting grace and peace. As in 1 Thessalonians (see commentary on 1 Thess 3:11), Paul does not reflect on how Jesus and God could jointly bestow gifts on the churches. He simply assumes that it is the case and that his audience will understand him. In later centuries commentators would struggle to spell out the implications of the mutual action of the Father and Son. In the fourth century, St. Ambrose saw the action of all three persons of the Trinity in this Pauline phrase:

> Behold we have it that there is one grace on the part of the Father and the Son, and that there is one peace on the part of the Father and the Son, but this grace and peace are the fruit of the Spirit, as the Apostle himself taught when he said: "But the fruit of the Spirit is charity, joy, peace, patience" [Gal 5:22].[6]

In other words, the Father and Son jointly give peace, but Paul says elsewhere that peace is a fruit of the Spirit (Gal 5:22). Thus, for Ambrose, the Father and Son grant peace to the churches through the indwelling of the Holy Spirit.

Thanksgiving (1:3–4)

[3]**We ought to thank God always for you, brothers, as is fitting, because your faith flourishes ever more, and the love of every one of you for one another grows ever greater. [4]Accordingly, we ourselves boast of you in the churches of God regarding your endurance and faith in all your persecutions and the afflictions you endure.**

OT: Ps 116
NT: 1 Thess 1:2–9; Phil 1:3–7

1:3   It was Paul's custom to follow his letter opening with a report of how he thanks God for the letter recipients, and often these thanksgivings hint at the main themes that will unfold in the rest of the letter (see commentary on 1 Thess 1:3). The letters to the Thessalonians are unique in having two thanksgiving

---

6. *On the Holy Spirit* 1.12.127, in *Saint Ambrose: Theological and Dogmatic Works*, trans. Roy J. Deferrari, FC 44 (Washington, DC: Catholic University of America Press, 1963), 80.

St. Augustine on the Divine Origin of the Thessalonians' Faith and Love

Augustine drew on both letters to the Thessalonians to argue that God makes it possible for humans to have faith and love.

There would be no merit in men's choosing Him unless the action of God's grace in choosing them had gone before. This is why in imparting his blessing to the Thessalonians the Apostle Paul declares: "And may the Lord make you to increase and abound in charity towards one another, and towards all men" [1 Thess 3:12]. He who gave this blessing to love one another is the same who gave us the love to love one another. Again, because some of them were sure to possess already the good dispositions he wished to be theirs, he went on to say in another passage, directed to the same Thessalonians: "We are bound to give thanks to God always for you, brethren, as is fitting, because your faith grows exceedingly and your charity each for the other increases" [2 Thess 1:3]. This he said so that they might not be elated over this great blessing which they enjoyed from God, as if it were something they possessed of themselves. Seeing, therefore, that your faith grows exceedingly and your charity for each other increases, as the Apostle says, we ought to thank God in your regard, and not praise you as if you possessed all this of yourselves.[a]

a. *Grace and Free Will* 18.38. In *The Teacher; The Free Choice of the Will; Grace and Free Will*, trans. Robert P. Russell, FC 59 (Washington, DC: Catholic University of America Press, 1968), 294.

sections (2 Thess 1:3–12; 2:13–14; 1 Thess 1:2–10; 2:13–16). In this case, the first thanksgiving stretches from verses 3 to 12, and 3–10 is a single sentence, which is broken up in translation for the sake of clarity. The beginning of the thanksgiving section might appear counterintuitive because Paul thanks God for something that the Thessalonians are doing: their **faith flourishes ever more** and their **love . . . for one another grows ever greater** despite the hardships they have endured (see also Rom 1:8; Phil 1:5; 4:10–20; Col 1:3–4; Philem 1:4–5). It only makes sense for Paul to pray this way if he thinks that their faith and love are ultimately attributable to God. At the same time, when Paul thanks God for their faith, he is also subtly encouraging them to continue to cultivate this divine gift.

Many modern commentators have argued that Paul's thanksgiving sounds detached and cold. Paul says, **We ought** (*opheilō*) **to thank God** and that this **is fitting** (*axios*), suggesting that 1:3–12 is not a spontaneous expression of gratitude for the faith and love of the Thessalonians but rather the mere fulfillment of a requirement (see also 2:13). As noted in the introduction, this has

The Obligation to Thank God

BIBLICAL BACKGROUND

New Testament scholars have sometimes alleged that the mention of the "obligation" and "fittingness" of thanking God (1:3; 2:13) sets a cold, formal tone. In so doing they reveal more about themselves than about 2 Thessalonians. People today often suspect that religion is spoiled by obligation, formality, and reciprocity.[a] The ancients, however, did not share these concerns. The Old Testament often speaks of the obligation to render thanksgiving to God.[b] For instance, in Ps 116, a prayer of thanksgiving to God for deliverance from death, the psalmist says, "I will offer a sacrifice of praise / and call on the name of the Lord. / I will pay my vows to the Lord / in the presence of all his people" (vv. 17–18).[c] The "vow" here involves asking God for help and promising to render praise if God comes to the rescue. In this and similar passages, thanking God is both an obligation and a joyful response to God's acts of faithfulness. The Thessalonians would have already been familiar with similar language even before their conversion. For instance, an inscription from Roman-era Macedonia gives thanks to the goddess Artemis by "repaying the vow" to her.[d] Rabbinic texts say similar things, such as the passage in the Mishnah that says "we are obligated to give thanks" to God for redeeming Israel from Egypt.[e] The late first-century Christian letter *1 Clement* describes Christian worship as the services that "we ought [*opheilō*] to perform" for God (40.1). The second-century *Shepherd of Hermas* says, "You who suffer for the name ought [*opheilō*] to glorify God" (Parable 9, 28.5). Similar language has endured in liturgies and hymns down to the present day. For instance, in

been one of the main arguments against Paul's authorship of the letter. First Thessalonians has a warm, spontaneous feel, it is argued, whereas 2 Thessalonians describes a relationship of dreary obligation.[7] In fact, the ancients did not associate obligation with cold reluctance as many people do today. Instead, ancient Christians, Jews, and pagans used the language of debt and obligation to describe the appropriate response to kindnesses shown by friends or gods, and these obliged responses are often clearly very heartfelt (see sidebar, "The Obligation to Thank God," above). Thanking God for the Thessalonians is both Paul's duty and—as Paul's boasting to the other churches suggests (1:4)—his delight.

1:4   Though the Thessalonians are confused about the timing of the day of the Lord, and some of their number have been disobeying Paul's teaching on the

---

7. E.g., Victor Paul Furnish, *1 Thessalonians, 2 Thessalonians*, ANTC (Nashville: Abingdon, 2007), 132.

the preface of the eucharistic prayer of the Latin Rite the priest says, "Let us give thanks to the Lord our God," and the people respond, "It is right and just" (*dignum et iustum est*). Greek liturgies similarly affirm that it is right and just (*axion kai dikaion*) to give thanks to God. A fourth-century catechetical lecture explains the "obligation" to praise God in the Eucharist:

> Truly, we ought to give thanks, because when we were unworthy he called us to so great a gift. While we were enemies he reconciled us, counting us worthy of the Spirit of sonship.... In giving thanks we do a deed that is "right and just."[f]

For Paul, like other ancient worshipers, the obligation to thank God does not detract from the purity or sincerity of that thanksgiving (see also 1 Thess 3:9; Phil 1:7).[g]

a. On the modern preference for spontaneity in approaching God, see Lori Branch, *Rituals of Spontaneity: Sentiment and Secularism from Free Prayer to Wordsworth* (Waco: Baylor University Press, 2006). On the modern suspicion of reciprocity between humans and God, see John M. G. Barclay, *Paul and the Gift* (Grand Rapids: Eerdmans, 2015), 51–65.

b. On this issue, see Roger D. Aus, "The Liturgical Background of the Necessity and Propriety of Giving Thanks according to 2 Thes 1:2," *JBL* 92 (1973): 432–38.

c. See also Pss 22:26; 50:14; 61:9; 66:13; 76:12; see Paul in Acts 18:18; 21:23–26.

d. *Epigraphes Anō Makedonias* 29.

e. *Mishnah Pesahim* 10:5.

f. This lecture has sometimes been attributed to St. Cyril of Jerusalem. Greek text from *Lectures on the Christian Sacraments: Greek Original and English Translation*, Popular Patristics Series 57 (Yonkers, NY: St. Vladimir's Seminary Press, 2017), 125 (my translation).

g. The nineteenth-century English translation of the medieval hymn *Victim Paschali* encourages the offering of fitting praises to the risen Jesus: "Christ the Lord is risen today; / Christians, haste your vows to pay; / Offer ye your praises meet [i.e., "fitting"] / At the Paschal Victim's feet."

importance of work (2:1–3:15), Paul begins the letter by noting their **endurance and faith** in the midst of **persecutions** and **afflictions**. We don't know the precise details of these hardships, though it is clear that the trouble is coming from people outside the church (1:6). In the Bible the language of affliction (*thlipsis*) sometimes describes the tribulations of the people of God in the last days prior to God's decisive intervention. As the book of Daniel puts it,

> It shall be a time unsurpassed in distress [Greek *thlipsis*]
>   since the nation began until that time.
> At that time your people shall escape,
>   everyone who is found written in the book.
> Many of those who sleep
>   in the dust of the earth shall awake;
> Some to everlasting life,
>   others to reproach and everlasting disgrace. (12:1–2)

Regardless of whether Paul has this passage in mind, he clearly envisions a similar scenario playing out: the Thessalonians currently suffer, but God will vindicate them and punish their tormentors. Readers familiar with the importance of faith, hope, and love in later tradition will notice that the trio of love, faith, and endurance appears here. Hope and endurance are closely linked in 1 Thessalonians, where Paul thanks God for their "endurance in hope" (1:3).

The Coming Judgment of Good and Evil (1:5–10)

[5]This is evidence of the just judgment of God, so that you may be considered worthy of the kingdom of God for which you are suffering. [6]For it is surely just on God's part to repay with afflictions those who are afflicting you, [7]and to grant rest along with us to you who are undergoing afflictions, at the revelation of the Lord Jesus from heaven with his mighty angels, [8]in blazing fire, inflicting punishment on those who do not acknowledge God and on those who do not obey the gospel of our Lord Jesus. [9]These will pay the penalty of eternal ruin, separated from the presence of the Lord and from the glory of his power, [10]when he comes to be glorified among his holy ones and to be marveled at on that day among all who have believed, for our testimony to you was believed.

OT: Dan 12:1–3; Mal 3:19–21
NT: Matt 5:2–12; 25:31–46; 2 Cor 5:10; Phil 1:27–30; 1 Thess 4:13–5:11
Catechism: judgment of the living and the dead, 678–79

Lurid descriptions of the suffering of the damned are common in †apocalyptic literature such as the book of Revelation. Paul, however, generally says very little about what happens to those who are not in Christ, typically making only brief comments about their "destruction" or "corruption" (e.g., Gal 6:8). This passage is a notable exception. Though the basic point of this section is clear enough, it presents a number of exegetical and theological difficulties that can make the flow of thought difficult to follow. For clarity's sake, here is a loose paraphrase of 1:5–9:

> Your endurance in the midst of afflictions is evidence that God will judge you to be worthy of the kingdom of God. What do I mean? At present you suffer at the hands of others, but God is going to put things right. He will punish those who afflict you and will give rest to those who are currently afflicted. When the Lord Jesus is revealed from heaven with his mighty angels in blazing fire, he will punish those who do not know God or obey the gospel of our Lord Jesus. These

people will pay the just penalty, which is eternal destruction away from the face of the Lord.

In this section Paul comforts the beleaguered congregation with the hope that God will bring justice to the world. Those who suffer for the kingdom will be given rest, but those who persecute them and oppose God will be destroyed.

Continuing the sentence that began in verse 3, Paul comforts the congrega- **1:5**
tion with the news that their current difficult situation is **evidence** that God will judge them **worthy of the kingdom of God**. Commentators disagree about which part of their situation constitutes the "evidence."[8] Some have suggested that the "evidence" is the persecution or perhaps their faith. The most likely suggestion is that the "evidence" is the same thing he is boasting about to the churches: the Thessalonians' "endurance and faith" in the midst of persecutions (1:4). According to 1 Thessalonians, believers are destined to endure afflictions (3:3). Moreover, joy in the midst of affliction makes one an imitator of the apostles and of Jesus himself, and for Paul this was a definite sign of the work of the Holy Spirit (1 Thess 1:2–6; see also Phil 1:28). This passage seems to be saying something similar: the Thessalonians have endured various attacks, and yet their faith and love continue to grow. This is an indication that God is with them and will judge them favorably (see Matt 5:2–12). Some scholars argue that this divine judgment has already taken place (see 1 Pet 4:17–19), noting that verse 5 could be understood to refer to a decision that has already occurred.[9] The main emphasis in this passage, however, is on the judgment that will occur when Jesus returns (see 1:6–10). The faithful endurance of persecution in the present is a strong indicator that the Thessalonians will be rewarded by God in the future.

The outcome of God's judgment of the Thessalonians is that they will be declared "worthy [*kataxioō*] of the kingdom of God."[10] The idea that humans could be found worthy before God may sound presumptuous to modern ears, but it is well attested in the New Testament. For instance, Luke 20:35 speaks of those who enter the life to come as those "who are deemed worthy [*kataxioō*] to attain to the coming age and to the resurrection of the dead." Sometimes it is said that suffering makes one worthy to enter into the kingdom. In the Gospels,

---

8. In the Greek it is not clear how v. 5 relates to the preceding. The words **This is** have been added to the NABRE for clarity.

9. E.g., I. Howard Marshall, *1 and 2 Thessalonians*, NCBC (Grand Rapids: Eerdmans, 1983), 173.

10. The NABRE assumes that worthiness is the result of the judgment rather than its content ("so that you may be considered worthy"). For a refutation of this interpretation, see Béda Rigaux, *Saint Paul: Les Épitres aux Thessaloniciens*, EBib (Paris: Lecoffre, 1956), 621. See commentary on 2 Thess 1:11 against translating *axioō* as "make worthy."

Jesus says that those who are persecuted for his sake will have a great reward in heaven, and that by taking up one's cross and giving one's life away one receives in return eternal life (Matt 16:24–27 and parallels). Jesus also teaches that those who endure to the end of the final †eschatological tribulations will be saved (Matt 24:13 and parallels). In Acts, Paul and Barnabas teach that "it is necessary for us to undergo many hardships to enter the kingdom of God" (14:22; see also 5:41). Paul has taught the Thessalonians that they must live a life "worthy of the God who calls you into his kingdom" (1 Thess 2:12), and in this passage Paul indicates that he thinks they are doing just that. For Paul, this is not a matter of earning a way into the kingdom. Instead, the faith that endures suffering is already a gift of God at work in the faithful (see commentary on 2 Thess 1:3). It is by God's grace that the Thessalonians are able to act in a way that makes them worthy of the kingdom.

1:6–7   Verses 6–7 describe an †eschatological reversal in which those who suffer now will find comfort while their tormentors are punished. It is **just** (*dikaios*) **on God's part to repay with afflictions those who are afflicting** the Thessalonians. Evildoers are to experience suffering proportionate with what they inflicted on others. The idea that those persecuting the Thessalonian converts should themselves be persecuted obviously conforms to a kind of justice, but not one that modern Christians often associate with God. This is a clear example of *ius talionis*, the principle that sins should be repaid in kind. This is a principle applied to the punishment of humans by humans in the Torah's famous "eye for an eye" legislation (Exod 21:23–24; Lev 24:20; Deut 19:21), but it appears more frequently in descriptions of God's judgment of humankind. Ever since the second century AD, some Christians have associated this form of justice with the Old Testament, supposing that Jesus and the New Testament proclaim love and mercy instead, but in fact the New Testament often teaches that God will punish evildoers in kind and give comfort to the oppressed.[11] Mary's Magnificat praises God for feeding the hungry and sending the rich away hungry (Luke 1:53). In Jesus's parable of the rich man and Lazarus (Luke 16:19–31), Abraham explains to the rich man why he must suffer in the afterlife while Lazarus is comforted: "My child, remember that you received what was good during your lifetime while Lazarus likewise received what was bad; but now he is comforted here, whereas you are tormented" (16:25; see Luke 6:20–26). Paul's Letters do not often discuss God's punishment of the wicked, but this passage is not unique (Rom 2:5–8; Col 3:25).

11. See Tertullian's comments regarding Marcion's discomfort with 2 Thess 1:5–10 in *Against Marcion* 5.16.

The positive flip side of the punishment of the afflicters is the comfort of the afflicted. The Thessalonians who have been afflicted will receive **rest along with us**—that is, along with Paul and his comrades, who also endure affliction in the present time. The word translated as "rest" (*anesis*) was used to describe relief from difficulties of various kinds and is a good antonym of "affliction" (*thlipsis*).[12] Paul uses it here in an eschatological sense: it refers to the definitive rest granted to those who have endured affliction for Jesus's sake. †Apocalyptic literature often contrasts the repose of the blessed with the torments of the wicked (Luke 16:19–31; *4 Ezra* 7.36–38). Hebrews reads the promise of the rest of the promised land †typologically to exhort readers to press on to God's eternal rest (chaps. 3–4). "Rest" in these texts refers not to sleeplike oblivion but rather to relief from the trials of this life. The promise of eschatological rest would become an important Christian hope in later tradition. For instance, a fifth-century burial epitaph from Thessalonica says, "Jesus Christ, who made all things through one word, grant rest [*anesis*] . . . to your servant Fortunatus."[13] Latin translations of this verse render *anesis* with the word *requies* (*requiem* when the object of a verb), a word that has become familiar to English speakers from the "requiem" mass, which beseeches God to give rest to the deceased.

The repayment of deeds will occur at the return of the Lord, which is described here using language drawn from Scripture, resulting in a more vivid portrait of eschatological events than is typical for Paul. Whereas 1 Thessalonians described Jesus's coming as something people will hear (the archangel's call and the trumpet of God), this passage focuses on what is seen: Jesus's coming is described as a **revelation** (*apokalypsis*) **. . . from heaven with his mighty angels**. It is as if the curtain separating earth and heaven will be pulled aside to unveil Jesus along with an angelic retinue ready to assist him in the judgment of the nations. Paul affirms that Jesus is already the Lord enthroned in heaven with the angels. But in the coming *apokalypsis* all nations will see what is in fact already true. Early Christian texts often portray angels accompanying Jesus in the last judgment (Matt 16:27; 25:31). Sometimes the angels are assigned specific tasks, such as announcing the time of the Lord's return (1 Thess 4:16), gathering people for the final judgment (Matt 13:41), recording or evaluating people's deeds (*Apocalypse of Zephaniah* 3.6, 9), or inflicting punishments (*2 Enoch* 10.1–3). In this passage no specific role is given to the angels other than to appear along with Jesus, thereby emphasizing the grandeur of the event.

12. See 2 Cor 2:13; 7:5; 8:13; *Acts of Thomas* 39.
13. *RIChrM* 180 (my translation).

Figure 9. *The Last Judgement* by William Butterfield in Keble College Chapel, Oxford.

In non-Christian texts, it is God who is accompanied by angels, but Paul places Jesus in the divine role, as he often does.

1:8   The words **blazing fire** could refer to the appearance of Jesus ("the revelation of the Lord . . . in blazing fire") or to the manner in which Jesus inflicts punishment ("with blazing fire inflicting punishment"). Recent translations and commentaries tend to favor the former (NRSV, NIV). Both possibilities find support in the biblical tradition, where variations of the phrase "blazing fire" describe both God's appearance (Exod 3:2; Dan 7:9) and the means by which God judges the world (Isa 29:6; Sir 21:9; *Psalms of Solomon* 12.4). It would probably be a mistake to draw too sharp a distinction between Jesus appearing in flames and judging with flames since it is his fiery presence that brings judgment. There is good reason to suppose, however, that this passage does describe Jesus using fire as a means of judgment. This passage echoes a number of Old Testament texts, especially LXX Isa 66:15, which says that God will repay evildoers with blazing fire, using an almost identical phrase (see sidebar, "Biblical Traditions in 2 Thessalonians 1:7–10," p. 149).[14] The earliest interpreters of this passage often understood the fire as an instrument of judgment. Irenaeus,

14. In many important manuscripts of 2 Thessalonians it is actually identical to the phrase in Isaiah.

Biblical Traditions in 2 Thessalonians 1:7–10

BIBLICAL BACKGROUND

The description of Jesus's return to punish evildoers and grant rest to the afflicted in 2 Thess 1:7–10 is adorned with biblical language describing God's presence and judgment of the nations.[a] Here are some of the passages that are most similar to 2 Thess 1:7–10, translated from the †Septuagint with close verbal parallels italicized.

I will choose mockery for them and I will *repay* their sins because I called them and *they did not obey me*. . . . Hear the word of the Lord, you who fear his word. Speak, our brothers, to those who hate and abominate us, so that *the name of the Lord may be glorified*. . . . The hand of the Lord shall be known to those who worship him, and he shall warn those who disobey him. For behold, the *Lord will come like fire*, and his chariots like the wind, to *render vengeance* with wrath and repudiation with a *flame of fire*. For by the fire of the Lord all the earth shall be judged. (Isa 66:4–5, 14–16 [my translation, here and below])

[Speaking of the coming judgment of evildoers:] And now go into the rocks and hide in the earth *from the face of* the fear of *the Lord and from the glory of his might* when he comes to break the earth! . . . The Lord alone will be exalted *on that day*. (Isa 2:10, 17; see also vv. 19–21)

Pour out your wrath on the gentiles *who do not know you* and on the families who have not called upon your *name* because they have devoured Jacob and destroyed him and laid waste to his pasture. (Jer 10:25; see also Ps 79:6 [LXX 78:6])

God is glorified in the council *of holy ones*, / great and terrible to all around him. (Ps 89:8 [LXX 88:8])

Marvelous is God *among his holy ones*. / The God of Israel himself will give power and strength to his people. (Ps 68:36 [LXX 67:36])

a. Rigaux, *Les Épitres aux Thessaloniciens*, 624.

for instance, links this blazing fire with the fire that John the Baptist said Jesus would bring.[15] It is also worth noting that the other Pauline judgment scene involving fire clearly makes fire a means of testing people (1 Cor 3:10–15). Of course, Paul's point here is not to reflect on the specifics of how Jesus will return but to comfort the Thessalonians with the hope that Jesus will unveil his glory and put the world right.

Jesus's return is to be a global event, so Paul widens the scope from Thessalonica to include the **punishment** of all **who do not acknowledge God** and

15. *Against Heresies* 4.33.11.

those who do not obey the gospel of our Lord Jesus. The word translated as "punishment" (*ekdikēsis*) could also be translated as "vengeance," though it lacks the negative connotation of the English word. *Ekdikēsis* appears frequently in the Greek Bible to describe God's just retribution for sins (see Isa 66:4–5, 14–16 in the sidebar, "Biblical Traditions in 2 Thessalonians 1:7–10," p. 149). In 1 Thess 4:6 Paul describes Jesus as the *ekdikos* ("avenger") of sexual sins. Some commentators argue that "those who do not acknowledge [literally, "know"] God" and "those who do not obey the gospel" refer to two groups of people: the former refers to Gentiles who are estranged from God (1 Thess 4:5; see Jer 10:25), whereas the latter refers to those who know enough to obey the gospel but do not.[16] It is also possible that these two phrases are parallel descriptions of all people who are estranged from God, whether Jew or Gentile. It is striking that Paul describes the gospel (*euangelion*, "glad tidings") as something that one must obey in order to escape divine wrath. In some forms of modern Christianity, "gospel" signifies the good news that God offers the free gift of salvation and will not judge people according to their deeds. In the Pauline Letters, however, the gospel makes both promises and demands. In 2 Corinthians Paul describes generosity to the needy as an act of obedience to the gospel (9:13). The gospel is the "power of God for the salvation of everyone who believes" (Rom 1:16), but it requires and empowers obedience (see Rom 1:5; 2:6–11). We see something similar in the Gospels, where the gospel of the kingdom requires all to repent and begin living in accord with the requirements of the kingdom (e.g., Mark 1:15).

1:9   Once again the fate of the wicked is described using the language of justice: they will **pay the penalty**, a common expression in classical Greek that occurs only here in the Bible.[17] The punishment is severe: **eternal ruin, separated from the presence** (literally, "from the face") **of the Lord**. This horrible fate is the reverse of the promise given to the Thessalonians that they will always be with the Lord (1 Thess 4:17; 5:10). The phrase "from the presence of the Lord and from the glory of his power" is taken from Isa 2, where it is repeated three times to describe the fate of the wicked in the last days (vv. 10, 19, 21 LXX). The prophet describes how "on that day" God will humble evildoers and put an end to idolatry. The wicked will flee from God's face, hiding themselves and their idols in the earth (2:9–21). In Paul's reappropriation of these words the wicked do not hide themselves; instead, Jesus sends them away. This is the closest the Pauline Letters ever come to describing eternal damnation, but, unlike many

16. Marshall, *1 and 2 Thessalonians*, 258.
17. The noun "penalty" (*dikē*) appears often in the †Septuagint (e.g., Deut 32:41).

other †apocalyptic writers, Paul does not describe how they suffer or use images of darkness, torture, or teeth gnashing. Instead, he cuts to the heart of what is arguably the core of these other portrayals: the wicked are estranged from the face of the Lord, left in horrible isolation. Many questions are left unanswered: Is Paul saying that this is the fate of those who have never had the opportunity to "obey the gospel"? What happens to people who die prior to Jesus's return? This passage is not interested in offering a systematic treatment or grappling with the problem of possible exceptions. Instead, like visual portrayals of the last judgment, it offers comfort and warning by portraying the two possible ends of humans in the starkest possible terms.

After discussing the relief that will be granted to those who are suffering **1:10** and the punishment of their afflicters, Paul concludes the description of the return of Jesus by stating that the purpose of his coming is his glorification. Paul describes this event using parallelism, a poetic device that is ubiquitous in the Old Testament. Jesus

> **comes to be glorified among his holy ones**
> **and to be marveled at on that day among all who have believed**.

"On that day," a phrase used often in the Old Testament to describe the time when God will finally put the world right (e.g., Isa 2:10–22), Jesus will receive glory from his people. They are described as both "his holy ones" (or "saints") and those "who have believed." They are those who believed Paul's **testimony** and have lived correspondingly holy lives. Paul typically uses the present tense to describe faith, but here faith is considered from the perspective of the Lord's return. When Jesus is present to the Church, they are those who "have believed" because they now see face-to-face.

Reflection and Application (1:5–10)

The idea that Jesus would consign some people to eternal punishment makes many modern Christians uncomfortable.[18] Even those who defend some form of the traditional doctrine of hell tend to avoid the suggestion that God actually damns anyone, preferring instead to say that people damn themselves by closing themselves off to divine love. Though misgivings about hell have perhaps reached their apex in our era, previous generations also struggled to reconcile

---

18. For a discussion of some of the shifts leading to modern discomfort with hell, see Charles Taylor, *A Secular Age* (Cambridge, MA: Harvard University Press, 2007), esp. 221–69, on "Providential Deism."

divine love that desires "everyone to be saved and to come to knowledge of the truth" (1 Tim 2:4) with biblical descriptions of God consigning some portion of humanity to eternal perdition.[19] In his homilies St. John Chrysostom occasionally chides the congregation for avoiding talk of eternal hell. While preaching on this passage he encourages his reluctant congregation to contemplate the day when they will stand before the judgment seat of Christ:

> Are you alarmed by the heaviness of these words? If you remain silent do you extinguish hell? If you speak about it do you light hell's fires? Whether you speak or not, the fire belches forth. Let hell be spoken of often so you will not fall into it. . . . "Remember," Scripture says, "your last days" and you will not sin [Sir 28:6].[20]

For Chrysostom, Christians who avoid talk of hell are like those who ignore the signs of a fatal disease. Better to get to the doctor and address the problem head-on.

One might well object that Chrysostom begs the central question. He assumes that eternal perdition is real and encourages his congregation to ensure they avoid it, but is it really true that "we must all appear before the judgment seat of Christ, so that each one may receive recompense, according to what he did in the body, whether good or evil" (2 Cor 5:10)? It is of course impossible to "prove" the reality of divine judgment, but from within the perspective of faith it is possible to see its fittingness. One way of conceiving of retributive justice is as a minimum requirement for God to be good. A good God cannot remain forever silent in the face of evil. As Joseph Ratzinger puts it, God's judgment of humankind

> implies that the unrighteousness of the world does not have the last word, not even by being wiped out indiscriminately in a universal act of grace; on the contrary, there is a last court of appeal that preserves justice in order thus to be able to perfect love. A love that overthrew justice would create injustice and thus cease to be anything but a caricature of love. True love is excess of justice, excess that goes farther than justice, but never destruction of justice, which must be and must remain the basic form of love.[21]

Of course, no one knows the fate of anyone else. The Church never asks us to accept that any particular individual is in hell, and indeed many Catholics are

---

19. In the ancient Church some, such as St. Gregory of Nyssa, argued that God uses postmortem suffering to cleanse sinners so that eventually all will be saved. See, e.g., *On the Soul and the Resurrection* 15.75–76.

20. *Homiliae in epistulam ii ad Thessalonicenses* (PG 62:477 [my translation]).

21. *Introduction to Christianity*, trans. J. R. Foster (San Francisco: Ignatius Press, 2004), 325.

in the habit of praying the Fatima prayer, which includes the words "Bring all souls to heaven, especially those in most need of thy mercy." But the "judgment of the living and the dead" means that, whatever surprises of divine mercy may be in store, God will not pass blithely in silence over the unjust acts by which we defy the gospel and hurt one another.[22]

Worthy of the Calling (1:11–12)

[11]**To this end, we always pray for you, that our God may make you worthy of his calling and powerfully bring to fulfillment every good purpose and every effort of faith,** [12]**that the name of our Lord Jesus may be glorified in you, and you in him, in accord with the grace of our God and Lord Jesus Christ.**

NT: Matt 22:1–14
Catechism: merit, 2006–11

At the conclusion of the thanksgiving section Paul explains how the return of the Lord described in 1:3–10 shapes the way he prays for them. Verses 11–12 are not a direct prayer, as is 1 Thess 3:11–13, but a summary or report of how he prays for them. **To this end** refers to the preceding description of the revelation of Jesus from heaven. In light of this coming event, Paul and his associates **always pray for** the Thessalonian church (see comment on "always" praying in 1 Thess 1:2 and 5:17). The purpose and content of the prayer extends to the end of verse 12. First, they pray that God will find them **worthy of his calling**. Scholars disagree on whether the divine calling (*klēsis*) is the invitation to enter the kingdom at the last judgment or the initial call that the Thessalonians received when they heard the gospel message. Pauline use of the word elsewhere tilts the scales in favor of the latter: for Paul, the "call" typically refers to the initial invitation to life in Christ (with the verbal cognate *kaleō*; see 2 Thess 2:14; 1 Thess 4:7).

Paul prays that on "that day," meaning the day of judgment, God would find the Thessalonians worthy of the call they had received. Unfortunately, however, Paul's point is obscured in most English translations. The NABRE and some other major English translations (e.g., NRSV, NIV) say that Paul prays for God to **make you worthy** (*axioō*) of the calling they received. This is a very odd translation: according to the major Greek lexicons, *axioō* can mean "find worthy" or "deem

1:11

22. The judgment of "the living and the dead" is perhaps best known from the creeds, but see Acts 10:42; 2 Tim 4:1; 1 Pet 4:5.

worthy," but not "make worthy."[23] Recent commentators have also supported the translation "make worthy," claiming that *axioō* was sometimes used this way.[24] These scholars offer little if any evidence in support of this claim because there simply isn't evidence of *axioō* being used to mean "make worthy," which is why the Greek lexicons do not mention it as an option.[25] Nevertheless, commentators allege that the context demands the translation "make worthy" because it wouldn't make sense for God to test people to see if they are worthy of the call. But this is an example of bad exegesis: starting with what we think the text must mean and then cramming Paul's Greek into that framework. When confronted with the use of a word that one finds confusing, rather than suggesting that it is used in a unique, idiosyncratic way (which would have made it unintelligible to the Thessalonians), it is better to reexamine our assumptions. What would it mean to be found worthy of the calling?

There is no doubt that according to 2 Thessalonians and throughout the Pauline Letters, God empowers the faithful to do the good, and so it is true for Paul that God "makes" people worthy of the kingdom. But by mistranslating the first part of Paul's prayer report, the NABRE misses an important part of what Paul is saying: when Jesus returns, there will be a judgment of people's deeds. God will assess whether people have obeyed the gospel to see if they have become "worthy" of the kingdom of God. God "calls" the Thessalonians and in the final assize expects to find them living worthily of that call. Some commentators have objected that it makes no sense for God to evaluate whether Christians have lived lives worthy of their calling, but this is exactly what Paul says on other occasions. In 1 Thess 4:7, for instance, he says that God calls them to live holy lives and warns of judgment if they do not (see also 1 Thess 2:12; 5:23–24; 2 Thess 2:14). Similarly, in this passage Paul reports that he prays that the Thessalonians would be found worthy of the call they received (for more New Testament examples of the concern to be found living worthily of God's call, see sidebar, "St. John Chrysostom on Living a Life Worthy of God's Call," p. 155).

In addition to praying that God would find the Thessalonians worthy, Paul prays that God would **powerfully bring to fulfillment every good purpose and every effort of faith**. These words would be clearer if Paul had added an explanatory pronoun or two: will God bring to fulfillment *God's* good purpose

---

23. LSJ; BDAG; *Brill Dictionary of Ancient Greek*. BDAG specifically notes that the translation "make worthy" lacks lexical support. The NRSV and some commentators make the same error with the related verb *kataxioō* in 2 Thess 1:5.

24. E.g., Fee, *First and Second Letters to the Thessalonians*, 265.

25. Werner Foerster ("ἄξιος, ἀνάξιος, ἀξιόω, καταξιόω," *TDNT* 1:379–80) cites *Epistle of Diognetus* 9.1 as a parallel, but *Diognetus* has no more claim to a special definition than 2 Thess 1:11.

St. John Chrysostom on Living a Life Worthy of God's Call

LIVING TRADITION

In 2 Thess 1:11 Paul reports that he prays that God will find the Thessalonians worthy of the calling they received. While preaching on this passage, John Chrysostom notes that Matthew's Gospel also speaks of the necessity to be found worthy of God's call.

> The one who was clothed in filthy garments was called, but he did not remain in the calling and for this reason was cast out [Matt 22:10–13]. . . . The five virgins were also called [Matt 25:1–13] . . . but they did not enter into the wedding banquet.[a]

In Matthew's parable of the wedding banquet (22:1–14), those who are initially invited (literally, "called") to the wedding of the king's son refuse to come and are so deemed not worthy (*axios*). The king then "calls" others to come to the wedding, and they come, but then one of them is found without a wedding garment—usually thought to represent good works—and is also cast out (see also Matt 10:37–39). Similarly, in the other Matthean parable (25:1–13), the five foolish virgins are called to join the bridegroom, but they are not ready and so remain locked outside. In these passages, as in 2 Thess 1:11, there is an invitation from God to enter the kingdom, but the invitation or calling is not a guarantee that those invited will be found worthy.

a. *Homiliae* (PG 62:481 [my translation]).

and effort of faith or *theirs*? The latter sense is more probable. The rest of the prayer focuses on the Thessalonians' lives, and the same seems to be true here as well. The phrase "effort of faith" (*ergon pisteōs*) also appears in 1 Thess 1:3 as "work of faith," where it refers to the deeds by which the Thessalonians enact their faith. Chrysostom suggests that the work of faith that Paul has in mind is "the patient endurance of persecutions."[26] The verb translated as "bring to fulfillment" (*plēroō*) could mean "fulfill" in the sense of bringing something to its fitting end (e.g., Luke 7:1). Paul prays that God would bring their good deeds to their intended outcome. In context, one would think especially of their recompense when Jesus returns. *Plēroō* frequently refers to payment, and, given the context of the last judgment, one might understand this passage similarly to Phil 4:18–19, where *plēroō* refers to God's repayment for good deeds.[27] If

26. *Homiliae* (PG 62:481 [my translation]).
27. MM. On this use of *plēroō* in Paul's Letters, see Nathan Eubank, "Justice Endures Forever: Paul's Grammar of Generosity," *JSPHL* 5, no. 2 (2015): 169–87, esp. 177–78.

this is correct, then Paul is praying that God would find the Thessalonians worthy and recompense their work of faith.

1:12   Paul prays that God would find the Thessalonians worthy and fulfill their deeds *so that* **the name of our Lord Jesus may be glorified in you**. The "name" of Jesus refers to his reputation, the general report about him. The first petition of the Our Father asks God to hallow the divine name, which means making its holiness known. The prophet Ezekiel says that when God's people fail to live up to their calling it brings dishonor to God's name, but when God's purposes are fulfilled in his people it brings him glory (36:22–32).[28] Here Paul prays that the name of Jesus would be glorified by the Thessalonians' being found worthy of their call. While Paul no doubt expects Jesus to be glorified in the Church in the present day (1 Cor 6:20; 10:31), the focus here is on Jesus's return, when he will be glorified by the holy ones (see 2 Thess 1:10). Even more surprising, Paul adds **and you in him**, presumably meaning that "you" (plural, referring to the Thessalonians) will be glorified in Jesus just as he is glorified in them. In what sense are the Thessalonians to be glorified? They would certainly expect to be vindicated before those who currently persecute them. In other letters Paul speaks of humanity lacking God's glory because of sin (Rom 3:23) but being transformed by the Holy Spirit to share in God's glory (2 Cor 3:18), culminating in the general resurrection, when Jesus "will change our lowly body to conform with his glorified body" (Phil 3:21).[29] This fuller understanding of the glorification of the faithful is not spelled out here, however. Paul concludes this section with another reminder that all of this is due to **the grace**—or, one might say, the "gift" (*charis*)—**of our God and Lord Jesus Christ**.

Reflection and Application (1:11–12)

Second Thessalonians is one of the lesser-known letters of Paul. Historians of Christian origins tend to focus on letters about which there is more confidence in Pauline authorship. Theologians, at least since the Reformation, have given disproportionate attention to Romans, Galatians, and other letters that seem relevant to the theology of "justification." Nevertheless, Paul's prayer in 2 Thess 1:11–12 has echoed down the centuries in the Church's prayers to become worthy of the kingdom (1:5, 11). Since antiquity, Greek liturgies have used the very language found in this passage (*kataxioō, axioō*) to pray that God would make

28. See also Isa 66 in the sidebar, "Biblical Traditions in 2 Thessalonians 1:7–10," p. 149.
29. Jeffrey A. D. Weima, *1–2 Thessalonians*, BECNT (Grand Rapids: Baker Academic, 2014), 486.

it possible for the people to be found worthy to serve him and enter eternal life.[30] In the liturgy of St. John Chrysostom, when the people enter the church it is prayed, "O Benefactor and maker of all creation . . . lead all your church to perfection and make us worthy [*axios*] of your kingdom."[31] Similarly, in the Liturgy of St. James it is prayed, "Lead all to perfection and make us worthy [*axios*] of the grace of your sanctification, gathering us in your holy, catholic, and apostolic church."[32] The Presanctified Liturgy of St. James includes a prayer that "we would be counted worthy [*kataxioō*] of the kingdom of heaven."[33] Another Greek prayer says, "Give to us grace and power so that we would be found worthy [*kataxioō*] to sing with understanding, and to pray without ceasing [1 Thess 5:17], in fear and trembling working out our salvation [Phil 2:12] through the help of your Christ."[34] Latin liturgies contain many similar prayers, though they translate the biblical *axios*-language with *dignus* and *meritum* and their cognates. In the Novus Ordo Mass one Advent prayer asks that "we may be found worthy [*dignus*] of the banquet of eternal life and merit to receive heavenly nourishment from his hands."[35] Another Advent prayer asks God to rescue us from our sins so that "with you to set us free, we may be worthy of salvation."[36]

Close attention to the language of human worthiness in these liturgies reveals another way they reflect Paul's Letters: like Paul, the great liturgies show a keen sense that humans are in themselves utterly *unworthy* to worship God. Paul's hope that the Thessalonians would be counted worthy of the kingdom was based not on anything impressive about them but rather on God's faithfulness to them and on signs that God's grace was taking effect in their lives (see 2 Thess 1:12). The great liturgies acknowledge that, in the strict sense, Christ alone is "worthy" (Rev 5:12) and that humans become worthy to worship God by grace. Here are a few examples from the Novus Ordo:

> Since we have no merits to plead our cause, come, we pray, to our rescue with the protection of your mercy.[37]

---

30. The liturgy draws on a deep well of tradition and the entirety of Scripture. I am not suggesting that these prayers were necessarily composed in conscious imitation of 2 Thess 1:11–12. But it is noteworthy that 2 Thess 1:11–12 is the only such prayer in the Bible. Other biblical passages speak of the need to be found worthy of the next age (Luke 20:35), but this passage records the only prayer that it would be so.

31. F. E. Brightman, ed., *Liturgies: Eastern and Western* (Oxford: Clarendon, 1896), 312 (my translation).

32. Brightman, *Liturgies*, 32 (my translation).

33. Brightman, *Liturgies*, 498 (my translation).

34. Brightman, *Liturgies*, 112 (my translation).

35. *The Roman Missal: Renewed by Decree of the Most Holy Second Ecumenical Council of the Vatican, Promulgated by Authority of Pope Paul VI and Revised at the Direction of Pope John Paul II*, 3rd ed. (Washington, DC: United States Conference of Catholic Bishops, 2011), 139.

36. *Roman Missal*, 144.

37. *Roman Missal*, 141.

Admit us, we beseech you, into their company [i.e., of the saints], not weighing our merits, but granting us your pardon.[38]

Lord Jesus Christ . . . look not on our sins, but on the faith of your Church.[39]

Lord, I am not worthy [*dignus*] that you should enter under my roof, but only say the word and my soul shall be healed.[40]

Paul is not the only biblical author to emphasize humanity's desperate need for grace, but no one stresses this idea as forcefully and influentially as he did, and yet he is perhaps also the most eloquent proponent of the hope that the faithful would become worthy of the kingdom. The liturgy offers training in understanding these two aspects of his thought, which are so often pulled apart.

---

38. *Roman Missal*, 642.
39. *Roman Missal*, 751.
40. *Roman Missal*, 337. See Matt 8:8.

Events Presaging the Day of the Lord

2 Thessalonians 2:1–17

The Thessalonian Christians seem to have worried that the day of the Lord had already come. One of the main reasons Paul wrote 2 Thessalonians was to address this confusion, and his response presents some of the most puzzling and fascinating material in all his letters. He assures them that certain events must take place prior to the Lord's return: a great apostasy, and the revelation of "the lawless one," a figure opposed to God who deceives many. After these events have played out according to the preordained timetable, Jesus will return.

Confusion about the Day of the Lord (2:1–2)

> ¹We ask you, brothers, with regard to the coming of our Lord Jesus Christ and our assembling with him, ²not to be shaken out of your minds suddenly, or to be alarmed either by a "spirit," or by an oral statement, or by a letter allegedly from us to the effect that the day of the Lord is at hand.

NT: 1 Thess 4:13–5:11; 2 Tim 2:14–19

This section continues the discussion of the Lord's return, which Paul refers to here as Jesus's *parousia* (**coming**) and as **the day of the Lord** (see commentary on 1 Thess 5:1–2). As in 1 Thessalonians, Paul links Jesus's return to the faithful being gathered to him (1 Thess 4:17; 5:10), which he describes here as **our assembling** (*episynagōgē*) **with him**. For Paul, the hope of the Lord gathering his people would have recalled the traditional belief that God would someday

2:1–2

reunite the scattered people of God (2 Macc 2:7; Mark 13:27), but he does not elaborate on this point here.

Paul asks them not to be **shaken out of your minds suddenly** or **alarmed** by a certain false teaching. The word translated as "suddenly" (*tacheōs*) could refer to how quickly after his last letter the Thessalonians accepted false teaching (see Gal 1:6) or to their lack of careful deliberation in accepting this new idea. The NABRE renders Paul's summary of this erroneous belief as **the day of the Lord is at hand** (*enistēmi*), which would mean the Lord is about to return. A translation that better reflects the grammar and Paul's use of the word elsewhere would be "the day of the Lord has come" (see NRSV, NIV).[1] In other words, the Thessalonians seem to have thought the †parousia had already occurred! When one considers the global spectacle of Jesus's return as described in 1 Thess 4:16–17, one might wonder how they could fall for such a silly error. But the idea that the parousia had already come was not as ridiculous as it first sounds. Throughout Paul's Letters †eschatology is characterized by both future hope and present realization. For Paul, Jesus's death and resurrection mark God's decisive victory and the beginning of the end of all things. Those who belong to Christ already taste the life of the world to come because they are united to their risen Lord. In some of Paul's Letters this current sharing in Jesus's victory is very strongly emphasized, while always affirming the future day of the Lord (e.g., Rom 6:1–14). In 1 Thessalonians, Paul says that the Thessalonians must live even now as "children of the day" (5:2–5).[2] Similar affirmations that the resurrection is in some sense already present are well attested in early Christianity. John's Gospel says that judgment and new life have already come (John 3:18; see 1 John 3:14), and in Luke, Jesus says, "The coming of the kingdom of God cannot be observed, and no one will announce, 'Look, here it is,' or, 'There it is.' For behold, the kingdom of God is among you" (Luke 17:20–21). Some pushed this idea even further and denied that there was any future coming. In the *Gospel of Thomas* (second century) the disciples ask, "When will the repose of the dead take place? And when will the new world come?" Jesus replies, "What you are looking for has come, but for your part you do not know it" (51).[3] Second Timothy 2:18 warns against certain men who "deviated from the truth" by claiming that "[the] resurrection has already taken place."[4] It is not

---

1. See the discussion in Jeffrey A. D. Weima, *1–2 Thessalonians*, BECNT (Grand Rapids: Baker Academic, 2014), 501–2.

2. Abraham J. Malherbe, *The Letters to the Thessalonians: A New Translation with Introduction and Commentary*, AB 32B (New Haven: Yale University Press, 2000), 429.

3. Bart D. Ehrman and Zlatko Pleše, *The Apocryphal Gospels: Texts and Translations* (Oxford: Oxford University Press, 2011), 323.

4. See also *Acts of Paul and Thecla* 14; Irenaeus, *Against Heresies* 1.23.5.

hard to imagine how a congregation still new to Paul's theology could become confused about the timing of the parousia, even to the point of thinking that it had already occurred.[5]

Why is Paul so concerned that they might accept this teaching? In addition to the fact that he regarded it as false, there are some hints that he worried that the Thessalonians would despair if they lost hope in the coming day of the Lord. As John Chrysostom puts it, "The faithful, having lost hope for anything great or splendid, might give up because of their troubles."[6] According to 2 Thess 1:3–10, the Thessalonian converts were experiencing significant afflictions because of their faith. If they came to believe that there was nothing more to hope for, no "justice" (see commentary on 2 Thess 1:6–7), then they would have had good reason to be "alarmed." To quote Chrysostom once more: those who teach that the day of the Lord has already come "might even catch Christ in a lie, and, having shown that there is to be no retribution, nor court of justice, nor punishment and vengeance for evildoers, they might make evildoers more brazen and their victims more dejected."[7]

Paul doesn't seem to be certain about who has been spreading the idea that the day of the Lord is already present, but he has suspicions. He warns them against becoming rattled by accepting this idea, whether delivered **by a "spirit," or by an oral statement, or by a letter allegedly from us**. The "spirit" here probably refers to a spirit of prophecy. Early Christian prophets were sometimes said to speak by means of spirits (1 John 4:1). Whatever is meant by the NABRE's quotation marks around the word "spirit"—they do not correspond to anything in the Greek—Paul did not doubt the reality of divinely aided prophecy in the Church (1 Cor 14). He encourages such activity, but he is anxious that it be done appropriately and subject to the discernment of the whole community (1 Cor 14:29). In 1 Thessalonians he says, "Do not quench the Spirit. Do not despise prophetic utterances," but also, "Test everything; retain what is good" (5:19–21). Someone might claim to have a prophetic word, but it is necessary to test such messages to see if they are genuine. As 1 John puts it, "Do not trust every spirit but test the spirits to see whether they belong to God, because many false prophets have gone out into the world" (4:1). Paul also warns against being deceived by an "oral statement" (literally, a "word"), which refers to Christian teaching or preaching. Finally, Paul warns them against receiving this idea from a letter. Some take this to mean that Paul is

---

5. This passage reads very differently on the assumption of non-Pauline authorship. See, e.g., M. Eugene Boring, *I & II Thessalonians*, NTL (Louisville: Westminster John Knox, 2015), 259–81.

6. *Homiliae in epistulam ii ad Thessalonicenses* (PG 62:469 [my translation]).

7. *Homiliae* (PG 62:469 [my translation]). See also 2 Pet 3:3–4.

aware of forgeries circulating in his name, but the vagueness of Paul's warnings in verse 2 suggest that he is concerned about the possibility—perhaps he has even heard a rumor about letters written in his name—but not that he knows about a particular forgery.[8]

Events Presaging the End (2:3–12)

---

[3]Let no one deceive you in any way. For unless the apostasy comes first and the lawless one is revealed, the one doomed to perdition, [4]who opposes and exalts himself above every so-called god and object of worship, so as to seat himself in the temple of God, claiming that he is a god— [5]do you not recall that while I was still with you I told you these things? [6]And now you know what is restraining, that he may be revealed in his time. [7]For the mystery of lawlessness is already at work. But the one who restrains is to do so only for the present, until he is removed from the scene. [8]And then the lawless one will be revealed, whom the Lord [Jesus] will kill with the breath of his mouth and render powerless by the manifestation of his coming, [9]the one whose coming springs from the power of Satan in every mighty deed and in signs and wonders that lie, [10]and in every wicked deceit for those who are perishing because they have not accepted the love of truth so that they may be saved. [11]Therefore, God is sending them a deceiving power so that they may believe the lie, [12]that all who have not believed the truth but have approved wrongdoing may be condemned.

OT: 1 Macc 1:41–61; Dan 8:9–11
NT: Mark 13:14–23; 1 John 2:18–23
Catechism: the Church's ultimate trial, 675–77

Paul explains how the Thessalonians can be certain that the day of the Lord has not yet come: certain other events must take place first. Paul says that he already taught these things while in Thessalonica (2:5), and indeed he does not attempt to explain them clearly or systematically here. The sequence of events is out of order, and the bewildering names and events come thick and fast; the lawless one, the restrainer, the mystery of lawlessness, and the rebellion. Here are the events described in this section rearranged in chronological order. Those who find the verse-by-verse commentary disorienting may want to turn back to page 163 for clarification.

---

8. Weima, *1–2 Thessalonians*, 504–6.

- At present, someone or something is holding back an enemy of God called "the lawless one," preventing him from doing evil. Though the lawless one is currently being restrained, the "mystery of lawlessness" is already at work in the world, and eventually the restraining power will be removed.
- After the restraining power is removed, "the apostasy" will take place and the lawless one will be revealed. The lawless one will pretend to be God, taking his seat in the temple, and, aided by the power of Satan, he will do mighty deeds that deceive many people. God allows this deception to take place as a form of judgment for those who do not love the truth.
- Finally, Jesus will return and destroy the lawless one.

The words **Let no one deceive you in any way** might indicate that Paul isn't   2:3–4
completely certain about the source of the error, but they also warn against any possible future confusion. Two events must occur before Jesus's return: the **apostasy** and the revelation of **the lawless one**. The Greek word *apostasia* refers to rebellion against authority, whether human or divine. The use of the article (*the* apostasy) and the fact that Paul has already instructed them about this (v. 5) suggest that he is describing an event they are already expecting, an event not fully described here. Many ancient Jewish and Christian texts describe a penultimate period in history when people will rebel against God (e.g., *4 Ezra* 5.1–13). In the Gospels, Jesus warns that prior to his return lawlessness will increase, with false prophets and messiahs appearing and deceiving many (e.g., Matt 24:3–13). We find similar warnings elsewhere in the Pauline Letters: 1 Timothy warns that "the Spirit explicitly says that in the last times some will turn away from the faith by paying attention to deceitful spirits and demonic instructions" (4:1), and 2 Timothy says that "there will be terrifying times in the last days" because of an increase in rebellion against God (3:1–5).[9] Paul seems to have something similar in mind here. Prior to Jesus's return he expects a widespread rebellion against God, including the defection of many to the lawless one because of the marvels he works (2 Thess 2:9–12).

The other event that will occur before the Lord's return is the revelation of the lawless one. It is not clear whether Paul expects the apostasy first and then this event, or if he expects them to happen together. The fact that this figure is to deceive many suggests that Paul sees these events happening at the same time prior to Jesus's return. For the sake of clarity I will combine everything that Paul says about this figure in verses 3–4 and 9. This figure is called "the lawless one" and **the one doomed to perdition**. A more wooden translation would be "the

9. See also 2 Pet 3:3–4; Jude 1:17–19.

man of lawlessness [*anomia*], the son of perdition [*apōleia*]," titles that echo biblical descriptions of evil. In Greek Isaiah, Isaiah excoriates the wickedness of the people, calling them "children of perdition [*apōleia*], lawless [*anomos*] offspring" (57:4). Daniel prophesies that in the last days many will be "lawless" (*anomos*) (12:10). The lawless one will be the culmination of human wickedness and opposition to God, a uniquely wicked person who leads others to wickedness (2 Thess 2:9). The title "son of perdition" indicates that he is destined to be destroyed, and perhaps also that he will bring about the destruction of others.[10]

The manner of the lawless one's appearance suggests that he appears as an imitation or parody of Jesus, a sort of "antichrist," though Paul never uses that word.[11] Three times Paul describes this figure being revealed (*apokalyptō* [2:3, 6, 8]), just as he spoke of the revelation (*apokalypsis*) of Jesus in 1:7. It would be equally accurate to describe the lawless one as "anti-God" because he **opposes and exalts himself above every so-called god and object of worship** (compare Dan 11:36–38). This figure exalts himself above all the gods of the nations and their shrines. Not content to stop there, he desires to take the place of the one true God, so he takes his seat **in the temple of God**, presenting himself as God.[12] Many of the "low points" in Scripture describe attempts to usurp God, beginning with our first parents' attempt to "be like God" (Gen 3:5 NRSV). The prophet Isaiah denounces the king of Babylon for saying, "I will ascend above the tops of the clouds; / I will be like the Most High!" (14:14). The prophet taunts him for his punishment at God's hands: "How you have fallen from the heavens, / O Morning Star, son of the dawn! / How you have been cut down to the earth, / you who conquered nations!" (14:12). Later Christians read this passage as a description of the fall of Satan and made the Latin translation of "morning star" (*lucifer*) into one of his names (see also Ezek 28:2–19). The Gospels portray the devil tempting Jesus to worship him (Matt 4:8–10; Luke 4:6–8), and the book of Acts portrays Herod being struck down by God for receiving divine honors (12:20–23). For worshipers of the one true God, any attempt to take God's place is the height of evil.

More directly relevant to this passage, there was a series of disasters in Jewish history involving rulers who interrupted or desecrated the temple in some way. In 167 BC the Seleucid king Antiochus IV Epiphanes, whose name suggested

---

10. This same phrase refers to Judas in John 17:12.

11. In Scripture only the Johannine Epistles use the word "antichrist" (1 John 2:18, 22; 4:3; 2 John 1:7), where it refers to a coming figure (1 John 2:18) as well as to all who deny that Jesus is the Christ (1 John 2:22) or that he came in the flesh (2 John 1:7).

12. The NABRE's "claiming that he is a god" is grammatically possible but contextually unlikely. From a Jewish perspective, pretending to be the One who resides in the temple is a claim to be God.

Figure 10. *Sermon and Deeds of the Antichrist* by Luca Signorelli.

that he was a manifestation of the divine, sought to interrupt Jewish worship and caused a pagan altar to be erected on the altar of burnt offering (1 Macc 1:41–61). In 63 BC the Roman general Pompey entered the holy of holies, though he did not take anything or attempt to set up false worship.[13] Perhaps the threat to Jewish worship that most closely resembles the lawless one came from the Roman emperor Caligula. Claiming to be divine, he sought to have his own image placed in the temple in Jerusalem in AD 40, not that long before 2 Thessalonians was written.[14] Inasmuch as images of deities represented their presence, this would have been tantamount to "seating himself in the temple of God, claiming he is God."

These events as well as later ones, such as the destruction of the temple in AD 70, left a deep imprint on the Jewish and Christian imagination, often forming the template for consummate evil.[15] Speaking of Antiochus Epiphanes, the book of Daniel describes a king desecrating the temple (8:11; 9:27; 12:11), "exalting himself and making himself greater than any god; he shall utter

13. Josephus, *Jewish Antiquities* 14.4; *Jewish War* 1.7.6; Tacitus, *Histories* 5.9.
14. Josephus, *Jewish War* 2.184–85; Tacitus, *Histories* 5.9; Philo, *The Embassy to Gaius*. Caligula's assassination prevented his wish from being carried out.
15. Naturally, those who read 2 Thessalonians as the product of a later follower of Paul will put more weight on these later events.

dreadful blasphemies against the God of gods" (11:36). The noncanonical *Psalms of Solomon* describes a certain Gentile ruler as a "lawless one" (*anomos*) who entered Jerusalem and perverted the people.[16] The Gospels take up the prophecy from Daniel, warning of the day when "the desolating abomination spoken of through Daniel" would be seen standing "in the holy place" (Matt 24:15; see Mark 13:14). As a reader of Daniel and a recipient of oral traditions about Jesus, Paul would have had good reason to expect a final, definitive version of these attempts to usurp God. The recent attempt of Caligula to be worshiped in the Jerusalem temple would have been a terrifying reminder of these prophecies.

"The temple of God," where the lawless one is to enthrone himself, could refer to the temple in Jerusalem, which was still standing during Paul's life, though since antiquity some have suggested that it refers not to a particular building but to the Church, which Paul refers to as God's temple (1 Cor 6:19).[17] The identification of the temple with the Church eventually led early Protestants to identify the pope as the antichrist, one who enthrones himself in the Church as divine. Most modern commentators, however, conclude that this passage refers to the Jerusalem temple.[18] The historical analogues listed above all concern the Jerusalem temple, as do the parallel prophecies in Daniel and the Gospels (see Matt 24:15; Mark 13:14), and the description of this figure sitting down lends itself more naturally to the physical temple in Jerusalem. Moreover, the threat to worship in Jerusalem from Caligula was a very recent memory for Paul.

This description of the lawless one opposing God in the last days by entering "the temple of God" raises a number of questions. Did Paul still think of the structure in Jerusalem as God's place of residence, even after coming to believe that those in Christ are the temple of God? Readers of Paul after the temple was destroyed faced another question: How could the lawless one fulfill Paul's end-time scenario if there was no temple left to desecrate? While interesting to ponder, these questions may attach too much literal, predictive weight to Paul's description. The image of a supremely wicked person opposing God in this way is the traditional image, and it need not possess strict predictive accuracy (see Reflection and Application on 2 Thess 2:3–12).

2:5   Just when we would expect Paul to finish his sentence by describing the return of the Lord ("For the apostasy comes first . . . *then the Lord will return*"), he interrupts himself to chide the Thessalonians for so quickly forgetting what he had taught them: **do you not recall that while I was still with you I told**

---

16. See chaps. 2, 8, and 17. The figure spoken of is probably Pompey.
17. Béda Rigaux, *Saint Paul: Les Épitres aux Thessaloniciens*, EBib (Paris: Lecoffre, 1956), 660–61.
18. See the discussion in Weima, *1–2 Thessalonians*, 518–23.

you these things? This is a rhetorical question: the Greek grammar assumes a positive answer. He knows that they must remember his previous instruction on this matter. He is therefore frustrated that they have been rattled by the claim that the day of the Lord is already present. The tense of the verb translated as "I told you" (*legō*) suggests that he repeatedly spoke on this matter when he was in Thessalonica. This fact may also help to explain the somewhat disjointed and elliptical nature of this passage. Paul is reminding them of the implications of things they have already been taught. He is not sketching this †eschatological scenario for the first time.

In the present time, something—or someone—is keeping the revelation of 2:6–7
the lawless one at bay.[19] The Thessalonians **know** what it is because Paul has already told them. This leaves it to us to try to work out what he means. Paul describes this restraining activity using both a neuter participle, *to katechon* (**what is restraining**), and then a masculine participle, *ho katechōn* (**the one who restrains**). This thing or person (or both) has the task of restraining the lawless one until it/he is **removed from the scene**, and then the lawless one will be **revealed**. The idea that †eschatological scenarios play out according to a mysterious preordained schedule is well attested in the New Testament (e.g., Mark 13:32; Titus 1:3; 1 Tim 2:6). The million-dollar question is the identity of the restraining force. Tantalizingly vague biblical passages tend to encourage speculation, and this one is no exception. Modern commentators can hardly hope to improve on Augustine's approach to this passage:

> Since the Thessalonians know the reason for Antichrist's delay in coming, St. Paul had no need to mention it. But, of course, we do not know what they knew; and, much as we would like, and hard as we strive, to catch his meaning, we are unable to do so. The trouble is that the subsequent words only make the meaning more obscure: "For the mystery of iniquity is already at work; provided only that he who is at present restraining it, does still restrain until he is gotten out of the way. And then the wicked one will be revealed." What is to be made of those words? For myself, I confess, I have no idea what is meant. The best I can do is to mention the interpretations that have come to my attention.[20]

Augustine wrote this sixteen hundred years ago, and today we are no closer to a definitive identification of the restraining power. All the commentator can

---

19. I take "now" (*nun*) to modify "what is restraining," not "you know" as in the NABRE. See Gordon D. Fee, *The First and Second Letters to the Thessalonians*, NICNT (Grand Rapids: Eerdmans, 2009), 286–87.

20. *The City of God* 20.19, in *The City of God, Books XVII–XXII*, trans. Gerald G. Walsh and Daniel J. Honan, FC 24 (Washington, DC: Catholic University of America Press, 1954), 298.

do is, like Augustine, "mention the interpretations that have come to my attention." Here are four of the best interpretations of the restrainer, in ascending order of plausibility.[21]

1. The Roman Empire and the Roman emperor are "what is restraining" and "the one who restrains," respectively.[22] This view assumes that Paul had a positive view of the empire and its authority as a divinely instituted means of restraining evil. Though this view had some patristic support and Paul does tell the Roman Christians to respect the governing authorities (Rom 13:1–7), it would be odd, to say the least, just a few years after an emperor attempted to install an idol of himself in the temple, to identify the Roman emperor as the one who holds such behavior in check. Similar passages in early Jewish and Christian literature tend to cast Rome as a tool of evil (e.g., Rev 13).

2. The preaching of the gospel and Paul prevent the coming of the lawless one. Citing Matt 24:14 ("This gospel of the kingdom will be preached throughout the world as a witness to all nations, and then the end will come"), some since antiquity have argued that the gospel must be preached to all nations before this event can occur. This suggestion is on thin ice in taking a line from the Gospels and using it to solve an obscure statement from Paul without any support in Paul's Letters. Also, at this point in his life Paul probably believed that he would live to see the Lord's return (see commentary on 1 Thess 4:17) and would therefore not expect to be "removed from the scene."

3. Citing Augustine's agnosticism with approval, Eugene Boring argues that "the restrainer" refers to nothing in particular: "The author of 2 Thessalonians himself probably did not have in mind a specific power, principle, or person that was presently restraining the advent of the Lawless One. He likely intended his depiction to be provocatively obscure."[23] In support of this view is the fact that after two millennia of trying we still don't know what Paul meant. Boring's suggestion is much more persuasive if one takes the view that Paul is not the author and that the reference to teaching the Thessalonians about this matter (2:5) is fiction for the sake of verisimilitude. If Paul is the author, however, he probably taught the Thessalonians about the restraining power and expected them to remember what it was.

21. For longer discussion including more proposals, see Weima, *1–2 Thessalonians*, 567–77.
22. See Tertullian, *The Resurrection of the Flesh* 24.
23. Boring, *I & II Thessalonians*, 276.

4. Others argue that the restraining force is probably supernatural and that there is only one figure that fits: an angel, probably the archangel Michael. God could not be "removed from the scene," and the devil would not be expected to restrain the power of evil. Angels, however, are often assigned important tasks in eschatological scenarios, including opposing Satan and defending God's people. The archangel Michael is mentioned more than others (see commentary on 1 Thess 4:16). In the book of Daniel, Michael opposes evil forces, keeping them from amassing too much power (10:13, 21; 12:1), and in the †Septuagint version of Dan 12:1, Michael is said to "pass by" or "disappear" just before the final tribulation: "At that hour, Michael, the great angel who stands over the sons of your people, will disappear [*parerchomai*]" (my translation).[24] In 2 Thess 2:6–7, the neuter participle ("what is restraining") would refer to Michael's restraining activity, and the masculine participle ("the one who restrains") to Michael himself. I suggest that this is the best proposal available, but, since we were not there when Paul instructed the Thessalonians face-to-face, we cannot know for certain.

Though the final onslaught of evil is currently held at bay, even now **the mystery of lawlessness is already at work**. The Latin translation of "mystery of lawlessness," *mysterium iniquitatis*, has come to refer to the mystery of the existence of evil in God's good creation.[25] The original meaning of the phrase is related but has important differences. In this passage, lawlessness is not said to be a mystery in the sense of a truth beyond human comprehension. Instead, lawlessness is currently a mystery in the sense that it is currently hidden but will be revealed. For Paul, "mystery" typically signifies a reality that has been revealed to the faithful by the Spirit, but not to the rest of humanity.[26] In this passage, this means that with the eyes of faith, the Church recognizes its current sufferings as "labor pains" (Mark 13:8) of the final tribulation. The Thessalonians know—or they ought to know—that the evil they currently experience is not a sign that the end has come but rather a sign that forces opposed to God are moving in the world.

And then—that is, after the present period during which the lawless one is held back—**the lawless one will be revealed** (*apokalyptō*), only to be destroyed   2:8

24. On this point and in support of this reading generally, see Colin Nicholl, "Michael, the Restrainer Removed (2 Thess. 2:6–7)," *JTS* 51 (2000): 27–53, esp. 42–50. Weima (*1–2 Thessalonians*, 574) notes that Rev 20:1–3 likewise speaks of an angel temporarily restraining evil (in this case, the devil) that will be unleashed in the final days.

25. See Catechism 385, 675.

26. E.g., 1 Cor 2:7; Col 1:26. See T. J. Lang, *Mystery and the Making of a Christian Historical Consciousness: From Paul to the Second Century*, BZNW 219 (Berlin: de Gruyter, 2015).

by Jesus. This verse compresses events, failing to mention for the moment the period during which the lawless one masquerades as God and deceives many. In verse 9, which is part of the same sentence in Greek, Paul goes on to describe the lawless one's activity. But here his appearance is described in terms of his inevitable doom: he appears only to be destroyed. This is one reason why he is the "son of perdition" (see 2:3): the victory has already been won. The †eschatological events will play out as preordained, but the powers of evil will fall to divine omnipotence.

Jesus's appearance is described as **the manifestation** (*epiphaneia*) **of his coming** (*parousia*).[27] The word "epiphany" is best known today from the Feast of the Epiphany, which celebrates the manifestation of Jesus to the world, including the adoration of the magi (Matt 2:9–11), his baptism (Matt 3:13–17 and parallels), and his first sign at the wedding in Cana (John 2:1–11). In the ancient world, *epiphaneia* often described the conspicuous and powerful appearance of God or gods.[28] It is language that would have already been very familiar to recent Gentile converts. For instance, Paul's younger contemporary Plutarch speaks of the goddess Rhea saving a man by appearing to him in a dream, which is described as the "epiphany of the goddess."[29] Stronger than *parousia*, *epiphaneia* was often associated with the display of extraordinary power. The addition of this word stresses the visibility of the event.[30] Jesus will be made visible to the world, unmasking the lie of the lawless one. By stressing the splendid conspicuousness of Jesus's coming, Paul soothes the Thessalonians' worry that the event has already occurred.

Jesus will rout the lawless one effortlessly, **with the breath of his mouth**, not because of the weakness of evil, but because of Jesus's incomparable might (see Rev 19:11–16). This description echoes Isa 11's prophecy of a coming king from the line of Jesse, King David's father:

> But a shoot shall sprout from the stump of Jesse,
>   and from his roots a bud shall blossom.
> The spirit of the Lord shall rest upon him:
>   a spirit of wisdom and of understanding,
> A spirit of counsel and of strength,
>   a spirit of knowledge and of fear of the Lord,
>   and his delight shall be the fear of the Lord.

---

27. See the discussion of *parousia* in the commentary on 1 Thess 4:15.

28. E.g., 2 Macc 14:15. The Pastoral Epistles use *epiphaneia* to describe Jesus's future coming, as well as his past coming. See 1 Tim 6:14; 2 Tim 1:10; 4:1, 8; Titus 2:13.

29. *Lives: Themistocles* 30.3. Antiochus IV, mentioned above, took the name "Epiphanes" to claim that he was a manifestation of the divine. Second Maccabees describes the Jews praising God because he "always comes to the aid of his heritage by manifesting [*epiphaneia*] himself" (14:15).

30. Malherbe, *Letters to the Thessalonians*, 434.

> Not by appearance shall he judge,
>   nor by hearsay shall he decide,
> But he shall judge the poor with justice,
>   and decide fairly for the land's afflicted.
> *He shall strike the ruthless with the rod of his mouth,*
>   *and with the breath of his lips he shall slay the wicked.* (11:1–4 [italics
>   added])

Though the Messiah had already come, Paul still searched the Scripture to understand his future coming, finding in this passage a description of Jesus's future, public triumph.

After rushing to describe the destruction of the lawless one, Paul backs up to   2:9–10
say more about the deceit that will precede ultimate victory. At his appearance or **coming** (*parousia*), the lawless one wields diabolical power. More precisely, **Satan** works in him to enable him to do mighty deeds, **signs**, and **wonders**. Paul was proud of his own mighty deeds, signs, and wonders (Rom 15:19; 2 Cor 12:12—the same three Greek words) because he saw them as markers of apostolic ministry, and of course Jesus's ministry was distinguished by the performance of miracles. Yet the New Testament also describes miracles as part of the deceptive strategy of end-time impostors. Jesus warns that in the last days false christs and false prophets will perform deceptive wonders (Mark 13:22; Matt 24:24; see also Rev. 13:11–13). The purpose of the lawless one's wonders is to **lie** and seduce people to their ruin. This does not mean that the signs will be mere parlor tricks—those do not require diabolical assistance. They will target **those who are perishing** (*apollymi*), drawing them to the son of perdition (*apōleia*). These people are vulnerable because **they have not accepted the love of truth**. The phrase "have not accepted" or "have not received" implies that "the love of truth" was offered but turned down. By rejecting the divine offer, those who are perishing condition themselves to accept lies that will destroy them. What was offered was not merely "the truth" in the sense of a few facts or a bit of information but "the love of truth"—that is, a commitment to the truth that orders one's life and also shields one against deleterious lies.

In response to people's love of falsehood, God sends them **a deceiving power**   2:11–12
so that they may believe the lie and so **be condemned**. The present tense **God is sending them** could indicate that Paul has shifted focus from the future coming of the lawless one to the present, but it is more likely that he is speaking from the perspective of the event itself. These people accept "the lie"—that is, the deception of the lawless one. There is individual choice—people opt for

"the lie" rather than the truth—but God also seems to work to confirm this choice in order to bring these people to judgment. This description does not fit the "free will" versus "determinism" dichotomy often discussed today, but it follows a familiar biblical pattern: people turn away from God, and in return God causes them to suffer the full weight of their decision. For instance, in Rom 1:18–27 Paul says that God hands idolaters over to be enslaved by their sexual passions. In Ps 81 God says, "My people did not listen to my words; / Israel would not submit to me. / So I thrust them away to the hardness of their heart" (vv. 12–13).[31]

How could God, who is Truth itself (John 14:6), be an agent of deceit?[32] Wouldn't we expect Paul to say that God wants to rescue those who believe the lie (1 Tim 2:4)? Throughout his letters Paul assumes that people are responsible for their actions, that evil is at loose in the world and is capable of seducing people to their ruin, and that God is sovereign over all things. Paul never reflects in a philosophical-theological mode on how to hold these things together. Holding to divine sovereignty does require him to see every diabolical deception as taking place with divine permission. The Catholic tradition maintains that God never forces people to sin but only allows it. As Augustine puts it while commenting on this passage, "'God will send' [*mittet*] means that God will allow [*permittet*] the devil to do these things."[33]

Reflection and Application (2:3–12)

Two main paradigms have dominated interpretation of this passage since antiquity.[34] The first, favored by many in the ancient Church, reads this passage as a straightforward prediction of a distinct historical event that will occur in the days shortly before the Lord's return, including a single historical lawless one or antichrist. Some who follow this approach have sought to identify the lawless one with particular figures in history such as the emperor Nero and various other emperors, or various ancient heretics. Martin Luther and John

31. See also 1 Kings 22:23; Ezek 14:9; compare 2 Sam 24:1 and 1 Chron 21:1.
32. God as Truth is a Johannine description, but the Pauline Letters assume that truth characterizes God.
33. *City of God* 20.19 (my translation). *The Catechism of the Council of Trent* says of biblical texts such as Exod 7:3 and Rom 1:26, 28, in which God is said to hand people over to sin, "These and similar passages, we are not at all to understand as implying any positive act on the part of God, but his permission only" (trans. Theodore Alois Buckley [London: George Routledge, 1852], 574).
34. This reflection is indebted to Kevin L. Hughes, *Constructing Antichrist: Paul, Biblical Commentary, and the Development of Doctrine in the Early Middle Ages* (Washington, DC: Catholic University of America Press, 2005). See also Anthony C. Thiselton, *1 & 2 Thessalonians through the Centuries*, BBC (Chichester: Wiley-Blackwell, 2011), 213–17.

Calvin accused the pope of being the antichrist.[35] Some Catholics returned the favor by alleging that Luther was himself the leader of the great apostasy and therefore a good candidate for being the antichrist.

The second paradigm of interpretation, associated most of all with Augustine, focuses on the existence of antichrists in the present day: everyone who opposes Christ by inciting apostasy and demanding from others the loyalty owed only to God is a lawless one.[36] Augustine accepted that there will be trials in the last days, but he avoided attempts to predict what the last days will be like, noting that there is hostility toward God throughout history. These two streams of interpretation reflect two aspects already present in 2 Thessalonians and related biblical passages. Paul speaks of a future lawless one, but he also says the mystery of lawlessness is already at work. First John says the antichrist is coming, but also that many antichrists have already appeared (2:18). After two thousand years of mistaken attempts to identify the antichrist with particular individuals, one could certainly argue that it is safer to stick to the Augustinian approach, regardless of what is revealed in days to come.

Recent magisterial teaching maintains that "before Christ's second coming the Church must pass through a final trial that will shake the faith of many believers (cf. Lk 18:8; Mt 24:12)," but also stresses the presence of antichrist today: "The Antichrist's deception already begins to take shape in the world every time the claim is made to realize within history that messianic hope which can only be realized beyond history through the eschatological judgment."[37] In other words, whenever human powers, whether secular or religious, claim to bring to fruition the final ends of humankind, they are setting themselves up in God's place, in effect "claiming to be God." One example of this identified by the Catechism is political ideologies that claim to fulfill every need of humankind, offering, as it were, "salvation."

Hold Fast to the Traditions (2:13–15)

[13]But we ought to give thanks to God for you always, brothers loved by the Lord, because God chose you as the firstfruits for salvation through sanctification by the Spirit and belief in truth. [14]To this end he has [also] called

---

35. According to Thiselton (*1 & 2 Thessalonians*, 217), Joachim of Fiore (1135–1202), a Catholic, had already suggested that a pope would be the lawless one.
36. See especially *City of God* 20.
37. Catechism 675–76.

you through our gospel to possess the glory of our Lord Jesus Christ.
¹⁵Therefore, brothers, stand firm and hold fast to the traditions that you
were taught, either by an oral statement or by a letter of ours.

NT: 1 Thess 2:13–14
Catechism: Tradition, 74–83

2:13–14   As in 1 Thessalonians, Paul repeats his thanksgiving (see 1 Thess 2:13–14; 2 Thess
1:3).[38] Throughout this section there is also a conspicuous repetition of language from 1 Thess 2. He addresses them as **brothers loved by the Lord**, words
reminiscent of Moses's description of the tribe of Benjamin (Deut 33:12), which
was Paul's own tribe. God **chose** them, which recalls the formal reaffirmation
of the relationship between God and Israel in Deuteronomy: "The Lord chose
you today that you should be his peculiar people . . . to keep all his commands"
(LXX 26:18 [my translation]). It is unlikely that the Thessalonians would have
caught the biblical echo, but this suggests once again that Paul considered these
former pagans to be recipients of the inheritance of Israel.

In some important ancient manuscripts it says not that God chose them **as the
firstfruits** [*aparchēn*] but rather that God chose them "from the beginning [*ap'
archēs*]." The difference in Greek is only one letter. If the latter reading is right,
Paul is saying that God had chosen them from the very beginning of creation to
belong to him, despite the fact that this surprising reality had only recently been
revealed. If the NABRE is correct to accept the former reading, Paul's point is
that the Thessalonians are like a portion of a harvest that is the first or the best
and is offered to God. There are reliable ancient manuscripts attesting to both
readings. One can never be certain in such cases, but there is good reason to
think the NABRE got it right. Though it is no doubt true according to Pauline
theology that God chose the Thessalonians from before creation (e.g., Eph 1:4),
nowhere else does Paul use the phrase "from the beginning [*ap' archēs*]." He
does, however, apply the label "firstfruits" metaphorically on a number of occasions (Rom 8:23; 11:16; 16:5; 1 Cor 15:20, 23; 16:15).[39] His point here would
be that they are but the beginning of a larger harvest of converts who will be
holy, devoted to God. Though they are currently a beleaguered minority, Paul
hints that there will be (or are already) more who follow in their path. Paul
draws here, as elsewhere (Rom 11), on the Old Testament teaching on firstfruits,
but it was also common in pagan antiquity to set aside firstfruits to the gods,

---

38. On the obligation to give thanks ("ought"), see commentary on 2 Thess 1:3. On praying "always,"
see commentary on 1 Thess 1:2 and 5:17.

39. For a longer argument, see Fee, *First and Second Letters to the Thessalonians*, 301–2.

so Paul's encouragement would have been understandable regardless of their knowledge of the Scriptures.[40]

Paul says they are the firstfruits **for salvation** (see commentary on "salvation" in 1 Thess 5:9) and mentions two means by which God set them aside for this end: their salvation is **through sanctification by the Spirit and belief in truth**. God's sanctifying Spirit has been given to them (see commentary on 1 Thess 4:3–8) to make them holy so they will be found worthy when the Lord returns. They in turn offer their "belief" or "trust" in the truth, in contrast to those mentioned in 2:9–12, who prefer lies. The main idea of the second half of verse 13 is restated in a slightly different way in verse 14: God **called you through our gospel**. "Through our gospel" means here "through Paul's preaching," as Thomas Aquinas paraphrases.[41] The call comes from God (1:11; see also 1 Thess 2:12; 4:7; 5:24) through the instrument of Paul's missionary activity. As Paul puts it in 2 Corinthians, "We are ambassadors for Christ, as if God were appealing through us" (5:20).

In the Thessalonian correspondence the language of divine calling is always linked to sanctification—it is a call to become like God—and this passage contains perhaps the most arresting articulation of this idea (see also 1 Thess 2:12; 4:7; 5:23–24; 2 Thess 1:11). The purpose of the call is for them **to possess the glory of our Lord Jesus Christ**.[42] What does the "glory" of Christ refer to here, and how could the Thessalonians come to possess it? In the Old Testament the glory (Greek *doxa*) of God is God's visible radiance, the splendor that surrounds him in the heavenly throne room (Isa 6:1; Ezek 1:28) and that will one day be revealed to all people (Isa 40:5), though the earth is already full of divine glory (Isa 6:3; Ps 8) in the sense that it attests to the greatness of the Creator. In 2 Thess 1:9 Paul describes the fate of the damned as being estranged from the "glory" of the Lord, cast away from his brilliance (Rom 3:23). This verse adds to this idea, claiming that the saved come to possess Christ's glory for themselves, which would mean that they participate or share in that glory. This could mean sharing in the honor of his rule over all things, but the link to sanctification suggests that it means what later Church Fathers would call "theosis" or divinization, being transformed to become like God. Theosis is already implied by sanctification, and Paul's later letters often link salvation to participation in divine glory (Rom 2:7; 2 Cor 3:18; Phil 3:21).[43]

---

40. E.g., Plutarch, *De Pythiae oraculis* 16.
41. *Super ad Thessalonicenses II reportatio* 2.3.58 (my translation).
42. The word translated as "possess" (*peripoiēsis*) appears in 1 Thess 5:9 ("gain" salvation).
43. See Catechism 456–60, 1996–99.

2:15   Sometimes verse 15 is quoted as a freestanding statement about the importance
of tradition, but it is important at least in the first instance to read it for what it was
originally: a final instruction designed to protect the Thessalonians from wandering
into error again. After reassuring the Thessalonians that the day of the Lord has
not yet come (2:1–12) and that they are on the path to salvation (2:13–14), Paul
attempts to prevent this sort of confusion from taking root again: **stand firm and
hold fast to the traditions that you were taught**. The word translated "tradition"
(*paradosis*) can have the sense of handing something down, such as the traditions
handed down (*paradidōmi*) about Jesus's death (1 Cor 11:23–26) and resurrection
(1 Cor 15:1–11) in the early years of Christianity. Paul saw the traditions he handed
down as having divine origins because they came ultimately from the Lord (see
commentary on 1 Thess 2:13). Standing firm and holding fast suggests a contrast
to the Thessalonians' current "shaking" with fear (2 Thess 2:2). By holding lightly
to what they had been taught, they made themselves vulnerable to the idea that
the day of the Lord had already come, and in 3:6–13 we discover another tradition
to which the Thessalonians need to cling: working to support oneself.

Paul specifies two forms of tradition that they should hold to, **either by an
oral statement or by a letter of ours**. The phrase "oral statement" translates *logos*
("word"), referring to Paul's preaching and teaching. The Thessalonians are to
hold fast to what Paul taught regardless of whether they received it when he was
with them or by letter. Paul's oral teaching and his letters are to be the authoritative
guards against possible sources of confusion mentioned in 2:2: spirits,
oral teaching from other sources, and letters supposedly from Paul. One of the
three sources of information mentioned in verse 2 is conspicuously absent here:
the utterances of "spirits." Why doesn't Paul ask them to hold fast to authentic
prophetic utterances as well? In 1 Thess 5:20–21 he instructed them not to despise
prophecies but to test all things and hold on to the good. Since that time
the Thessalonians do not seem to have done well at weighing ideas and holding
to the good. It may be that he preferred to direct the "shaken" converts to the
truths that would help them discern true prophecies from false in the first place.

Reflection and Application (2:13–15)

Scripture and Tradition. Catholics have sometimes appealed to 2 Thess 2:15
to defend the view that there are two sources of revelation: Scripture (written
tradition) and oral tradition.[44] Since the Second Vatican Council, Catholic
teaching has stated strongly and repeatedly that there is only one source of

---

44. Rigaux, *Les Épitres aux Thessaloniciens*, 689.

revelation—God—and that Scripture and Tradition are the two modes of transmitting divine revelation.[45] Why does this matter? A 1962 lecture given by a young Joseph Ratzinger on the eve of the Council helps to explain what is at stake.[46] For one thing, speaking of Tradition as a discrete "source" of revelation encourages the erroneous idea that all Church teaching was already formulated in the first century and was then passed down orally to be defined publicly at some point in the future. Professor Ratzinger rightly objects, "History can name practically no affirmation that on the one hand is not in Scripture but on the other hand can be traced back even with some historical likelihood to the Apostles."[47] In other words, it is impossible for historians to defend the view that everything the Church now teaches was known by Tradition in the apostolic period. It is clear that doctrine has developed in the Church through the centuries "through the contemplation and study made by believers, who treasure these things in their hearts" (*Dei Verbum* 8). Moreover, treating Scripture and Tradition as the "sources" of revelation can lead to a serious theological error. This approach narrows the concept of revelation to a finite list of truths, whereas the Fathers and medieval theologians taught that revelation is divine self-gift that always exceeds our knowing.[48] As the Council's declaration on divine revelation, *Dei Verbum*, would go on to put it, there is one "divine wellspring" of revelation from which flows both Scripture and Tradition.[49] This is why sacred Tradition is rightly said to be "living": it reflects the people of God's ongoing search for the face of the Lord.

Tradition and Traditions. Broadly speaking, the New Testament describes two kinds of tradition (Greek *paradosis*): traditions that distract from the truth, and holy traditions that guide one into it.

> Stand firm and hold fast to the traditions [plural of *paradosis*] that you were taught. (2 Thess 2:15)

> We instruct you . . . to shun any brother who conducts himself in a disorderly way and not according to the tradition [*paradosis*] they received from us. (2 Thess 3:6)

> I praise you because you remember me in everything and hold fast to the traditions [plural of *paradosis*], just as I handed them on to you. (1 Cor 11:2)

---

45. See especially *Dei Verbum* (Dogmatic Constitution on Divine Revelation) 9; Catechism 74–83.

46. Translated into English by Jared Wicks, "Six Texts by Prof. Joseph Ratzinger as *peritus* before and during Vatican Council II," *Gregorianum* 89 (2008): 233–311.

47. Wicks, "Six Texts by Prof. Joseph Ratzinger," 274.

48. See Henri de Lubac's explanation of the quotation of 1 John 1:1–4 in the opening of *Dei Verbum* in his commentary on the latter in *La Révélation divine*, 3rd ed., Traditions chrétiennes (Paris: Cerf, 1983).

49. See Matthew Levering, *Engaging the Doctrine of Revelation: The Mediation of the Gospel through Church and Scripture* (Grand Rapids: Baker Academic, 2014).

You have nullified the word of God for the sake of your tradition [*paradosis*]. (Matt 15:6)

In her book on the importance of tradition in Scripture, Edith Humphrey points out that English Bibles since the King James Version tend to use the word "tradition" only in negative contexts.[50] When Jesus condemns *paradosis* that nullifies the word of God, the KJV and many English Bibles since are happy to use the translation "tradition." But when the same Greek word is used in a positive context, it is translated as "instruction" or "teaching" or some other word. The New International Version largely follows the KJV in casting a sinister light on "tradition," as does the New Living Translation.[51] The tendency of English Bibles to make "tradition" something to be avoided arises from and reinforces a Reformation suspicion of tradition, and it also obscures the fact that these passages speak not just of "teaching" but of something handed down and treasured. It would be a mistake, however, to assume that traditions are always a good thing. As Thomas Aquinas notes in his commentary on 2 Thessalonians, traditions are *not* to be kept if they are contrary to the teaching of the faith.[52] Indeed, Paul himself tells the churches in Galatia not to listen to anyone who teaches something contrary to the gospel (Gal 1:8).

Prayer for Strength (2:16–17)

[16]**May our Lord Jesus Christ himself and God our Father, who has loved us and given us everlasting encouragement and good hope through his grace,** [17]**encourage your hearts and strengthen them in every good deed and word.**

NT: 1 Thess 3:11–13
Lectionary: 2 Thess 2:1–3a, 14–17; Memorial of Saint Augustine

2:16–17   In a prayer very similar to 1 Thess 3:11–13, Paul asks **our Lord Jesus Christ** and **God our Father** to console the Thessalonians and empower them to do good deeds.

50. Edith Humphrey, *Scripture and Tradition: What the Bible Really Says* (Grand Rapids: Baker Academic, 2013), 25–44.
51. To be more precise, the 1984 NIV exacerbates the tendency of the KJV by leaving no positive uses of "tradition." The 2011 NIV contains one positive use of "tradition" (1 Cor 11:2). The NLT contains one positive use (2 Thess 3:6).
52. *Super ad Thessalonicenses II reportatio* 2.3.60.

Divine Assistance in Doing Good according to 2 Thessalonians 2:16–17

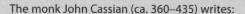

LIVING TRADITION

The North African bishop St. Fulgentius (468–533) writes:

> To be sure, divinely given grace works in a man so that his heart, upon receiving the gift of faith and love, may both bring forth worthy speech and persevere in zeal for doing good. This is divinely given to the faithful, as the blessed Apostle both shows and prays for when he says, "Now may our Lord Jesus Christ himself, and God our Father, who has loved us and given us everlasting consolation and good hope through grace, comfort your hearts and establish you in every good work and word."[a]

The monk John Cassian (ca. 360–435) writes:

> The endurance with which we are able to put up with the temptations hurled at us depends not so much in our power as in the mercy and guidance of God. The blessed Apostle thus teaches, "No temptation has come upon you but what is common to humans. But God is faithful and will not allow you to be tempted beyond your ability, but with the temptation will provide an escape so you will be able to bear it" [1 Cor 10:13]. And the same Apostle teaches that God adapts and strengthens our souls for every good work. . . . "May the God of peace, who brought out of shadows the great shepherd of sheep, Jesus Christ, in the blood of the eternal covenant, adapt you in all goodness, working in you what is pleasing in his sight" [Heb 13:20–21]. And that the same may come to the Thessalonians he prays thus: "May the Lord Jesus Christ and God our Father who loved us and gave us eternal consolation and a good hope in grace exhort your hearts and confirm you in every work and good word" [2 Thess 2:16–17].[b]

a. *Fulgentius of Ruspe and the Scythian Monks: Correspondence on Christology and Grace*, trans. Rob Roy McGregor and Donald Fairbairn, FC 126 (Washington, DC: Catholic University of America Press, 2013), 109.

b. *Conlationes* 3.17 (my translation).

The prayer states that God has already **loved us and given us everlasting encouragement and good hope through his grace**. The encouragement or consolation is "everlasting" in the sense that it is has already been given but will never end. The "good hope" refers to the hope of their final salvation. Though this phrase does not appear elsewhere in Scripture, it was used occasionally by Jews and pagans to refer to the hope of life after death.[53] The words "through his grace" indicate again that this is a divine gift. Paul prays that God would **encourage your hearts and strengthen them in every good deed and word**.

53. See Povl Otzen, "'Gute Hoffnung' bei Paulus," *ZNW* 49 (1958): 283–85.

In modern English, "heart" refers to the source of a person's emotions, but "heart" here and in the Bible generally refers to the center of a person's being, the source of thinking and willing as well as feeling. God will strengthen them to speak the word, which could refer to their own evangelizing efforts. The encouragement and strength he prays for contrasts with their current state of confusion, and the mention of good deeds foreshadows the coming rebuke of those who have been idle.

Rebuke of the Idle

2 Thessalonians 3:1–18

After offering encouraging and complimentary remarks, Paul broaches the second major issue in the letter. Some in the Thessalonian church have refused to work for a living, despite Paul's repeated reminders to follow his example by earning their own food. This passage has sometimes been used as an excuse to ignore the needy, but Paul's concern is that Christians who are able should work to support themselves and for the good of others.

Request for Prayer (3:1–2)

¹Finally, brothers, pray for us, so that the word of the Lord may speed forward and be glorified, as it did among you, ²and that we may be delivered from perverse and wicked people, for not all have faith.

The NABRE translates the phrase *to loipon* as **finally**, but something like "As 3:1 for the other matters . . ." would be more accurate (see commentary on 1 Thess 4:1). Paul is not near the end of the letter but rather is about to turn to a second major issue: members of the church who refuse to work. Paul begins by asking them to pray that **the word of the Lord may speed forward and be glorified**. The "word of the Lord" refers to the gospel message (see 1 Thess 1:8, where Paul speaks of it echoing forward from the Thessalonians). It is the word *about* the Lord Jesus, but for Paul it is also the word *from* the Lord. The image of the word of the Lord running loose in the world is similar to various biblical descriptions of the efficacy of God's speech. Psalm 147 speaks of God's word running swiftly on the earth, having been sent by God (v. 15). In Isa 55 God speaks of his word going forth from his mouth and accomplishing what it is intended to accomplish (v. 11). As recent converts who probably did not have intimate knowledge of the Scripture, the Thessalonians might have thought first of the divine message as a triumphant runner: the image of the word "speeding forward" or "running" and being "glorified" could evoke the image of a runner winning a race and being praised.

3:2   Paul also asks them to pray that God would rescue him, Silvanus, and Timothy from people he refers to as **perverse and wicked**. The NABRE doesn't translate the definite article, but Paul says "*the* perverse and wicked people," which could mean that he is worried about a specific group.[1] Second Thessalonians is focused on the Thessalonians' own suffering and reveals very little about what was happening in Paul's life, but we know from 1 Thessalonians that Paul had endured many difficulties on this missionary journey through Macedonia (1 Thess 2:2). The request ends with the obvious observation that **not all have faith**. "Faith" (*pistis*) could refer to belief or trust in the gospel (Latin *fides qua creditur*) or to "the faith" itself, the gospel message (Latin *fides quae creditur*). Commentators sometimes suggest that if Paul is the author, he couldn't have meant the latter because talk of "the faith" is thought to be characteristic of later times, but Paul refers to "the faith" in this way already in Gal 1:23.

Additional Prayer for the Thessalonians (3:3–5)

> [3]But the Lord is faithful; he will strengthen you and guard you from the evil one. [4]We are confident of you in the Lord that what we instruct you, you [both] are doing and will continue to do. [5]May the Lord direct your hearts to the love of God and to the endurance of Christ.

3:3   Chapter and verse divisions as well as punctuation are later additions to the biblical text designed to make it easier to navigate, but sometimes these aids make it easy to miss connections in the original text. Verse 2 ends with the word *pistis* ("faith"), and the next word is *pistos* (**faithful**). The lack of faith on the part of those who are a danger to Paul is contrasted with the faithfulness of **the Lord**, who can be counted on to **strengthen you and guard you from**

---

1. Abraham J. Malherbe, *The Letters to the Thessalonians: A New Translation with Introduction and Commentary*, AB 32B (New Haven: Yale University Press, 2000), 444.

the evil one. "Strengthen" suggests that Jesus will empower the Thessalonians to resist evil, and "guard" indicates that Jesus will also act on their behalf. The phrase "from the evil one" (*apo tou ponērou*) is identical to the final words of the Our Father ("deliver us *from evil*") and can be translated either as "from the evil one" or "from evil." The preceding discussion of the deceit of Satan (2:9–12) suggests that the NABRE is correct to see a reference to the devil here (see Eph 6:16; Matt 5:37; 6:13; 13:19; John 17:15).

Paul expresses confidence that the Thessalonians **are doing and will con-** **3:4** **tinue to do** all the things that **we instruct you** (see 1 Thess 4:11). Paul does seem to have been pleased with the Thessalonians' progress to a certain extent (2 Thess 1:3–12), but the rhetorical effect of stating that he is confident in their continued obedience is to encourage and reinforce this behavior. As Theodoret puts it, Paul offers this encouragement in order to establish them in their good habits.[2] This statement of confidence also prepares for 3:6–12, where we learn that some of the Thessalonians were not following Paul's instructions on a particular matter. At the same time, Paul does not appear to be disingenuous in claiming to be confident they will follow his instructions.

This section concludes with a prayer that the **Lord** would **direct** their **hearts** **3:5** **to the love of God and to the endurance of Christ** (see 1 Thess 3:11). He has already commended them for their love and endurance (2 Thess 1:3–4), but he prays that they continue and increase on this path because, as John Chrysostom puts it, "There are many things that distract us from love."[3] The phrases "love of God" and "endurance of Christ" could be interpreted in a number of ways. "The love of God" may denote primarily God's love for them, but this would also imply their own response. The "endurance of Christ" could refer to Christ's own endurance or to their own endurance in imitation of Christ, or even to their patient endurance as they wait for Christ to return. The letter is filled with references to the hardship they were enduring, and just before this prayer Paul says that the Lord will strengthen them and protect them from the evil one (3:3). The most likely interpretation is that he prays that their hearts would be drawn to Christ's endurance in the face of suffering, so they would behave similarly.[4] A similar thought is expressed in 1 Thessalonians when Paul gives thanks that they have become imitators of the Lord by enduring tribulation with the joy of the Holy Spirit (1:6).

2. *Interpretatio in xiv epistulas sancti Pauli* (PG 82:669). Gordon Fee (*The First and Second Letters to the Thessalonians*, NICNT [Grand Rapids: Eerdmans, 2009], 311) labels 3:1–5 a *captatio benevolentiae*, a rhetorical technique that aims to charm listeners in order to persuade them.

3. *Homiliae in epistulam ii ad Thessalonicenses* (PG 62:493 [my translation]).

4. Béda Rigaux, *Saint Paul: Les Épitres aux Thessaloniciens*, EBib (Paris: Lecoffre, 1956), 700.

Those Who Refuse to Work (3:6–15)

---

[6]We instruct you, brothers, in the name of [our] Lord Jesus Christ, to shun any brother who conducts himself in a disorderly way and not according to the tradition they received from us. [7]For you know how one must imitate us. For we did not act in a disorderly way among you, [8]nor did we eat food received free from anyone. On the contrary, in toil and drudgery, night and day we worked, so as not to burden any of you. [9]Not that we do not have the right. Rather, we wanted to present ourselves as a model for you, so that you might imitate us. [10]In fact, when we were with you, we instructed you that if anyone was unwilling to work, neither should that one eat. [11]We hear that some are conducting themselves among you in a disorderly way, by not keeping busy but minding the business of others. [12]Such people we instruct and urge in the Lord Jesus Christ to work quietly and to eat their own food. [13]But you, brothers, do not be remiss in doing good. [14]If anyone does not obey our word as expressed in this letter, take note of this person not to associate with him, that he may be put to shame. [15]Do not regard him as an enemy but admonish him as a brother.

NT: 1 Thess 2:9; 4:9–12; 5:14
Catechism: work, 2427–28; daily bread, 2830; love for the poor, 2443–49
Lectionary: 2 Thess 3:6–10, 16–18; Memorial of Saint Monica

In this section Paul turns to the second major issue in the letter: apparently some in the congregation are refusing to work. Paul's concern regarding this issue goes all the way back to when he was in Thessalonica and founded the church. He and his associates worked to support themselves and taught the Thessalonians that they should follow this example (1 Thess 2:9; 4:9–12; 2 Thess 3:6–10). When he wrote 1 Thessalonians, Paul apparently did not yet see a crisis in this area, though his special attention to the issue and his encouragement to progress (4:11) suggest that perhaps he thought some in the congregation were reluctant to follow his instructions.[5] At some point after writing 1 Thessalonians, Paul received word (3:11) that some in the church were shirking this instruction.[6] In response, Paul fires off the most pointed rebuke of his otherwise warm Thessalonian correspondence.

New Testament scholars have often argued that the trouble with idleness was linked to †eschatological confusion: if the day of the Lord has already come, why

---

5. See also 1 Thess 5:14.
6. Those who are not persuaded that Paul wrote the letter will read this section as an expansion of 1 Thess 2:9–12 and 4:9–12 by a later writer.

bother working?[7] This argument has a certain appeal because it links the two major issues of the letter. Paul himself never links these two issues, however, and his warnings about the need to work began while he was still with them, seemingly before their eschatological confusion had set in. Other scholars have offered sociological explanations. The most plausible of these is the suggestion that the congregation was sharing possessions and some members were taking advantage. We know that Paul and other early Christians stressed the importance of sharing possessions and giving alms.[8] We also have evidence of some taking advantage of this generosity, accepting aid when it was not needed.[9]

After expressing confidence that the Thessalonians would obey his instruc-   **3:6** tion (3:4), Paul puts this to the test by commanding them to stay away from **any brother who conducts himself in a disorderly way**. The "disorder" Paul has in mind here is a refusal to work (see commentary on 1 Thess 5:14). Certain members are neglecting the apostolic tradition of working for a living, preferring instead to loaf and meddle in other people's affairs. Paul adopts a solemn tone, commanding the Thessalonians **in the name of [our] Lord Jesus Christ** to **shun** or stay away from these people (see below on 3:14).[10]

Paul restates the tradition that is being neglected by some with a "not X   **3:7–9** but Y" structure reminiscent of 1 Thess 2:1–8: the apostles did not take anyone's food without paying for it; instead, they worked tirelessly so they would not be a burden to any of the Thessalonians. We know that Paul was happy to accept financial assistance in other contexts (see commentary on 1 Thess 2:9–12). The apostles had the **right** or the "authority" to receive payment from the Thessalonians, a right that came from a command of Jesus himself (1 Cor 9:14; see also Matt 10:10; Luke 10:7). In this case, however, Paul deemed it necessary to forgo this right in order to give them a **model** to **imitate**. He did not **eat food received free from anyone**, and neither should they. This instruction is meant to prevent freeloading, not table fellowship.

Why was it so important to Paul that his converts work for a living instead of mooching off of others? Two reasons are given in this passage, both of which echo concerns mentioned in 1 Thessalonians. One reason is not to

---

7. E.g., the overconfident footnote in the NABRE: Paul admonishes "them about a specific problem in their community that has grown out of the intense eschatological speculation, namely, not to work but to become instead disorderly busybodies (2 Thes 3:6–15)."

8. On the importance of sharing possessions in Paul's Letters, see Nathan Eubank, "Justice Endures Forever: Paul's Grammar of Generosity," *JSPHL* 5, no. 2 (2015): 169–87.

9. E.g., *Didache* 1.5 and *Shepherd of Hermas* Mandate 2.5 warn against accepting alms without need. See various related suggestions in Victor Paul Furnish, *1 Thessalonians, 2 Thessalonians*, ANTC (Nashville: Abingdon, 2007), 177.

10. The NABRE places "our" in brackets because it is missing from some important early manuscripts.

burden others. To state the obvious, taking other people's food while refusing to work is self-centered and fails to attain to the other-oriented way of life to which Paul exhorted his churches (1 Thess 4:9–12). The second reason is that this behavior is disorderly and meddlesome. He describes those who refuse to work as behaving in an *ataktōs* ("disorderly") fashion (2 Thess 3:6), a word that suggests undisciplined or even illicit behavior. They are failing to "work quietly" (see 1 Thess 4:11)—that is, to be modest and unassuming—and are instead assuming that others should pick up their slack. He also accuses the idle of "minding the business of others" (2 Thess 3:11), which is a play on words in Greek. They should be workers (*ergazomai*), but instead they are busybodies (*periergazomai*)—that is, people who meddle in other people's affairs instead of minding their own business (see 1 Tim 5:13).

3:10 Paul reminds them of what he said when he was in Thessalonica: **if anyone was unwilling to work, neither should that one eat**. Despite the relative neglect of 2 Thessalonians, this line has become a proverb sometimes called the Golden Rule of work, which is not a bad description of the meaning of the saying here (see Matt 7:12). One should work and share resources as one wants others to do. Note that Paul's command is not addressed to the "unemployed," those willing to work but unable to find it, like the people standing around without work in the parable of the workers in the vineyard (Matt 20:1–16). It is addressed to those who could be gainfully employed but choose not to be, those who are "unwilling" to work. The verb translated as "should that one eat" is a third-person imperative, something common in Greek but notoriously difficult to translate into English. Some translations give the impression that Paul is commanding the church to stop the idle people from eating (RSV: "let him not eat"), but the command that Paul gave to the Thessalonians would have been addressed first and foremost to the idle people themselves, as is the similar command in verse 12. They are to stop burdening others and work with their own hands.[11]

3:11–12 Some unnamed person has informed Paul, Silvanus, and Timothy that some of the Thessalonians are being disorderly, acting like busybodies instead of working. There is no indication of how large or organized this group is. Paul commands them solemnly **in the Lord Jesus Christ** that they must **work quietly** and **eat their own food**. "Quiet" (*hēsychia*) refers not to suppressing noise but rather to living in an orderly way. The related verb *hēsychazō* appears in 1 Thess 4:11 when Paul admonishes them to aspire to "live a tranquil life." Instead of

---

11. The third-person imperative can be used as a functional second-person imperative (1 Tim 4:12). In this case the rest of the congregation is implicitly led to help reinforce Paul's injunction. But the command is given most directly to "such people" who do not work.

2 Thessalonians 3:10 among Monks and Ascetics

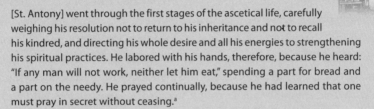

In the ancient Church 2 Thess 3:10 was often cited to show that it is necessary for those who have devoted themselves to prayer as monks or ascetics to work with their own hands rather than relying on the generosity of others. St. Athanasius (ca. 296–373), bishop of Alexandria, writes:

> [St. Antony] went through the first stages of the ascetical life, carefully weighing his resolution not to return to his inheritance and not to recall his kindred, and directing his whole desire and all his energies to strengthening his spiritual practices. He labored with his hands, therefore, because he heard: "If any man will not work, neither let him eat," spending a part for bread and a part on the needy. He prayed continually, because he had learned that one must pray in secret without ceasing.[a]

St. Basil the Great (ca. 329–379), bishop of Caesarea in Cappadocia, writes:

> [He should] not make a display of dress or shoes, as this is indeed idle ostentation. He should use inexpensive clothing for his bodily needs. He should not spend anything beyond actual necessity or for mere extravagance. This is an abuse. He should not seek honor nor lay claim to the first place. Each one ought to prefer all others to himself. He ought not to be disobedient. He who is idle, although able to work, should not eat; moreover, he who is occupied with some task which is rightly intended for the glory of Christ ought to hold himself to a pursuit of work within his ability. Each one, with the approval of his superiors, should, with reason and certainty, so do everything, even to eating and drinking, as serving the glory of God.[b]

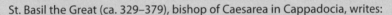

a. "Life of St. Anthony," in *Early Christian Biographies*, trans. Mary Emily Keenan, FC 15 (Washington, DC: Catholic University of America Press, 1952), 137.
b. *Letters: 1–185*, trans. Agnes Clare Way, FC 13 (Washington, DC: Catholic University of America Press, 1951), 58.

shirking their duties and minding other people's business, they ought to work in tranquility and earn their own living. The command in verse 12 is addressed only to **Such people**—that is, those individuals who are not working. Perhaps Paul was not entirely certain about who the offenders were. He does not name them or address them in the second person. Instead, he gives the command in a way that leaves anyone who is refusing to work feeling addressed.

With the words **But you, brothers**, Paul shifts from addressing the idle to   3:13 addressing the congregation as a whole. The idle are to work to earn their own bread, and the rest of the congregation is to remain steadfast **in doing good**. The

NABRE states that they should **not be remiss**, but a better translation would be "Do not weary in doing good."[12] "Doing good" (*kalopoieō*) could apply to any good deed, but this language often refers to material generosity, and the context suggests that this is the case here. Those who refuse to work are rebuked and told that they should not eat if they will not work, but the rest of the church should not take this as an excuse to stop doing good for others. As Abraham Malherbe puts it, Paul is "warning against overinterpretation of his directions."[13] This is not a matter of balancing contrary principles (self-reliance and generosity). Rather, the entire congregation is urged to increase in their care for others: the idle, by no longer making themselves a burden, and the rest, by continuing to do good deeds.

3:14–15   After so many attempts to convince the idle to start working, Paul realistically expects continued problems and gives the congregation instructions on how to handle those who do not obey. Verse 6 mentioned the need to avoid the idle, and here we find expanded instructions: they are **not to associate with** such people so that such people will become ashamed. The practice of excluding unrepentant sinners is well attested in early Christianity.[14] This is a drastic measure that could be devastating to members of what was already a beleaguered minority. The purpose of this action is not to destroy them, however, as verse 15 makes clear. The excluded members are to be regarded not as enemies but as "brothers," a label that indicates that the purpose of their exclusion is their reintegration. This also implies that those who continue to refuse to work will still be treated with respect, as one would a brother or sister. "He who admonishes his brother," Chrysostom comments, "doesn't do it in public; he doesn't make a show of the rebuke. Instead, he does it privately and with much care and sorrow."[15]

Reflection and Application (3:6–15)

The instruction Paul gives the Thessalonians about the necessity of work in 3:10 ("If anyone was unwilling to work, neither should that one eat") has become a well-known proverb. In the ancient Church it became a favorite argument against monks who refused to work (see sidebar, "2 Thessalonians 3:10 among Monks and Ascetics," p. 187); it has often been cited to show that trusting God with the future does not give license to laziness but rather provides freedom from worry.[16] It was even cited in Soviet propaganda as a reminder that every

12. BDAG.
13. *Letters to the Thessalonians*, 458.
14. E.g., 1 Cor 5:9–13; Matt 18:15–20; *Shepherd of Hermas* Mandate 4.1.
15. *Homiliae* (PG 62:496 [my translation]).
16. Catechism 2830.

citizen must work, though of course it was scrubbed clean of any mention of St. Paul.[17] Unfortunately, however, 2 Thess 3:10 is often cited by those who wish to argue against helping the needy, an idea that directly contradicts Paul's own teaching. This abuse of the Pauline proverb began already in antiquity, as St. John Chrysostom's sermons show. Chrysostom chides those in his congregation who quote the verse and start nosing into beggars' affairs to make sure they really need help.[18] In our own time, American politicians sometimes appeal to 2 Thess 3:10 as justification for cutting aid to the poor.[19] During the 2012 presidential election season I attended a public lecture given by a friend on principles for voting. The lecture, a distillation of the main points from the United States Conference of Catholic Bishops' document "Forming Consciences for Faithful Citizenship," mentioned care for the poor and vulnerable among the goals of any Catholic citizen. After the lecture one man raised his hand and objected, "In the Old Testament it says, 'If a man doesn't work, he shouldn't eat.'" He was mistaken about the source of the proverb, but his assumption that it teaches us not to help the poor is all too common.

The fact that so many have seen 2 Thess 3:10 as a good justification for neglecting the needy shows that this interpretation of the verse has a certain plausibility to it. It is worth taking the time, therefore, to show why this interpretation is wrong. Here is a list of arguments, beginning with general observations and gradually working down to specific points from 2 Thessalonians.

1. Those who cite this verse presumably believe that the Bible has something to say about how to live. If this is the case, one wonders why this particular verse should be given so much weight when there are so many other passages enjoining liberality. For example,

Give to the one who asks of you, and do not turn your back on one who wants to borrow. (Matt 5:42)

Religion that is pure and undefiled before God and the Father is this: to care for orphans and widows in their affliction. (James 1:27)

Is this not, rather, the fast that I choose:
releasing those bound unjustly,
untying the thongs of the yoke;

---

17. Samuel Kucherov, *The Organs of Soviet Administration of Justice: Their History and Operation* (Leiden: Brill, 1970), 198. See also the discussion of the verse in Max Weber's 1905 classic, *The Protestant Ethic and the Spirit of Capitalism*, trans. Talcott Parsons (London: Routledge, 2001), 105–6.

18. *De eleemosyna* 51.269.

19. An Internet search of key words from the verse reveals multiple examples.

> Setting free the oppressed,
>> breaking off every yoke?
> Is it not sharing your bread with the hungry,
>> bringing the afflicted and the homeless into your house;
> Clothing the naked when you see them,
>> and not turning your back on your own flesh? (Isa 58:6–7)

There are many, many more similar examples.[20] Second Thessalonians 3:10 should not be used as an excuse to ignore the rest of the Bible.

2. Those who cite this verse presumably believe that Paul in particular has something to say about how they should live their lives. If this is the case, then it might be helpful to check one's interpretation by what Paul says about the poor on other occasions. To take one particularly clear example, see 2 Cor 9:13:

> Through the testing of this ministry [i.e., the collection to aid poor Christians in Jerusalem] you glorify God by your obedience to the confession of the gospel of Christ and by the generosity of your sharing with them *and with all others*. (my translation)

For Paul, generosity to all people brings glory to God and shows obedience to the gospel.

3. Those who refuse to help the needy because of 2 Thess 3:10 are acting on the assumption that the person asking for help is in need because he or she is lazy or dishonest. Most of the time, however, we do not have the slightest idea what led a person to the point of asking others for help. John Chrysostom unmasks the lack of charity in this assumption:

> You say the beggar is an impostor. Man, what are you saying? For the sake of a single loaf of bread or a garment you call him an impostor? Then they say the beggar will sell it immediately. Do you manage all your affairs well? Is laziness the only reason people fall into poverty? Is no one poor from shipwreck? From lawsuits? From robbery? From dangers? From illnesses? From other problems? But if we hear someone mourning these things and crying out, naked, and looking to heaven with long hair and ragged clothes, immediately we call him impostor, cheat, liar! Are you not ashamed? Whom do you call an impostor?[21]

More often than not we do not know why a person is in need, and it is cruel to assume the worst. Chrysostom frequently preaches against those who are

---

20. For a good introduction to this issue, see Gary A. Anderson, *Charity: The Place of the Poor in the Biblical Tradition* (New Haven: Yale University Press, 2013).

21. *In epistulam ad Hebraeos* (PG 63:93–94 [my translation]).

overly inquisitive about the goodness of those to whom they give. Seeking to give only to those we deem worthy is to "take away the greater part of almsgiving, and will in time destroy the thing itself. And yet that is almsgiving: it is for the sinners, it is for the guilty. For this is almsgiving [*eleēmosynē*], to have mercy [*eleeō*] not on the successful, but on those who have done wrong!"[22] Moreover, most of us, if we are honest, will admit that we often waste money on ourselves. Why not let someone else waste our money once in a while?[23]

4. Paul's command to work in 2 Thess 3:10 is directed primarily toward Christians in Thessalonica who are refusing to work, not to hardworking people who need to stop giving to beggars. These idlers were able-bodied Christians who appear to be living off the generosity of others. Paul wants them to get to work. He is not saying that aid should be withheld from beggars or other people in need. This point bears repeating: Paul is not saying what many people today seem to think he is saying. The best interpretation of verse 10 is Paul's restatement of the point in verse 12: Lazy people, start working! Those who pass judgment on the industriousness of strangers miss Paul's point entirely.

5. There is good reason to believe that the laziness in Thessalonica was made possible by the mutual support of the Christians there: they are eating other people's bread.[24] Paradoxically, then, the favorite verse of those who oppose charity actually attests to the early Christian habit of sharing possessions. Moreover, Paul wanted them to keep helping one another even after some had taken advantage, as verse 13 shows. Indeed, for Chrysostom, the key to proper interpretation of this passage is to hold verse 13 together with verses 10–12:

> I say these things not to encourage idleness. No way! Rather, I earnestly wish all to work, for idleness teaches every evil. But I exhort you not to be unmerciful or cruel, since Paul . . . when he said "If any will not work, neither should he eat," didn't stop there but added, "But you, do not be weary in doing good." You say, "No, these statements contradict each other. For if he commanded them not to eat, how can he urge us to give?" . . . But these commands complement each other. For if you are ready to be merciful, the poor man will be set free from his idleness, and you will be set free from your cruelty.[25]

22. *In epistulam ad Hebraeos* (PG 63:88 [my translation]).

23. On a number of occasions I have heard Walter Hooper tell the story of C. S. Lewis's defense of giving to beggars in Oxford. Hooper noticed Lewis giving alms and asked him if he worried that the beggar would spend the money on booze. Lewis responded, "Well, if I keep the money, *I'm* going to spend it on booze."

24. See commentary on 1 Thess 4:9.

25. *In epistulam ad Hebraeos* (PG 63:94 [my translation]).

The apparent tension between verse 10 and the many biblical exhortations to generosity vanishes upon closer examination. In both cases Christians are to be motivated by love of neighbor, the love that works hard not to burden others (1 Thess 2:9; 2 Thess 3:8), and the love that shows mercy to those in need.

6. Contrary to what non-Catholics sometimes imagine, the Magisterium very rarely dictates how particular passages of Scripture should be interpreted. This passage is an exception. In his 1931 encyclical *Quadragesimo Anno*, Pope Pius XI warns against "the unwarranted and unmerited appeal made by some to the Apostle," which twists this verse to argue that only the gainfully employed should have access to money, food, and housing.[26] It is wrong to use this verse as a justification for ignoring the needy because

> the Apostle is passing judgment on those who are unwilling to work, although they can and ought to, and he admonishes us that we ought diligently to use our time and energies of body, and mind and not be a burden to others when we can provide for ourselves. But the Apostle in no wise teaches that labor is the sole title to a living or an income.[27]

Pope Pius confirms what exegesis and the testimony of the Fathers has already shown: Paul directs the lazy to work, and everyone else to be generous.

Prayer for Peace and the Lord's Presence (3:16)

[16]**May the Lord of peace himself give you peace at all times and in every way. The Lord be with all of you.**

3:16   Prayers for peace and the presence of the Lord are common in the biblical tradition (Num 6:26; Ruth 2:4) and in Paul's Letters (Rom 15:33). The prayer for peace **at all times and in every way** reflects the turmoil currently experienced by the Thessalonian church. They were suffering persecution and significant theological confusion and fear, as well as the obstinate refusal of some to follow Paul's teaching about work. In the immediately preceding lines it became apparent that the congregation would soon experience painful tensions as they disciplined the members of the church who refused to work. Paul thus prays that they would have peace on all of these fronts. There is some debate regarding

26. *Quadragesimo Anno* 57.
27. *Quadragesimo Anno* 57.

whether this prayer is the conclusion of what came before, as the NABRE's paragraph break suggests, or is the beginning of the end of the letter.[28] The very fact that we are unable to decide may indicate that the prayer helps to transition from the difficult issue discussed in 3:6–15 to the close of the letter.

Final Greeting (3:17–18)

[17]This greeting is in my own hand, Paul's. This is the sign in every letter; this is how I write. [18]The grace of our Lord Jesus Christ be with all of you.

Like many other ancient letter writers, Paul dictated his letters to an †amanuensis. At the end of Romans, Paul's amanuensis reveals himself and offers greetings: "I, Tertius, the writer of this letter, greet you in the Lord" (16:22). Though Paul "wrote" Romans in the sense that he composed the letter, Tertius was responsible for transcribing what Paul said. Sometimes letter writers would take the stylus from the amanuensis and write a few lines in their own hand. This could function simply as a personal touch, similar to handwriting a note or signature at the bottom of a typed letter, or as a mark of authenticity.[29] Letter writers did not always draw attention to the change of handwriting, since it was obvious to the recipients. On some occasions, however, Paul does draw explicit attention to the fact that he has taken the pen, perhaps in order to make his presence felt or to ensure that those who heard the letter read aloud in the church would be aware of the shift (see 1 Cor 16:21; Gal 6:11; Col 4:18; Philem 1:19). On this occasion, after noting that **This greeting is in my own hand**, he adds: **This is the sign in every letter; this is how I write**. Paul does not end every letter with these words, so the "sign" cannot be the words of the greeting. Rather, the sign is probably the change of handwriting.[30] Why does Paul draw attention to his handwriting in this way? Most modern commentators would concur with Jerome, who said that Paul wanted "to remove suspicion that the entire epistle he sent was a forgery."[31] The possible existence of false letters was mentioned in 2:2. By drawing attention to his handwriting Paul offers them a guard against

3:17

---

28. See the discussion in Jeffrey A. D. Weima, *1–2 Thessalonians*, BECNT (Grand Rapids: Baker Academic, 2014), 632.

29. See the discussion in Weima, *1–2 Thessalonians*, 636–38. See also Stanley K. Stowers, *Letter Writing in Greco-Roman Antiquity*, LEC 5 (Philadelphia: Westminster, 1989), 61.

30. As noted by Chrysostom, *Homiliae* (PG 62:469).

31. Jerome, *Commentary on Galatians*, trans. Andrew Cain, FC 121 (Washington, DC: Catholic University of America Press), 261.

any possible future forged letters. The use of the singular also shows that Paul is the principal author, though the letter is from Silvanus and Timothy as well (see commentary on 2 Thess 1:1).

3:18   It was Paul's custom to close his letters with a prayer for the gift or **grace** of Jesus to be with the recipients. It is easy to read too much into small details in Paul's Letters, but the repetition of **all of you** may be significant here, following closely on the prayer for the Lord to be with "all of you" in verse 16 (see 1 Cor 16:24; 2 Cor 13:13). Difficult times are ahead, including the probable exercise of ecclesial discipline in admonishing the idle members. It is fitting, therefore, that Paul stresses that he prays for the grace of Jesus to be with all of them, including those who are about to be disciplined for being idle busybodies.

Suggested Resources

Commentaries from the Tradition

John Chrysostom. "Homilies of St. John Chrysostom, Archbishop of Constantinople, on the Second Epistle of St. Paul the Apostle to the Thessalonians." In *Saint Chrysostom: Homilies on Galatians, Ephesians, Philippians, Colossians, Thessalonians, Timothy, Titus, and Philemon*, edited by Philip Schaff, translated by James Tweed and John Albert Broadus, 377–98. *NPNF¹* 13. New York: Christian Literature Company, 1889.

Gorday, Peter, ed. *Colossians, 1–2 Thessalonians, 1–2 Timothy, Titus, Philemon*. ACCS 9. Downers Grove, IL: InterVarsity, 2000.

Scholarly Commentaries

Malherbe, Abraham J. *The Letters to the Thessalonians: A New Translation with Introduction and Commentary*. AB 32B. New Haven: Yale University Press, 2000.

Richard, Earl J. *First and Second Thessalonians*. SP 11. Collegeville, MN: Liturgical Press, 1995.

Weima, Jeffrey A. D. *1–2 Thessalonians*. BECNT. Grand Rapids: Baker Academic, 2014.

Midlevel Commentaries

Boring, M. Eugene. *I & II Thessalonians*. NTL. Louisville: Westminster John Knox, 2015.

Gaventa, Beverly Roberts. *First and Second Thessalonians*. IBC. Louisville: John Knox, 1998.

Gupta, Nijay K. *1–2 Thessalonians*. NCC. Eugene, OR: Cascade, 2016.

Popular Commentary

Wright, N. T. *Paul for Everyone: Galatians and Thessalonians*. Louisville: Westminster John Knox, 2004.

Glossary

amanuensis: a secretary or one who writes what another dictates. Paul ordinarily dictated his letters to an amanuensis but would sign a final greeting in his own hand. See Rom 16:22, where the amanuensis greets the Roman Christians, and Gal 6:11, where Paul writes a message in his own hand.

apocalyptic (from the Greek *apokalypsis*, meaning "revelation"): a genre of literature in which divine mysteries impinging on human events are revealed. The biblical books of Daniel and Revelation are two canonical examples. The word "apocalyptic" can also describe a worldview that shares the main concerns of such literature.

cosmology (from the Greek *kosmos*, meaning "world"): one's understanding of the structure and nature of the world.

cultic: referring to worship, especially as expressed in ritual or sacrifice.

eschatology, eschatological (from the Greek *eschatos*, meaning "last"): a term referring to the end time and last things, such as the return of Jesus and the resurrection of the dead.

paraenesis: exhortation or moral instruction.

parousia: a Greek word meaning "presence" or "arrival." In the New Testament it often refers to the future advent or coming of Jesus.

Septuagint (abbreviated LXX): the oldest Greek translations of the Hebrew Bible and other ancient Jewish Scripture.

Shema: a Jewish confession of faith from Deut 6:4–5.

textual variant: a discrepancy between manuscripts of a text.

typology, typological: the study of how biblical persons, things, and events prefigure later ones, especially the coming of Jesus.

Index of Pastoral Topics

Index of Sidebars